CONVERSATIONS ON MIND, MATTER, AND MATHEMATICS

D0209672

JEAN-PIERRE CHANGEUX

ALAIN CONNES

Conversations on Mind, Matter, and Mathematics

EDITED AND TRANSLATED BY

M. B. DeBevoise

PRINCETON UNIVERSITY PRESS

PRINCETON, NEW JERSEY

Copyright © 1995 by Princeton University Press
Published by Princeton University Press, 41 William Street,
Princeton, New Jersey 08540
In the United Kingdom: Princeton University Press,
Chichester, West Sussex

Originally published in French under the title *Matière à Pensée*,
copyright © 1989 by Editions Odile Jacob

Glossary of Neurobiological Terms on pp. 247–51 copyright © 1983
by Libraire Àrthème Fayard and © 1985 by Jean-Pierre Changeux

Library of Congress Cataloging-in-Publication Data
Changeux, Jean-Pierre, and Connes, Alain.
Conversations on Mind, Matter, and Mathematics / Jean-Pierre Changeux
and Alain Connes
p.   cm.
Translation of *Matière à Pensée*.
Includes bibliographical references and index.
ISBN 0-691-08759-8

This book has been composed in Times Roman
Designed by Jan Lilly

Princeton University Press books are printed on
acid-free paper and meet the guidelines for permanence and
durability of the Committee on Production Guidelines
for Book Longevity of the Council on
Library Resources

Printed in the United States of America

10   9   8   7   6   5   4   3   2   1

Contents

TRANSLATOR'S NOTE   vii

PREFACE TO THE ORIGINAL FRENCH EDITION   xi

1. MATHEMATICS AND THE BRAIN   3
   Introductory Remarks   3
   The Hierarchy of the Sciences in Question   6
   Invention or Discovery?   11
   Mathematics Has a History   18
   Is Mathematics Merely a Language?   22

2. PLATO AS MATERIALIST?   25
   The Intellectual Ascesis of the Materialist   25
   The Psychoanalysis of Mathematics   30
   Is a Mathematical Object a Cultural Representation Like
       Any Other?   32
   The Darwinism of Mathematical Objects   35
   Beliefs in Mathematics   38

3. NATURE MADE TO ORDER   41
   Constructivist Mathematics   41
   The "Unreasonable Effectiveness" of Mathematics   47
   Einstein and Mathematics   51
   The Usefulness of Mathematical Models in Biology   57
   The Auscultation of Quantum Mechanics   64

4. THE NEURONAL MATHEMATICIAN   74
   Illumination   74
   The Brain and Its Multiple Levels of Organization   82
   The Cellular Level   90
   From Elementary Circuits to Mental Objects   97
   The Neuropsychology of Mathematics   105
   Transition among Levels by Variation-Selection   107
   Mental Darwinism and Mathematical Creation   116

5. DARWIN AMONG THE MATHEMATICIANS   122
   The Utility of the Darwinian Schema   122
   Coding Stable Forms   127

The Organization of Long-Term Memory   138
Reasoning by Analogy   142
Linking Representations within Frameworks of Thought   143
The Natural Selection of Mathematical Objects   146

6. THINKING MACHINES   153

Are Intelligent Machines Possible?   153
Gödel's Theorem   154
Turing's Thinking Machine   162
The Theory of the S-Matrix in Physics as Analogue to
  Functionalism in Psychology   165
Is the Human Brain a Computer?   168
A Self-Evaluating Machine that Can Suffer   173

7. THE REAL AND THE RATIONAL   179

The Nature of Mathematical Objects Revisited   180
The Construction of Mathematics by the Child   192
Order in the World   196

EPILOGUE: ETHICAL QUESTIONS   210

In Search of the Natural Bases of Ethics   210
Social Life and the Frontal Lobe   216
Prosocial Behavior in the Child and Its Cultural Imprint   219
The Functions of Morality   222
In Defense of a Revisable, Rational, and Natural Morality   224
The "Enlargement of Sympathy" and the Function of Aesthetics   226
Ethics and Mathematics   233

GLOSSARY OF MATHEMATICAL TERMS   237

GLOSSARY OF NEUROBIOLOGICAL TERMS   247

INDEX   253

Translator's Note

THE PRESENT work is a revised and expanded edition of *Matière à Pensée*, first published in Paris to admiring reviews in 1989. The original edition consisted of a mostly unedited transcript of the authors' conversations. Because the French text is frequently choppy and elliptical, as actual conversation often is, and in many places hard to follow, my aim here has been to smooth out the language, to make the technical arguments both more precise and more accessible to general readers, and to soften the many sharp shifts and turns of debate as it initially unfolded—without, however, sacrificing the spontaneous quality of principled, passionate quarreling that gives this a prominent place in the literature of friendly dispute for the sake of truth and knowledge.

Quoted passages in the original work have almost all been paraphrased and attributed to their authors by name in the body of text, without further citation. The arguments of many of the authors mentioned in passing (Plato, Descartes, Spinoza, Kant, Bentham, Mill, and so on) remain well enough known to educated readers that specific references are either unnecessary or easily located elsewhere. Reference to modern research in mathematics and neurobiology poses difficulties of a different sort. Rather than carry over the footnotes found in the French edition (which are to some extent arbitrary and in any case often incomplete, and so of limited usefulness) or annotate the text more fully, I have dispensed with notes almost entirely: specialists will know where to look in the scientific literature; lay readers by and large will not care. Those who do may consult the excellent book by Jean-Pierre Changeux that Alain Connes mentions at the outset, published in English as *Neuronal Man: The Biology of Mind* (Pantheon, 1985; Oxford, 1986); also Peter Baumgartner's and Sabine Payr's informative collection of interviews with leading figures in computer science, neuropsychology, and philosophy,

Speaking Minds: Interviews with Twenty Eminent Cognitive Scientists (Princeton, 1995). On the mathematical side, interested readers are invited to consult the classic work by Jacques Hadamard, *The Psychology of Invention in the Mathematical Field* (Princeton, 1945), currently available in paperback from Dover Books; and the volume of papers edited by Thomas Tymoczko, *New Directions in the Philosophy of Mathematics* (Birkhäuser, 1986), forthcoming shortly in a revised and expanded paperback edition from Princeton. To further assist nonspecialist readers in grasping the authors' technical points, the English edition contains extensive glossaries of mathematical and neurobiological terms. A very small number of new notes has been added to call attention to especially useful recent summaries in English; old references have been retained in the few cases where direct quotation in the original text is reproduced.

At the urging of the Press, the authors graciously agreed to a final conversation for the purpose of tying up a number of ends left loose in the French transcript. Held in late 1993, it has been added to the main body of the text as the seventh and penultimate chapter, "The Real and the Rational." The concluding chapter of the original edition, "On Ethical Questions," was based on a written essay by Jean-Pierre Changeux followed by a very brief reply from Alain Connes, recast in the format of face-to-face dialogue of the previous chapters. This fiction has been preserved in the present edition, and the chapter itself in the form of an epilogue.

In editing these conversations I am grateful to have had the advice of Michel Baudry, Leon Cooper, and William Thurston, all of whom looked at a rough draft of the translation early on, and the generous cooperation of the authors themselves, who carefully checked the final result and made extensive corrections in response to suggestions for revision. I owe particular thanks to three of my colleagues at Princeton University Press: Trevor Lipscombe, whose shrewd comments on a later draft substantially improved it, and Lauren Oppenheim and Heidi Sheehan, without whose help in seeing the completed manuscript through production the book might have fallen even farther behind schedule than for various reasons it had already done.

I trust it does not need to be said that any infelicities and defects that may have eluded the scrutiny of these kind persons are my responsibility alone.

M. B. DeBevoise
Princeton, August 1994

Preface to the Original French Edition

MATHEMATICIANS and biologists get along fairly well for the most part, but they do not really talk to each other. Their training and interests are so different that conversation sometimes seems impossible. But it matters very much that they do talk, because while no one will deny that we do mathematics with our brain, no one has yet managed to build a machine that reproduces the faculties of reason and invention of our own cerebral machine. Thus the central question of our book: will it be possible one day to artificially create genuine intelligence out of matter?

Before this question can be answered, it is necessary to define what we mean by mathematics. What is the nature of mathematical objects? Do they exist independently of the human brain—which discovers them? Or are they only the result of cerebral activity—which constructs them? Recent developments in the neurosciences—the sciences of the nervous system—have added new pieces to an ancient puzzle that goes back at least as far as Plato, who placed it at the heart of his dialogues. Granting that mathematics is the same whether it is done in Paris, Moscow, or San Francisco, one may nonetheless ask whether its universality extends to the point that it could be used to communicate with hypothetical beings on other planets. So successful is mathematics in describing the world around us that its effectiveness sometimes seems (as Wigner famously remarked) altogether unreasonable. But might not this phenomenon merely be evidence of the fascination that created objects exert upon their creators? Of the mathematician as Pygmalion?

The answers to these questions are to be found, for the most part, in the organization and function of the brain. The brain is a network of neurons—a network of extreme complexity, to be sure, possessing exceptional properties. These properties are the result of certain architectural principles and elementary functions that anatomists and physiologists are now subjecting to intensive analysis. Once understood, they will profoundly influence the design of intelligent machines. But the brain also owes its special characteristics to the fact that it is an evolving system. While everyone is familiar with Darwin's theories about the evolution of living species, it is not generally recognized that the development of the brain itself, both during the embryonic stage and then after birth, constitutes an evolution in the course of which the connections among nerve cells are themselves subject to a process of selection. The fact that this process continues through further stages of evolution, at higher levels of organization, may account for the unfolding of thought and mathematical reasoning, perhaps even for imagination.

Developments in both mathematics and the neurosciences have increasingly come to have a social impact, so much so that they now begin to pose ethical problems. What do we mean when we talk of ethics in the first place? Can morality be given natural foundations, foundations that are to be sought in the social functioning of the human brain? Can ethics be based on universal principles similar to those of mathematics?

Our book takes the form of a dialogue, because neither one of us knows enough about the other's field to take it upon himself to answer the many questions that arise in each one. The dialogue form has the advantage of allowing each of us to sharpen his views in response to the other's. On certain points we agree; on others—and not necessarily the least important ones!—we disagree. For the reader, the third partner in our conversation, these questions remain open for him or her to pursue at will, free to agree or disagree with either of us— or both!

Jean-Pierre Changeux and Alain Connes
Paris, June 1989

CONVERSATIONS ON MIND, MATTER,
AND MATHEMATICS

1. *Mathematics and the Brain*

INTRODUCTORY REMARKS

JEAN-PIERRE CHANGEUX: The first question we need to address is the nature of mathematical objects. Before tackling this question, which is fundamental to our discussion, we should perhaps say a few words about what brings us together in the first place.

Biology and mathematics have several things in common, it seems to me. My first real experience of mathematics, preparing for college, was made more difficult than it might have been by the fact that biology in those days was almost universally discredited by teachers of mathematics. Their poor opinion of the subject was shared, in turn, by some of the most renowned mathematicians. If you read René Thom, for example, you will find he denies that advances in biology have had any practical consequences, either by improving health or increasing longevity. He denies too that biologists have any need for theory. It may be that this urge to discredit biology is to be explained by the tendency of mathematicians to prefer rapid comprehension to slower, more wide-ranging, more imaginative—but possibly deeper—forms of reflection. At all events my first reaction was hostile. No doubt it disguised a desire to gain a better understanding of mathematics, and possibly one day to make a contribution of my own.

It was only in the context of my later research in molecular biology, and more recently in neurobiology, that I was to have the occasion to put mathematical tools to real use. Jacques Monod was an exceptional teacher in this regard. Together we were able to develop several models of specialized regulatory molecules called allosteric proteins. Mathematics permitted us to formulate our ideas in a precise way and to develop quantitative predictions. Today, in my work as a neurobiologist, mathematical tools are indispensable for constructing rigorous models of brain function.

(The problem of how the brain actually works is currently the object of a great deal of attention in cognitive science, which as you know is a field of multidisciplinary research that's been developing at the intersection of neuroscience, psychology and mathematics over the last couple of decades. Progress both now and in the years to come will almost surely continue to depend on close collaboration among theoreticians and experimentalists.) In a larger sense, my interest in mathematics springs from a curiosity about how the brain creates and uses mathematical objects, which is to say about the relation between mathematics and the brain. This question alone is enough to justify our conversation, I think.

But we shouldn't overlook the fact that mathematics also plays a central role in social life. Western culture itself is characterized by a sort of mathematical myth: the belief, descended perhaps from Pythagoras, in the explanatory and almost transcendent virtue of mathematics. In many areas, from syntactic structure to laws of inheritance, it is typically assumed that a mathematical description provides a satisfactory "explanation." As a practical matter, the computer and its many applications confer upon mathematics a unique, and growing, power. The Wall Street crash of 1987, to name just one example, was due in large part to computer-driven "program trading" designed to maximize the profits of investors. In this as in other cases, the computer seems to be taking the place of the human brain—but without matching its performance! This problem, marginal though its impact may be upon our work as scientists, leads us nonetheless to reflect upon the relation between mathematics and ethics, and to ask, in particular, whether a universal moral code of human society can be founded on the basis of mathematical rigor. More specifically still, would research into the neurocognitive bases of moral behavior be consistent with such a program, or would it represent an entirely separate enterprise?

These, at any rate, are some of my motivations as a biologist for entering into this conversation. What are yours as a mathematician?

ALAIN CONNES: I entirely share your enthusiasm for inquiring into the relationship between mathematics and the brain, and especially into the nature of mathematical objects. You cited René Thom in speaking of the historically antagonistic relationship between mathematics and biology. There's no question about his originality as a mathematician. But it would be a mistake to regard him as a spokesman for mathematical opinion. We'd do better to talk about someone like Israël Gelfand, who's had a considerable influence upon mathematics and who at the same time has devoted a great part of his scientific activity to biology. More than half of his published articles are devoted to this subject, and he regularly conducts two seminars, one in mathematics, the other in biology.

Reading your book *Neuronal Man*, I was surprised to realize just how much is understood about the brain. I was struck especially by the existence of perceptual maps—far more numerous in humans than in other animals—that connect the retina to different parts of the brain associated with different interpretive functions. I was impressed too by Shepard's mental rotation experiments, in which a subject is asked if two objects are the same after rotating them in three-dimensional space. They show that the response time is proportional to the angle of rotation, and thus that cerebral function obeys physical laws. But it seems to me important that we try to go beyond the field of biology in studying the brain. Mathematics provides a far more propitious ground for this research, I believe, because it is absolute, universal, and therefore independent of any cultural influence.

CHANGEUX: You're committing yourself to a certain position, you realize—

CONNES: Let me explain. On the one hand, every language expresses notions that depend on poorly defined premises—poorly defined to the degree they are culturally influenced. Mathematical objects, on the other hand—and this is what I hope to be able to show—enjoy a much greater purity. Precisely because they are untainted by cultural associations, they should enable us to form a better idea of how the brain actually functions.

But obviously my interest in the matter is prejudiced. I'd like to know enough about biology to be able to draw conclusions from it. That might be useful to me in my work as a mathematician. Your book prompted me to reflect upon the way in which the brain assimilates a new theory, or familiarizes itself with a new activity, such as playing chess or the piano. It made me reconsider certain quite fixed ideas I'd had about learning, and caused me to correct various misconceptions. For example, when one works in an area of mathematics where problems are neither too difficult nor too diffuse, it sometimes happens that one succeeds in mastering a precise technique. Because mathematics is so abstract, there's a danger one may come to believe that this mastery is permanent—that one no longer has to practice it in order to summon it whenever one wants. Your book made me see that this ability is probably localized in a specific area of the brain, and, for this very reason, is liable to atrophy: if the corresponding system of neurons isn't excited from time to time by using the technique that's been mastered, it wastes away.

CHANGEUX: In other words, past mathematical experience leaves a material trace.

CONNES: Exactly. It's as though it were necessary from time to time to open a drawer that's been closed for years, to prevent what's inside from disintegrating through disuse.

THE HIERARCHY OF THE SCIENCES IN QUESTION

CHANGEUX: I'd like us to touch on three themes to begin with: first, the relation of mathematics to the other sciences; next, the question of realism and constructivism; and finally, the relation between numbers and experience.

As for the status of mathematics vis-à-vis the other sciences, there are two schools of thought: that of Descartes and Leibniz on the one hand, and that of Diderot on the other. Both schools are alive and well today. For Descartes and Leibniz, mathematical truth illuminates the world and permits the whole of human knowledge to be unified: whatever the object of study, it always winds up leading back to mathematics in the end! The hierarchy of the sciences implied by this view constitutes the basis of the educational system in France even today. Diderot, though he was close to d'Alembert and other mathematicians of comparable distinction, rejected such a notion: mathematics, he argued, adds nothing to experience, serving only to place a "veil" between human beings and nature. And as early as 1623 we find Francis Bacon lamenting the fact that logic and mathematics, which he took to be the natural "servants of physics," should be misled by a false certitude into trying to impose a law of their own.

CONNES: It's common—and justified, it seems to me—to regard mathematics as a necessary language for the formalization of nearly all the other sciences. No matter whether the formalization is quantitative or qualitative, it will always be done using mathematics.

CHANGEUX: That's pretty much Descartes' and Leibniz's position.

CONNES: Yes, except that for them everything leads back to mathematics in the end, as you say. Physicists are fond of telling a story that suggests just the opposite. A physicist goes off to a conference. After a week his suit's gotten soiled and rumpled, so he goes out to look for a dry cleaner. Walking down the main street of town, he comes upon a store with a lot of signs out front. One of them says "Dry Cleaning." So he goes in with his dirty suit and asks when he can come back to pick it up. The mathematician who owns the shop replies, "I'm terribly sorry, but we don't do dry cleaning." "What?" exclaims the puzzled physicist. "The sign outside says 'Dry Cleaning'!" "We don't clean anything here," replies the mathematician. "We only sell signs!"

The point of the story, of course, is that words by themselves aren't enough. Physicists may use mathematics as a language, but the actual content of their science can't be reduced to mathematics alone.

CHANGEUX: Mathematics is a more rigorous language—no more, no less.

CONNES: There's more to it than that. For one thing, a result in physics can't be reduced to its mere mathematical expression. The physicist often employs imprecise hypotheses that originate in what might be called "physical intuition." These allow one, in particular, to neglect certain quantities or make approximations that a mathematician would have a hard time guessing at. For example, it took some twenty years (between roughly 1930 and 1950) for physicists to work out the method of renormalization in quantum field theory. This consists in calculating a perturbative expansion whereby all terms of second order and above yield divergent integrals. Motivated by the extraordinary precision of experimental results in spectroscopy at the end of the 1940s—the discovery of the fine structure of atomic emission spectra and so forth—physicists were desperately searching for a way to draw a finite result from these divergent integrals. Restricting the domain of integration to energies of the order of mc^2, where m is the mass of the electron and c the speed of light, they were able by means of unjustified subtractions to obtain a finite result very close to the experimental result. This technique was progressively improved by Tomonaga, Schwinger, Feynman and Dyson, until finally agreement with the experimental result was achieved with a degree of precision corresponding to the thickness of a human hair divided by the distance between Paris and New York.

What was the role of physical intuition in their reasoning? Renormalization is a device that consists, for purposes of calculation, in changing the mass of the electron and replacing it by a quantity that depends on the order of magnitude of the energies in question, but diverges when this order of magnitude tends toward infinity. To take a very simple comparison, if a balloon filled with helium leaves the ground at an instant $t = 0$, calculating its acceleration by the Archimedean law doesn't yield the experimentally observed result. The presence of a field—the ambient air—is effectively equivalent to replacing the bare mass of the balloon in the calculation by a much greater effective mass. From this comparison one can guess that the electron, placed in the electromagnetic field, possesses an effective mass quite different from its bare mass, which is to say the one that enters into the mathematical equation. Thanks to this intuition physicists have been able to develop a method—renormalization—that is, of course, formulated in mathematical language but that would hardly have been discovered by mathematicians confronted with the same problem. Moreover, this intuition authorizes physicists to take liberties with mathematical rigor. Feynman's integral, for example, even though it doesn't presently correspond to any precise mathematical object, serves nonetheless as the daily bread of theoretical physics.

The second thing I want to draw your attention to is this: mathematics, in connection with physics, doesn't only play the role of a language used to express results. It surely does have this function when it's a case of modeling a rather primitive theory; but at a more developed stage, as in the case of quantum mechanics, the generative character of mathematics comes to play a crucial role as well. What physicist wouldn't feel troubled contemplating the extraordinary fact that Mendeleev's periodic table of the elements can be recovered using only Schrödinger's equation and Pauli's exclusion principle? It's this sort of thing that leads the mathematician to believe that physics can be reduced to a certain number of equations. Very often, however, it's the physicist's intuition that makes it possible to understand these equations in the first place.

CHANGEUX: You mean it's the experimental context in physics that permits mathematical objects to be created. After all, an equation doesn't just fall out of the sky one fine day! It's a part of the history of a physicist's relationship with his object. Over time one forges a mathematical tool adapted to the problem one's set for oneself.

CONNES: No, that's not what I mean. It may happen that a mathematician manipulates objects that have a physical meaning. But if one's not fully conscious of the manner in which these objects have historically been introduced, one runs a great risk as a mathematician of committing errors that a physicist wouldn't make. To say that mathematics forms a language that contains exactly what physicists have discovered would amount to a kind of exaggerated authoritarianism. Now, it may be that physicists balk at expressing their insights in a sufficiently precise mathematical manner for fear of impoverishing them. But certain recent developments in the interpretation of quantum mechanics, for instance, show that the attempt at mathematical formalization may make it possible to avoid paradoxes that often are due to some inadequacy in the language used by physicists, or to a lack of reflection upon the logic itself.

CHANGEUX: Mathematical language is plainly an authentic language. But is it therefore the *only* authentic language?

CONNES: It is unquestionably the only *universal* language. To see why this is so, let's imagine how we might try to communicate with an alien intelligence on another planet or in another solar system. It's obvious that these beings wouldn't speak any of the languages we do; moreover, they probably wouldn't live in an atmosphere composed of the mixture of oxygen and nitrogen that supports human speech.

CHANGEUX: But in order for us to communicate with them, would their mathematics have to be the same as ours?

CONNES: I'm convinced it would have to be. I believe furthermore that mathematics would be the best way of communicating with them. Imagine if we were to try transmitting the list of integers, say from 1 to 100. We'd send the following signal: a dash, followed by a long silence, then two dashes and a long silence, then three dashes and a long silence, and so on. Once this list was transmitted, we would communicate to them the law of addition. The only elements subject to variation are the number of dashes and the interval of time separating one from the other. To communicate $3 + 2 = 5$, for example, the message would be: three consecutive dashes, a silence, two consecutive dashes, a double silence, and five dashes. Of course we'd have to take care to avoid ambiguity, but in principle it would be possible to communicate the addition and multiplication tables in this way, at least within reasonable limits. The main problem would be how to make sure they had understood. One way would be to send them an incomplete addition. The trouble is that we'd have to wait thousands of years to receive an answer! A positive response would nonetheless provide incontestable proof of the existence of another intelligence beyond our solar system. Having established this much, we could then move to a higher level. We could transmit the series of prime numbers, let's say from 1 to 1,000, and ask them for the next one. A precise scheme for communication along these lines has been given, in fact, by Freudenthal.

CHANGEUX: As you say, we'd have to wait a long time before being able to decide the question. And even if the message were to get through, what would it prove? I'm afraid I can't agree with you when you claim that these beings wouldn't speak any of the languages we speak, but that they would use the same mathematics. In all probability there are a small number of fundamental cerebral processes common to the use of every human language, including mathematics. If these extraterrestrials were to use "human mathematics," that would mean they possessed a nervous system, a brain, very similar to ours.

INVENTION OR DISCOVERY?

CHANGEUX: Let's move on to the nature of mathematical objects. Here there are two diametrically opposed positions: "realism" and "constructivism." For the realist, who traces a direct line of intellectual descent from Plato, the world is populated by Ideas having a reality distinct from sensible reality (figure 1). A great many contemporary mathematicians call themselves realists. Dieudonné explicitly remarks the connection with Plato. No less distinguished a mathematician than Cantor talks about mathematics as the creation of a God whose highest perfection is manifested in the ability to create an infinite set. This is pure *mathesis divina*—pure metaphysics! It's amazing to hear serious scientists say such things. Even Descartes appeals to metaphysics in connection with geometry when he speaks of a triangle as an "immutable and eternal" figure, whose existence is independent of the mind that imagines it. For the constructivist, on the other hand, mathematical objects are creatures of reason that exist solely in the mind of the mathematician, not in some platonic

Figure 1. Plato's Allegory of the Cave
    Engraving from the seventeenth century illustrating a celebrated passage from Plato's *Republic*, in which Socrates and Glaucon inquire into the "reality" of the shadows projected on the walls of the cavern compared with that of the objects casting them. For Plato, appearance is only the shadow of reality, Ideas having an existence independent of the rest of the world. (Plate by Jean-Loup Charmet, Prints Division, Bibliotèque Nationale, Paris)

world independent of matter. They exist in the neurons and synapses of the mathematicians who produce them, and in those of other people who understand and employ them. We find this point of view, albeit taken to an extreme, in empiricist philosophers such as Locke and Hume. Hume, for example, holds that ideas are mere copies of sense impressions. For him, the objects of geometry arise exclusively from experience. Where do you situate yourself in relation to these two quite opposite points of view?

CONNES: I think I'm fairly close to the realist point of view. Take prime numbers, for example, which, as far as I'm concerned, constitute a more stable reality than the material reality that surrounds us. The working mathematician can be likened to an explorer who sets out to discover the world. One discovers basic facts from experience. In doing simple calculations, for example, one realizes that the series of prime numbers seems to go on without end. The mathematician's job, then, is to demonstrate that there exists an infinity of prime numbers. This is, of course, an old result due to Euclid. One of the most interesting consequences of this proof is that if someone claims one day to have found the greatest prime number, it will be easy to show that he's wrong. The same is true for any proof. We run up therefore against a reality every bit as incontestable as physical reality.

The mathematician fashions what may be called *thought tools* for the purpose of investigating mathematical reality. These are not to be confused with mathematical reality itself. The decimal system, for example, is a familiar thought tool, but it would be wrong to attribute significance to the numerals that appear in a number. (Consider that very soon we will be celebrating the year 2000. The importance of this number is a purely cultural phenomenon: in mathematics, the number 2,000 is utterly devoid of interest!) Among the many methods at the disposal of the mathematician for exploring mathematical reality, I think especially of axiomatization. It allows classification problems to be posed for mathematical objects defined by very simple conditions. Thus it is known, for example, how to determine exactly the list of all finite fields. A finite field is a finite set provided with a law of addition and multiplication such that every nonzero number has a reciprocal. The rules governing addition and multiplication are the same as the usual ones for the addition and multiplication of rational or of real numbers. It can be shown that for every prime number p and every integer n there exists one and only one finite field having p^n elements, and that any finite field belongs to that list. A theorem of this sort gives assurance that a particular region of mathematics has been explored in its furthest recesses, at least as far as the list of objects is concerned—entirely explored, without material support.

CHANGEUX: It seems to me, to the contrary, that mathematical objects exist materially in your brain. You examine them inwardly by a conscious process, in the physiological sense of the term.

Because these objects have a material reality, it's possible to study their properties. You've mentioned the case of mental rotations, and the case of objects our brain treats in a physical manner. Our brain is a complex physical object. As such, it constructs "representations" corresponding to physical states. In the head of a mathematician, mathematical objects are material objects— "mental objects," if you like—with properties that are analyzable by a reflexive process. This process may very well make appeal to other rather more ordinary mathematical objects, which you call "tools." But I don't consider them radically different in kind, even though their level of complexity, or abstraction, may differ. At bottom, mathematical work requires the cerebral faculties of reasoning and logic, which seem to me directly linked to the organization of our brain and which already existed, at least partially, in the brain of *Homo erectus* when he devised techniques for carving stone tools (figure 2). These "mathematical objects" correspond to physical states of our brain in such a way that it ought *in principle* to be possible to observe them from the outside looking in, using various methods of brain imaging, such as PET (positron emission tomography) scans, MRIs (magnetic resonance images), or EEGs (electroencephalographic recordings). Their resolution in time and/or space isn't sharp enough to really let us do that, but the basic idea is sound.

CONNES: It might also be an illusion—like believing that if we only knew more about the chemistry of ink and paper we would have a better understanding of the works of Shakespeare. If one accepts the existence of a mathematical reality independent of the human brain, it becomes necessary to sharply distinguish this reality from the manner in which it is apprehended. It's clear that in apprehending it our brain forms a mental image, as it does of a physical object, at least for ordinary geometry based on real numbers and Euclidean space. But by means of the axiomatic method, to mention only one among many, the mathematician can venture well beyond this familiar country. How is a mental image formed in such regions? Let's take an example. We know the complete classification of local fields. We know how to determine all such

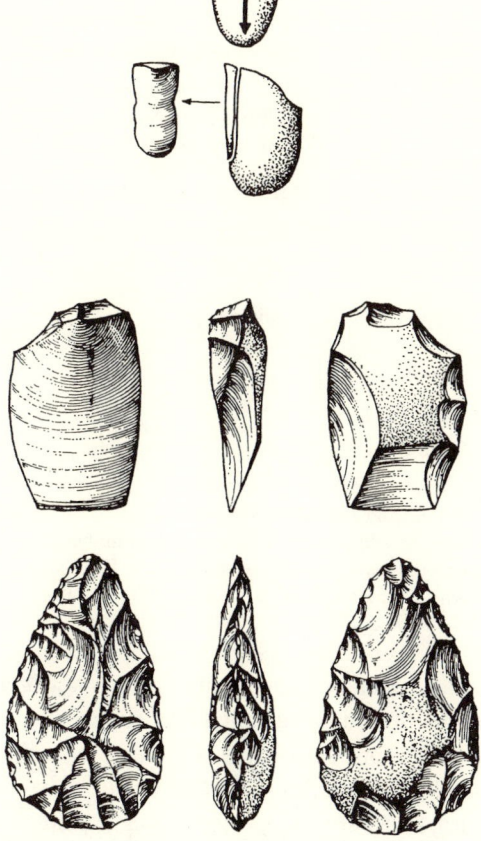

Figure 2. Archeological Evidence of the Evolution of Cognitive Abilities

The ancestors of *Homo sapiens* developed methods for carving tools from stone that required both motor skill and a high degree of precision in carrying out manual tasks. The faculties of representation and of logical reasoning were already very developed in *Homo erectus*, who about four hundred thousand years ago fabricated these tools and domesticated fire; a mild asymmetry between the impressions of the left and right hemisphere on the bones of the skull suggests that *Homo erectus* already had the use of speech. (After A. Leroi-Gourhan, *Le geste et la parole* [Paris: Albin Michel, 1964])

Real number in dyadic notation	10,010110100010 . . .
Addition of two real numbers	10,0101101000100 . . . + 1,1001001100110 . . . = 11,1110110101010

. . . 0010001011010,01	*p*-adic number (*p* = 2)
. . . 0010001011010,01 . . . 0110011001001,1 +	Addition of two *p*-adic numbers (*p* = 2)
. . . 1000100100011,11	

Figure 3. Addition of Real and *P*-adic Numbers
This figure compares the addition of two real numbers in dyadic (i.e., base 2) notation and the addition of 2-adic numbers. The connectivity of the real numbers is established by identities of the form 0,00111111 . . . = 0,0100000 . . .

fields: a local field is a locally compact space with a law of addition and a law of multiplication such that every nonzero element has a reciprocal. The simplest example is the field of real numbers, which underlies physical models. But there are others, which at first glance look very strange, called *p*-adic fields, where *p* is a prime number (figure 3). I won't give the complete list of such fields: so far only two local fields have been used in physical models, the fields of real and complex numbers; for the others, the usual mental images based on physics don't help. You can calculate with numbers such as the *p*-adics, but instead of working from left to right it's as though you were working from right to left. The size or magnitude of a number no longer corresponds to the usual notion. These calculations can be carried out by a computer as well as by the human brain, but it's difficult to come up with a simple physical model that supplies a mental image for them. My own view is that the adaptative capabilities of the brain actually permit it to develop an intuition that doesn't arise from physical reality but that is nonetheless well suited to the mathematical problem at hand.

CHANGEUX: It seems to me you don't distinguish clearly enough between mathematical objects themselves and their properties. These objects are new constructions, conceived by the mathematician in advance of examining all their properties. Initially they take the form of "conjectures," or "postulates," which may or may not be provable. It's at this stage of conjecture, in the initially postulated structure, that we're confronted with the nature of mathematical objects. John Stuart Mill was perhaps the first to argue that in defining a number we enunciate a *physical* fact. There's nothing surprising in the integers possessing this or that property, because they are contained in the definition that the mathematician proposes, working from intuition. But it takes time to recognize these properties. Axiomatization, logic, and all the related cerebral functions therefore play a crucial role in the task of *analysis* and *deduction*: they serve as a *logical apparatus*. But one of the most striking features of the human cerebral machine is its ability to create new mental objects, above and beyond the ability to analyze properties that often seem, at least in retrospect, to be extremely simple.

CONNES: In elementary school, children are taught addition, multiplication, and division of real numbers. It would be far more difficult to teach them to manipulate p-adic numbers, for example. Why? Because they'd be forced to leave behind all contact with physical reality—one of the most important hurdles that has to be cleared in learning how to do mathematics. Once you lose the immediate sense of magnitude, you have to rely solely on calculation. You run up against a reality that's no longer the tangible reality of an isosceles or some other triangle, but something much stronger. For instance, if you perform a calculation in two different ways, without arriving at the same result, you experience a very real sense of frustration. For me, this is what mathematical reality is all about: there exists, quite inexplicably, a coherence independent of our system of sensory perception, which guarantees that if one works correctly, one will always detect mistakes—a coherence that entirely surpasses the coherence yielded by sensible intuition, the direct intuition of phenomena.

CHANGEUX: The fact that this coherence hasn't yet been explained doesn't prove that it's *unexplainable*—still less, as you claim, that it's independent of our system of reasoning.

MATHEMATICS HAS A HISTORY

CHANGEUX: I therefore remain doubtful that mathematical objects exist "somewhere in the universe," independently of all material and cerebral support, as you would have it. It would be useful, I think, if we were to try to achieve a certain distance from the work of the mathematician, and, in particular, from the objects that he constructs. This requires setting mathematical objects in the historical context in which they appeared. Mathematics is taught in school as a coherent set of propositions, theorems, axioms. One forgets that these have appeared successively in the course of the history of mathematics and of human society—in short, that they are cultural objects subject to evolution. Putting mathematical objects back in historical perspective "secularizes" them, shows them to be more contingent that they appear. One comes to see that theories succeed one another, and that some of them manage to cast new light without invalidating their predecessors. This is the case, for example, with non-Euclidean geometries. The axioms of Euclidean geometry form a coherent whole. Here we find ourselves unmistakably in the presence of that remarkable coherence that so astonishes you, that seems to you to render the whole of mathematics independent of material support, to use your own term. This independence was finally shown to be illusory with the development of non-Euclidean geometries during the nineteenth century—

CONNES: But they did nothing to disturb the coherence of Euclidean geometry! Your example can be used, to the contrary, to show the power and fecundity of axiomatic tools. At first Euclidean geometry was understood through physical experimentation. Euclid proposed a certain number of axioms by means of which deductive proofs could be carried out. One of them looked as though it might be superfluous: the axiom of a unique line parallel to a given line passing through a given point. For a time it seemed possible to show that it wasn't needed, that it followed from the others. Amazingly, however, it was precisely as a result of trying to show the necessity of this axiom that non-Euclidean geometries were discovered. For a good part of the nineteenth century, these geometries were considered esoteric by mathematicians— Gauss even hesitated to publish his results for fear of being disbelieved—until Poincaré realized that non-Euclidean geometry was an extraordinary tool, even for solving problems in number theory, which he had worked on separately from his interest in geometry. Using this tool he was able to derive his theory of Fuchsian functions. How then were non-Euclidean geometries arrived at? Not because someone established that the space in which we live fails to conform to Euclidean geometry, but simply because of an axiomatic problem and the attempt to characterize the geometry by a small number of axioms.

CHANGEUX: That hardly proves the immateriality of mathematical objects! For me, the axiomatic method is the expression of cognitive faculties, which themselves are a function of cerebral faculties connected with the use of human language. For what characterizes language is precisely its *generative* character.

CONNES: Here we come upon a characteristic peculiar to mathematics that is very difficult to explain. Often it's possible, though only after considerable effort, to compile a list of mathematical objects defined by very simple conditions. Intuitively one believes that the list is complete, and searches for a general proof of its exhaustiveness. New objects are frequently discovered in just this way, as a result of trying to show that the list is exhausted. Take the example of finite groups. The notion of a finite group is elementary, almost on the same level as that of an integer. A finite group is the group of symmetries of a finite object. Mathematicians have struggled to classify the finite simple groups, that is to say the finite groups that (like the prime numbers to some extent) can't be decomposed into smaller groups. This is an extremely difficult problem. Galois showed that for $n \geq 5$ the group of even permutations of a set of n elements is simple. The French mathematician Claude Chevalley constructed series of finite simple groups that resemble what we now call Lie group series. It then became possible therefore to hope that no finite simple groups existed beyond these and the ones discovered by Mathieu in the nineteenth century. In trying to demonstrate this, and thanks in particular to the work of our colleague J. Tits, some twenty groups were discovered that weren't contained in Chevalley's list. They are known as the *sporadic groups*. Fifteen years ago the last finite simple group—the "Monster"—was discovered by purely mathematical reasoning. It is a finite group with a considerable number of elements:

$$808017424794512875886459904961710757005754368000000000$$

It has now at last been shown, as a result of heroic efforts, that the list of twenty-six finite simple sporadic groups is indeed complete (figure 4).

CHANGEUX: I don't see how exhausting all the possibilities shows that the object in question is somehow an "ideality" that preexists man. Take a regular object, a cube or a pyramid of rock salt, for example. It's obvious that its properties will rapidly be exhausted. That doesn't prove, Descartes notwithstanding, that its properties are of an "immutable and eternal" sort that don't in any way depend upon our brain. When the mathematician elaborates rules of logical coherence, rules of exclusion—in short, a formalism—he is constructing a universal language that permits him to recognize properties of the object he constructed in the first place. In the end he "discovers" only the consequences of what he himself has conjured up! He reveals what the philosopher Gilles-Gaston Granger calls its "formal content." No one—no one who's not a religious believer at least—is going to say that the Word comes before Matter.

The finite simple groups are as follows:

* Cyclic groups of prime order
* Alternating groups of degree 5 or more
* Chevalley's groups and Tit's group
* The twenty-six sporadic groups

THE SPORADIC GROUPS

Group	Order	Investigator
M_{11}	$2^4.3^2.5.11$	Mathieu
M_{12}	$2^6.3^3.5.11$	Mathieu
M_{22}	$2^7.3^3.5.7.11$	Mathieu
M_{23}	$2^7.3^2.5.7.11.23$	Mathieu
M_{24}	$2^{10}.3^3.5.7.11.23$	Mathieu
J	$2^7.3^3.5^2.7$	Hall, Jenko
Suz	$2^{13}.3^7.5^2.7.11.13$	Suzuki
HS	$2^9.3^2.5^3.7.11$	Higman, Sims
McL	$2^7.3^6.5^3.7.11$	McLaughlin
Co_3	$2^{10}.3^7.5^3.7.11.23$	Conway
Co_2	$2^{18}.3^6.5^3.7.11.23$	Conway
Co_1	$2^{21}.3^9.5^4.7^2.11.13.23$	Conway, Leech
He	$2^{10}.3^3.5^2.7^3.17$	Held/Higman, McKay
Fi_{22}	$2^{17}.3^9.5^2.7.11.13$	Fischer
Fi_{23}	$2^{18}.3^{13}.5^2.7.11.13.17.23$	Fischer
Fi_{24}	$2^{21.3^{16}}.5^2.7^3.11.13.17.23.29$	Fischer
HN	$2^{14}.3^6.5^6.7.11.19$	Harada, Norton/Smith
Th	$2^{15}.3^{10}.5^3.7^2.13.19.31$	Thompson/Smith
B	$2^{41}.3^{13}.5^6.7^2.11.13.17.19.23.31.47$	Fischer/Sims, Leon
M	$2^{46}.3^{20}.5^9.7^6.11^2.13^3.$ $17.19.23.29.31.41.47.59.71$	Fischer, Griess
J	$2^3.3.5.7.11.19$	Janko
$O'N$	$2^9.3^4.7^3.5.11.19.31$	O'Nan/Sims
J_3	$2^7.3^5.5.17.19$	Janko/Higman, McKay
Ly	$2^8.3^7.5^6.7.11.31.37.67$	Lyons/Sims
Ru	$2^{14}.3^3.5^{34}.7.13.29$	Rudvalis/Conway, Wales
J_4	$2^{21}.3^3.5.7.11^3.23.29.31.37.43$	Janko/Norton, Parker, Benson, Conway, Thackray

Figure 4. Finite Groups

Definitions: a finite group G is specified by a finite set G and a law of multiplication, that is, a map from $G \times G$ to G denoted $(g_1, g_2) \to g_1 g_2$ such that: 1) $g_1 (g_2 g_3) = (g_1 g_2) g_3$ for all $g_i \in G$; 2) there exists an $e \in G$ such that $eg = ge = g$ for all g in G; 3) for all $g \in G$ there exists $g_{-1} \in G$ such that $g g_{-1} = g_{-1} g = e$. A homeomorphism of a group G_1 in a group G_2 is a map f of the set G_1 to the set G_2 such that $f(g_1 g_2) = f(g_1) f(g_2) \; \forall \; g_1, g_2 \in G$. A finite group G is simple if and only if every homeomorphism of G to another group G' is either constant or injective.

IS MATHEMATICS MERELY A LANGUAGE?

CHANGEUX: When we speak, we manipulate concepts. You describe a series of logical steps, that is to say mental or cerebral procedures, operating on concrete objects that you picture to yourself. One thinks of the Greek geometer who drew simple figures in the sand and studied their properties. Nothing in what you say persuades me of the reality of these objects outside our brain and its projections. Even if you were to succeed in specifying their number or their nature in a perfectly coherent and organized manner, I wouldn't be convinced. Your arguments tend, to the contrary, to empty mathematical objects of all reality—"reality" in the platonic sense of the term. You maintain that mathematics is one among several elementary languages, constituting perhaps the purified synthesis of these languages, a sort of universal language. But no one imagines for a moment that Chinese or Russian came into existence prior to the emergence of the human species on earth—why then entertain such a metaphysical proposition with regard to mathematics?

CONNES: You say that nothing proves the reality of these objects outside our brain. Let's compare mathematical reality with the material world that surrounds us. What proves the reality of the material world, apart from our brain's perception of it? Chiefly the coherence of our perceptions, and their permanence—more precisely, the coherence of touch and sight that characterizes the perceptions of a single person, and the coherence that characterizes the perceptions of several persons. And so it is with mathematical reality: a calculation carried out in several different ways gives the same result, whether it's done by one person or several. The truth of Euclid's theorem about prime numbers doesn't depend on such-and-such a mode of perception. While it's true that mathematics is used as a language by the other sciences, reducing it to a mere language would be a serious mistake—which is why the comparison with Chinese or Russian seems to me unjustified. The exploration of mathematical reality began in areas where the mental imagery connected with the real world is very simple, as in the case of Euclidean geometry. Next, whether as a result of axiomatic procedures or of specific problems suggested by number theory, access was obtained to regions far more removed from material reality. The reality one meets with in such regions, however, is every bit as solid as that of daily life. It's just harder to grasp.

Your resistance to this idea leads me to suggest the following allegory. Imagine I live in a village that I am unable to leave, a dozen kilometers away from which there stands an immense tower. If I were the only blind man in the village, my neighbors would spend a great deal of time describing this tower to me. They wouldn't doubt its existence in the slightest. But I could deny it altogether, spending just as much time trying to explain to them that it's only a mental construction useful for explaining certain visual phenomena that don't concern me. And so it is, unfortunately, that so long as one isn't confronted with mathematical reality, there's no risk in denying its existence.

CHANGEUX: I'd say that this "coherence of perception" of the outside world is due instead to your cerebral apparatus—but at a lower *level of abstraction* than that of mathematical objects. That universal properties can be recognized in mathematical objects no more proves their independence of the human brain than the existence of the word "state" or of the word "happiness"—except that mathematical concepts have a more precise and restrictive definition, on account of which they possess better defined, more "universal" properties.

It needs to be said too that you frequently rely on metaphor. You compare mathematical research to the exploration of a continent, or of a village with its streets and tower. While this metaphor brings the discussion down from the level of abstract mathematics to a lower level, a more concrete and more vivid level, it's one that can't possibly be taken literally. A metaphor has no demonstrative value whatsoever. What's worse, you play upon multiple *and* contradictory senses of the words "realism" and "reality." "Realism" is, first of all, the platonic doctrine according to which *Ideas* belong to a world distinct from the material world, existing on a higher plane than individual sentient beings, who constitute mere reflections and images of them. But realism is also the doctrine according to which being is independent of the actual knowledge that conscious subjects have of it. A "realist," in this sense, is someone who postulates a difference in kind between being and thought: that is, being can neither be deduced from thought nor explained adequately and exhaustively in logical terms. Alas, your metaphors take you directly from the first to the third of these senses, when these senses are contradictory!

For my part, I mainly use the word "realism," or the term "reality," in a nonplatonic sense as a sort of compromise between the two other definitions. For me, matter in all its different states, humanity included, exists independently of human thought and of the actual knowledge that conscious subjects have of it. But human thought, which is itself the expression of a particular state of matter, seeks to describe this "in itself," this *ultima actualis*; it tries, in the light of experience, to give an evolutionary (though not necessarily exhaustive) definition of itself. I make therefore a very clear distinction between the reality of matter and what you call "mathematical reality." The existence of this latter sort seems to me connected with human thought, which itself is a product of the evolution of the human species.

2. Plato as Materialist?

THE INTELLECTUAL ASCESIS OF
THE MATERIALIST

CHANGEUX: Your claims about the nature of mathematical objects seem a bit paradoxical: you defend a platonist point of view, all the while insisting upon the materialist basis of your position. Perhaps then we should first of all take a closer look at what materialism, or rather the materialist method, involves. As J. T. Desanti has shown, it involves an attempt at explanation based on a minimum of laws, limited if possible to those of physics and chemistry. Materialism therefore supposes an *emendatio intellectus*, to use Spinoza's term, a reshaping of understanding that takes the form of an act of self-discipline—an "intellectual ascesis," if you will—by which one tries to eliminate the mythic residues of platonism, and all remaining traces of transcendence left by other metaphysical doctrines.

The materialist program aims at reintegrating man with nature. In Desanti's terms, this requires constructing models of reality that invariably contain a meticulously assembled submodel. This submodel, which links the larger model to those aspects of physical reality that it seeks to explain, he calls the *knowledge acquisition apparatus*. For the neurobiologist, of course, the apparatus that permits reality to be captured, that permits scientific models to be constructed, is the brain. Desanti, a philosopher of mathematics, unambiguously poses the problem of the nature of mathematics in neurobiological terms. But he considers this a utopian project, and calls the construction of an adequate model of the knowledge acquisition apparatus itself "chimerical." Accordingly he concludes that a weak materialist epistemology is the best that can be hoped for. His surrender is due to an ignorance of neuroscience, sadly frequent among philosophers, but also, it should be said, to the limitations of neuroscience, and of cognitive science more generally, at the time Desanti was writing—limitations that, I must admit, have yet to be completely overcome.

I defend, by contrast, a strong (though I like to think enlightened) materialist epistemology. I defend it for the simple reason that it seems to me the best one available to the informed scientist. It isn't by any means a new program. Its earliest formulation is due to Democritus, the pre-Socratic philosopher who, according to legend, always wore a smile (figure 5). Scientists throughout history have had the courage to adopt this way of looking at the world in spite of the persecution they experienced: Vanini, burned at the stake by the Inquisition in 1619 at Toulouse, the anatomist Vesalius, and, of course, Galileo—to name only three of the many victims of a special form of intolerance that has survived until the present day.

Therefore it's necessary for us to examine the internal workings of the knowledge acquisition apparatus, and to try to describe its products. Following Desanti, we may define cerebral function as proceeding by means of a mechanism of abstraction that constructs types and classes of objects out of the sensible material that the world provides. One of the main tasks facing the neurobiologist is to show how the human brain generates objects—among them, mathematical objects. If this can be done, the case for a strong materialist epistemology can begin to be made. What's your reaction to a program of this sort?

CONNES: Let me summarize my point of view. I hold on the one hand that there exists, independently of the human mind, a raw and immutable mathematical reality; and, on the other hand, that as human beings we have access to it only by means of our brain—at the price, in Valéry's memorable phrase, of "a rare mixture of concentration and desire." I therefore dissociate mathematical reality from the tool we have for exploring it. I grant that the brain is a tool of investigation, that it has nothing of the divine about it, that it owes nothing to any transcendence whatsoever. The better we understand how it functions, the better we can use it. But for all that mathematical reality will not be affected in the least, any more than the list of prime numbers—only the sum of our knowledge will be altered. If I were indifferent to the materi-

Figure 5. Democritus

Born sometime between 470–456 B.C. at Abdera, an Ionian colony where Greek and oriental cultures came into contact, Democritus lived to a great age (at least 90—according to some accounts, 109). A contemporary of Socrates, he was (with Leucippus) the founder of atomism and (as Nietzsche argued) the first rationalist thinker to have succeeded in eliminating all mythic elements from his thought. He is traditionally represented with a smile, the sign of his joy at having triumphed over irrational fears and superstitions. (Musée du Louvre: after a color engraving in the Réunion des Musées Nationaux based on the 1692 portrait by Antoine Coypel) alist point of view, I could easily claim that a better understanding of the physical and biological function of the brain contributes nothing to the understanding of the human mind. But that's not at all my position. That the two should go together seems to me perfectly reasonable.

CHANGEUX: The word "independent" needs to be defined precisely. In the context of platonic realism, it signifies immateriality. How can you assert that these mathematical objects exist independently of the human brain—that they are immaterial—and at the same time declare yourself a materialist? I have a hard time, for example, imagining that integers exist in nature. If they did, why wouldn't we see "$\pi = 3.1416$" written in gold letters in the sky, or "6.02×10^{23}" appear in the reflections of a crystal ball? Atoms exist in nature—but Bohr's atom doesn't! A hen might be able to reckon the number of eggs she's laid, or, likelier perhaps, form some idea of the space they take up in the nest; but surely she doesn't know how to count to one hundred, or how to define the properties of the integers. Mathematics seems to me to constitute instead a formal language with its own syntax and semantics, one that's simplified to the maximum degree possible and that's peculiar to the human species.

CONNES: We've got to be careful, I think, not to confuse mathematical reality with evidence of mathematical regularities in the world. When I speak of the independent existence of mathematical reality, I expressly do *not* locate it in physical reality. A certain number of physical models, it's true, use mathematics to describe natural phenomena, but it would be a grievous error to try to reduce mathematics to these phenomena. The mathematician develops a special sense, I think—irreducible to sight, hearing, or touch—that allows him to perceive a reality every bit as constraining as physical reality, but one that's far more stable than physical reality for not being located in space-time. Exploring the geography of mathematics, little by little the mathematician perceives the contours and structure of an incredibly rich world. Gradually he develops a sensitivity to the notion of simplicity that opens up access to new, wholly unsuspected regions of the mathematical landscape.

CHANGEUX: Your principal argument, then, is simplicity. But wouldn't it also be fair to say, for example, that the theme of Beethoven's Seventh Symphony is a melody of extreme simplicity?

CONNES: Yes, but in that case the rest of the symphony isn't necessary. That's the difference.

CHANGEUX: But it's your brain that produces the necessity! *You're* the one who creates this simplicity, every time you're confronted by your mental representations (whether they're representations of ideas or of natural objects), every time you recognize the adequacy or inadequacy of these representations with the aid of the special sense you mention—which I consider a product of our cerebral faculties. What proof is there that this simplicity has an immaterial origin?

CONNES: The difference with a symphony by Beethoven is the following: in mathematics one can prove—truly prove, once a problem has been properly posed (as in the case, for example, of finite fields)—that the complete list of objects searched for has been found. But there's no theorem that permits the rest of Beethoven's symphony to be deduced from its first theme.

CHANGEUX: That's an important difference, it's true. But we find this "generative" property of mathematics in another form: in musical notation—in particular in Bach, but also in Boulez and other contemporary composers. It also constitutes one of the characteristic traits of human language, the simplest expression of which is syntax. Concepts themselves can actually be said to possess a certain generativity. Consider, for example, the concept of liberty. Even though it's not a mathematical concept, it nonetheless had considerable generative power at the time of the French Revolution, and it retains that power today. How many new concepts, how many new rights and laws has it given birth to! Over the last two centuries it has triggered waves of social realignments and challenges to the structure of the state throughout the world. For all that, no one will say that "liberty" exists in nature independently of humanity. The mathematical demonstration you offer is clearly much more rigorous, closed, complete, coherent, and so on, than what history has been able to draw from the concept of liberty. But isn't this concept comparable in its abstraction to that of the integers? Leaving aside, of course, the different consequences that each entails, why should we suppose their *natures* are so profoundly different?

CONNES: Again, let's not confuse the tool with the reality that it's being used to study. The concept of liberty has been developed over time by the human mind to account for certain features of human behavior. I don't doubt their reality! In much the same way, the mathematician fashions tools such as the axiomatic method, or concepts such as general topology or probability, in the hope of being able to better understand the prime numbers, for example. But the progressive elaboration of concepts and methods of investigation doesn't alter the reality of these numbers in the slightest. It simply permits us to understand them better. Your unwillingness to admit the existence of mathematical reality arises in part from a confusion between conceptual tools and reality, and in part from the existence of a very partial physical illustration of mathematics.

CHANGEUX: I can hardly be accused of confusing conceptual tools with "reality"—in the sense in which I employ the word. For me, such tools serve to study the semantic *properties* of objects produced by the mathematician's brain, which I regard as having an authentic physical reality. On the other hand, I don't consider the axiomatic *method* to be a concept. It is a cerebral *process*—unlike the concept of an integer, which is just that: a concept, a simplified mental representation, whose properties are easily recognized. To my way of thinking, "liberty" is an authentic concept that's not in any sense comparable to the axiomatic method.

THE PSYCHOANALYSIS OF MATHEMATICS

CONNES: One of the essential things a mathematician does is recognize the internal coherence and generative character belonging to certain concepts. It happens that very simple concepts can suggest all sorts of ideas or models. Investigating these, one truly has the impression of exploring a world step by step—and of connecting up the steps so well, so coherently, that one knows it has been entirely explored. How could one *not* feel that such a world has an independent existence?

CHANGEUX: "Feel," you say? Do you consider mathematics to be more a matter of feeling than of reflection?

CONNES: More a matter of intuition—laboriously constructed intuition, I should add. My attitude derives partly from the frustration I often experience when faced with partial and contradictory solutions to a problem. But it also derives from direct contact with mathematical objects, which gives rise to an intuition that's obviously distinct from our intuition of natural phenomena. Realism and materialism don't strike me as being the irreconcilable doctrines you assert them to be. (The term "realism," by the way, is to be preferred to your misleading "platonism.") What price is there to pay for accepting the independent existence of mathematical reality as a working hypothesis? None at all that I can see—still less considering the additional advantage it offers of enabling us to entertain the possibility that mathematical concepts can be communicated from one civilization to another.

CHANGEUX: The real price to be paid is that it makes it harder to understand how our knowledge acquisition apparatus produces mathematical knowledge! I wonder actually to what extent the independence you insist upon isn't due simply to the fact that we're talking about a very particular kind of cultural object—particular in that they can be transmitted from one person to another, regardless of culture: a sort of universal semantics, limited (as far as we can tell) to the universe of human beings. The fact that these objects can assume written form, can be traced in the sand (as in ancient Greece) or recorded on magnetic computer diskettes (as today), may seem to suggest that they're independent of the human brain. Not at all—they are *cultural representations*, capable of thriving, propagating, proliferating, and transmitting themselves from brain to brain via many different types of communication media. They have specific properties: in particular, that special coherence, or interior necessity, you're fond of emphasizing, which gives them the *appearance* of autonomy.

This appearance is what fascinates you—but this is nothing more than the fascination that the created object exerts upon its creator! It finds expression in scientific practice itself, and all that implies in the way of *subjectivity*. But can we really say that undergoing psychoanalysis helps us make progress in understanding the basic mechanisms of cerebral function, or of the people with whom we come into contact? Alas, no. Psychoanalysis hasn't led to significant advances in our knowledge of the brain, its architecture, or its physico-chemical nature. I fear that the "feeling" you have of "discovering" this wholly platonic "reality" amounts to nothing more than a purely introspective—and therefore subjective—analysis of the problem. Just the same, I admit that mathematics constitutes a cerebral production of a particular kind. We could agree, I think, on a definition of this sort: that mathematical objects are abstract concepts (though of a different kind than concepts such as liberty), and that they do indeed have unique properties—but these properties don't in the least imply their immateriality, any more than platonic realism does.

CONNES: Our discussion turns on the definition of the word "reality." For me, reality is defined by the coincidence and permanence of perceptions, whether those of a single individual or of several individuals within a group.

CHANGEUX: This collective perception is a necessary, but not a sufficient, condition, because it includes optical illusions as well as collective hallucinations. If mere coincidence of perceptions sufficed to define an objective reality, then the Huichol Indians in Mexico, who eat hallucinogenic mushrooms on their annual pilgrimage into the mountains and who *all* have the feeling of *actually* going to heaven, would appear to the rest of us to have actually departed from this earth.

IS A MATHEMATICAL OBJECT A CULTURAL REPRESENTATION LIKE ANY OTHER?

CHANGEUX: Shouldn't we say instead that a mental object is defined by its internal coherence, by a certain number of properties *exclusive* of those of any other mental object, and by the fortunate fact that it can be mutually perceived by the members of a social group? Fortunate though this fact may be, there's nothing extraordinary about it—human beings all have the same (or virtually the same) brain! What's more, as I've already stressed, mathematics has a history, having developed over the course of human social development. If mathematical objects existed in the universe in some atemporal way, as Pythagoras and Plato imagined, it should have been possible for human beings in every century to recognize them. Plainly that's not been the case. Mathematics has evolved, as much in its content as in its writing and symbolism. How do we account for this constant process of renewal, which you yourself refer to? It's hard to imagine that a new physical theory could call into question the existence of the "immutable and eternal" objects of a *mathesis universalis*! If they're as universal and as independent of our brain as you suggest, why do they evolve? The history of mathematics isn't at all linear—it's made up of an unending succession of controversies, splits, reexaminations, divergences, and realignments. Isn't it far likelier that what we're dealing with here is a special kind of cultural object that's produced and used at each stage of the development of our civilization, and periodically refashioned in response to the evolution of other cultural objects, not all of which are necessarily mathematical objects?

CONNES: Mathematical knowledge obviously has a historical character, just as geographical exploration does. Think of the mathematicians whose heroic efforts led to the discovery of finite simple sporadic groups. Don't you suppose a list of their names would produce the same impression on the average person as a list of the names of the great explorers who opened up new continents? To go back to my example, the existing proof of the exhaustive classification of the finite groups is too long for a nonspecialist to be able to completely verify it alone with utter certainty. This domain belongs therefore to a "fringe" of mathematical results that haven't yet been entirely settled. By contrast, the list of finite fields is relatively easy to grasp, and it's a simple matter to prove that the list is complete. It is part of an almost completely explored mathematical reality, where few problems remain. Cultural and social circumstances clearly serve to indicate which directions need to be pursued on the fringe of current research—the conquest of the North Pole, to return again to my comparison, surely obeyed the same type of cultural and social motivations, at least for a certain time. But once exploration is finished, these cultural and social phenomena fade away, and all that's left is a perfectly stable corpus, perfectly fitted to mathematical reality, which we try to pass on to future generations. This is a slightly simplified view of things, I grant you, but that shouldn't prevent us from acknowledging the distinction between charted mathematical territory and the tools used for surveying it.

CHANGEUX: You refer to the acquisition of knowledge. Our knowledge of the universe in general conforms to the pattern you describe. Certainly no one at this late date is going to challenge the fact that the earth moves around the sun!

CONNES: Once a mathematical theorem has been proved—Euclid's theorem about prime numbers, for example—no one's going to doubt it any longer.

CHANGEUX: Of course not. This is another point on which we can agree, I think. But I find especially striking your use of the notion of a "fringe," more specifically, a fringe of *unsettled* mathematical results—the notion that an initially small number of relatively simple mathematical objects gradually became enlarged over time. The "stabilization" phenomenon you mention seems to me to be tied to the cultural environment—which is why I regard mathematical objects as cultural objects. Only a fraction of the mathematical objects produced by the brains of mathematicians throughout history has been retained, then selected, and ultimately engraved in memory—first in the brains of their colleagues, later in written texts or computer programs. Certain authors even go so far as to say that mathematics was born the day when Greek philosophers began to draw figures in the sand, when they were able to use a memory other than their short-term memory, which couldn't store so many complex objects. And so a cultural heritage was able to take shape year after year in a simple fashion, gradually reducing itself to a minimum coherent structure, at which point it constituted what you call a "corpus."

This corpus thus came about as a result of the development of human cerebral faculties. The development of human cerebral faculties permitted a dialogue to be established between short-term working memory, which gives private access to mathematical objects, on the one hand, and, on the other hand—in addition to long-term memory—an external, noncerebral memory that stores them for future public access. Human beings have therefore been able to use mathematical objects extracerebrally in order to produce new ones, compare them with earlier ones, pass them through the "sieve of reason," and return them to the common pool of objects once it's clear that that's where they belong. It seems to me, as an outsider, that this sort of contingent evolution is at the heart of mathematics. If it is, shouldn't we define mathematical objects as cultural objects? As public representations of mental objects of a particular type that are produced in the brains of mathematicians and are propagated from one brain to another—until finally they reach the brains of biologists?

THE DARWINISM OF MATHEMATICAL OBJECTS

CONNES: The exploration of mathematical objects is certainly subject to cultural influence. This isn't enough, however, to justify the term *cultural object*. I think that the principal difficulty lies in the distinction between what I call "raw" mathematical reality and what we have both agreed to call "thought tools." On my view, these are tools devised by mathematicians to understand mathematical reality. I don't deny that they make up part of our cultural heritage. Consider what might be called "the study of asymptotic behaviors." Now, it may be that mathematical reality is too complex to be readily perceived: there exists, for example, no simple formula that gives the nth prime number. The asymptotic problem consists in finding a formula that gives the approximate order of magnitude of the nth prime number. It can be proved that the nth prime is of the order of n multiplied by the logarithm of n—thus revealing a new aspect of mathematical reality. But one must distinguish the thought tool from the mathematical reality it explores. A mathematician can very well *invent* a new thought tool. But so long as it doesn't enable him to succeed in revealing a new part of mathematical reality, previously unknown to his contemporaries, they will regard the newly invented tool with a certain skepticism. What I'm trying to get at is this: imagination isn't the only thing you need in order to do mathematics!

CHANGEUX: We've arrived at an interesting point in our conversation. You yourself brought up the evolution of mathematical knowledge. I bring it up again because it fits in with what we've been saying about a general evolution of knowledge, of cultural objects in their diverse forms. As you concede, there is every reason to think that mathematical objects—like all objects of knowledge—first appeared by a sort of mental mutation, by the chance cerebral experiments of mathematicians, and that they were then used and exploited by reason to the point, one might say, of being ground down. What's left is a residue—I employ the Darwinian term intentionally—of objects that have been selected both for their fitness and for their coherence with the existing whole. In this way a process of *rigidification* takes place. Coherence and rigidity seem to me, however, to be a posteriori results of evolution—it's exactly here that I part company with you.

Permit me, if you will, to compare the evolution of mathematical objects to biological evolution. Even if vertebrate evolution appears to display a continual "progress" from fish to amphibians, from reptiles to mammals, and finally then from apes to humans (figure 6), no one today—apart from certain religious fundamentalists—entertains the idea that evolution has unfolded with man, in all his perfection, as its final purpose. I won't go so far as to compare your attitude with that of these fundamentalists, but when you speak of the mathematician as progressively "revealing" a mathematically structured universe, I detect a sort of *finalism* that's surprising to find in a theoretical scientist. When one examines a macromolecule in a biology lab and asks how it

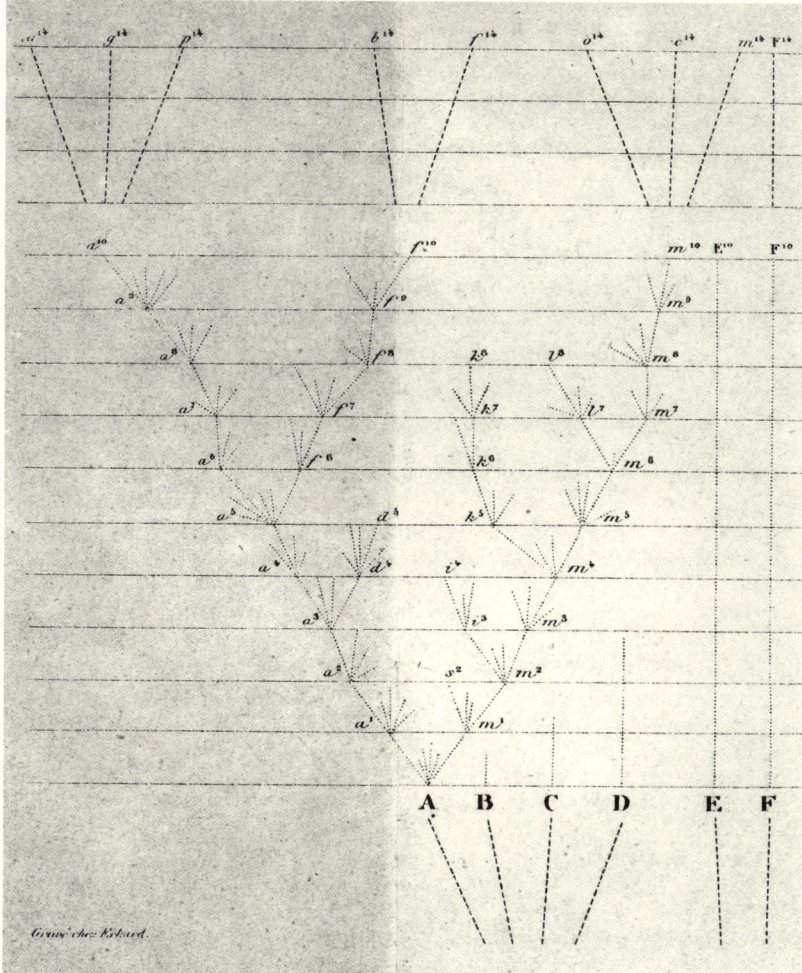

Figure 6. Darwin Tree

The original figure from Darwin's *The Origin of Species by Means of Natural Selection* (1859) illustrating the effects of natural selection on the descendants of a common ancestor.

comes to exhibit enzymatic activity, how it comes to furnish a material basis for heredity, one is posing what the evolutionary biologist Ernst Mayr calls "the question of the next cause." One is asking, in effect, what purpose it serves. This does *not* amount to supposing that the molecule has been conceived by an all-powerful Being for the purpose of doing this or that, or that it belongs to a rational universe conceived by an infinitely intelligent Mind. These metaphors, deriving from Aristotle, are permanently ingrained in the jargon of the laboratory. I imagine that mathematicians, like all scientists, use them in talking about their work as well. But no one takes teleological arguments seriously any more, at least not in biology. Spinoza long ago warned against the danger of using arguments of this sort in reasoning about the world, and the rigor of his philosophical method stands as a model for us still. It strikes me as curious the extent to which the coherence and rigidity you mention in speaking of mathematical objects resemble the coherence of mammalian organs and the rigidity of the mammalian skeleton—don't forget that for a long time it was believed that the universe, and living beings in particular, were divine creations whose "discovery" by the naturalist supplied evidence of the preestablished harmony of the world!

CONNES: Let's be clear about the term "evolution." In mathematics, as in every other discipline, knowledge evolves; but the underlying reality doesn't change. Once established by proof, the list of finite simple groups, for example, will never change—it really *is* the product of a discovery. I can't see that teleology has anything to do with it. To affirm the existence of a mathematical reality independent of perception certainly doesn't amount to making a teleological claim. I wouldn't dare for a moment assert that such-and-such a mathematical object is evidence of any sort of finalism whatsoever. No mathematician would make such an argument!

BELIEFS IN MATHEMATICS

CONNES: In no way, then, can my position be characterized as teleological—nor do I think I can change it.

CHANGEUX: And why not?

CONNES: I *cannot.*

CHANGEUX: Are you sure that you haven't entered into this debate with certain preconceived notions?

CONNES: I've told you what I believe—what I strongly believe.

CHANGEUX: Be careful, you've just used the word "believe" again!

CONNES: Of course I did. One part of our discussion, after all, is metaphysical—

CHANGEUX: And it's a fundamental part.

CONNES: To the extent that it leads us to clarify our notion of reality, yes. It's humility, finally, that forces me to admit that the mathematical world exists independently of the manner in which we apprehend it, that it isn't localized in time and space. But the manner in which we apprehend it is subject to rules very similar to those of biology. The evolution of our perception of mathematical reality causes a new sense to develop, which gives us access to a reality that is neither visual, nor auditory, but something else altogether.

CHANGEUX: Perhaps here, once more, we can find common ground. When you say that our brain develops a *new* sense, you sound more like a constructivist. Speaking as a neurobiologist, I don't by any means exclude the possibility that our cerebral apparatus possesses a flexibility and a capacity for reorganization that enables it to apprehend novel objects—objects it wasn't in a position to perceive at the time it was first formed, some millions of years ago, on the plains of central Africa. In principle this aptitude ought to be capable of producing a new "sense," as it were. But that doesn't necessarily imply that a totally organized mathematical system exists in nature waiting to be gradually discovered.

Your position seems to me to conceal a contradiction. You acknowledge, on the one hand, that mathematics evolves according to a model that conforms to the one advanced by biologists. On the other hand, however, you maintain that the mathematical corpus constitutes a *mathesis universalis*, an immense, coherent and stable whole, only the rudiments of which are known to us.

Once again I'm reminded of Ernst Mayr's reflections about causality in the life sciences. He opposes the "next cause"—the "how does it happen?" of the biologist or physiologist—to the "last cause"—the "why?" of the metaphysician. His answer is clear: the science of the "why?" isn't theology, it's evolutionary biology. And the "why?" of the existence of mathematics has as much to do with the evolution of our knowledge acquisition apparatus—our brain—as it does with the evolution of mathematical objects themselves. So when you speak of a new sense that forges itself, that provides access to cultural objects as they evolve in their turn, I think we find ourselves in agreement.

3. Nature Made to Order

CONSTRUCTIVIST MATHEMATICS

CHANGEUX: Despite our differences, some of which have assumed a rather extreme form, the two of us have managed to agree on at least a couple of points: the definition of mathematical objects as cultural representations of a very particular type, and the fact that mathematical knowledge evolves. For the moment we continue to differ on the larger question whether mathematical reality exists in the universe prior to its existing in the brain of the mathematician, but perhaps one of us—you, as a creationist mathematician, or I, as an evolutionary biologist—will modify his position during the course of these discussions. According to you, the mathematician merely discovers this *mathesis universalis*—this corpus whose special existence you *believe* in (as you know, I use the word "believe" deliberately!)—step by step. But not all mathematicians share this belief. As early as the eighteenth century one finds Kant expressing the view that the ultimate truth of mathematics lies in the possibility of its concepts being constructed by the human mind. A number of mathematicians in our own century, known as constructivists for their view that a mathematical object exists only insofar as it can be constructed, have carried on a lively debate with formalists—almost as lively as our own!

One of them, Allan Calder, even goes so far as to suggest that constructivist mathematics insists on more rigorous criteria of acceptability than nonconstructivist mathematics, and that the constructivist approach yields deeper analysis and more powerful theorems. It's really quite remarkable that certain mathematicians defend propositions nearer to the ones I advance as a neurobiologist than to yours. Calder is even more direct than I was in describing your experience as a creative mathematician and the subjectivity of your attitude. Looking back at several generations of mathematicians trained in the formalist school, he accuses them of suffering from a "mental block" that makes it difficult for them to take an "objective view" of mathematics, to the point that some of them seem actually to regard constructivism as a cancer threatening to destroy mathematics. One finds a great deal of passion, even irrationality, in the debate among mathematicians—so much so that Calder ends up sounding the same note on which I concluded our last conversation, namely that belief in the existence of a mathematical truth outside the human mind requires an act of faith that the majority of formalist-minded mathematicians are not aware of making. At this point we find ourselves quite removed from the *emendatio intellectus* so dear to Spinoza!

CONNES: The distinction between constructivism and formalism is a methodological distinction more than anything else. Constructivists may be compared to mountain climbers who proudly scale a peak with their bare hands, and formalists to climbers who permit themselves the luxury of hiring a helicopter to fly over the summit. Each approach has its advantages, depending on the problem being attacked. Without going so far as to adopt constructivist methods, it's sometimes necessary, even in present-day mathematics, to temper the effects of an established axiomatization, in particular those of the axiom of choice. By way of example, let's take a specific problem that I've encountered in my own work, and that has occasioned two very different points of view. It belongs to a fairly old debate over the problem of measurability, in the Lebesguian sense, of real-valued functions. It turns out to be provable that nonmeasurable functions can't be constructed using the countable axiom of choice alone. From this it follows that mathematical reasoning that uses only the countable axiom of choice will never run into the problem of nonmeasurability.

Now let's examine the formalist point of view. When set theory is developed on the basis of the uncountable axiom of choice, it can be proved that any set is well ordered. Yet any well-ordering of the reals is essentially nonmeasurable, and so, of course, nonconstructible. The uncountable axiom of choice considerably simplifies the theory of cardinal numbers, and therefore gives a fairly crude glimpse of part of mathematical reality. In particular, some sets between which no bijection (or one-to-one correspondence) can actually be constructed are nevertheless considered to be isomorphic (that is, to have the same cardinality). For example, if one assumes the uncountable axiom of choice, the Penrose set of quasi-crystals can be shown to have the cardinality of the continuum, even though it's impossible to construct an effective bijection between this set and the continuum. To revert to the image I used a moment ago, the uncountable axiom of choice gives an aerial view of mathematical reality—inevitably, therefore, a simplified view. Now it's true that most mathematicians have been trained in the tradition of set theory, and that this supposes the uncountable axiom of choice, the simplifying function of which few of them understand. But this simplification affects only a tiny proportion of current mathematics, and in general it's a welcome thing. Clearly, then, different approaches reveal different aspects of mathematical reality—there's nothing contradictory in that. For similar reasons, constructivism can't be said to cast doubt again upon the existence of an independent mathematical world.

CHANGEUX: But constructivists maintain that it does. They can't be accused of obscurantism: after all, they *do* know the mathematical world. But for them that world exists only insofar as they can build it step by step.

CONNES: I don't think you'll find a constructivist who doesn't accept the list I gave previously of finite simple groups. It's important to understand that the majority of fundamental mathematical objects are by their very nature constructible, which explains why their existence isn't questioned by the constructivists. With regard to method, however, the difference between the two schools can be considerable. Take, for example, the very useful proof tool called ultraproducts. If the result to be proven isn't formulated using ultraproducts, we know from mathematical logic that there exists a proof that doesn't use ultraproducts. Nonetheless, for certain problems, it's much easier to arrive at the proof using this tool. We can show, for instance, that the fields obtained in making ultraproducts of p-adic fields are the same as those obtained in making ultraproducts of formal series over the finite fields Fp. This can be very useful for solving certain equations. In such cases, it's clearly the constructivist point of view, in forbidding the use of ultraproducts, that's conservative and limited. But be that as it may, I don't believe that the existence of a mathematical world independent of us, which escapes sensory apprehension, has been cast into doubt again as you suggest.

CHANGEUX: That's because you believe the constructivist/intuitionist distinction is more methodological than ontological—constructivists see it the other way around. In the end, however, your subjective experience as a mathematician and your vehement profession of faith—because you admit that's what it is—may reveal a deeper truth not necessarily involving appeal to anything immaterial; a truth that you feel, that you perceive, that you imagine—but that we can't seem to be able to agree on, perhaps for lack of an overarching concept that might help us bridge our differences.

This question of the existence of a mathematical world constitutes our major point of disagreement. Granting your position for the sake of argument, I've tried to see where this world could be, to see what *evidence* of it there is in nature. If you form the hypothesis that this mathematical world exists outside of us, and if you call yourself a materialist, then it seems to me you're obliged to give it a material basis. I don't see how this mathematical world could be present in nature in any form other than the organization of matter itself (excepting, of course, what is stored in books and in the memories of mathematicians). Now, it's undeniable that regularities are found everywhere in nature: in the movement of the planets (figure 7), the organization of atoms in a rock salt crystal, or the double-helix configuration of desoxyribonucleic acid. Do you believe that these regularities are the expression of a universal mathematics that constitutes, in effect, an ideal "skeleton" around which matter organizes itself? Or do you think, to the contrary—as I maintain—that these regularities

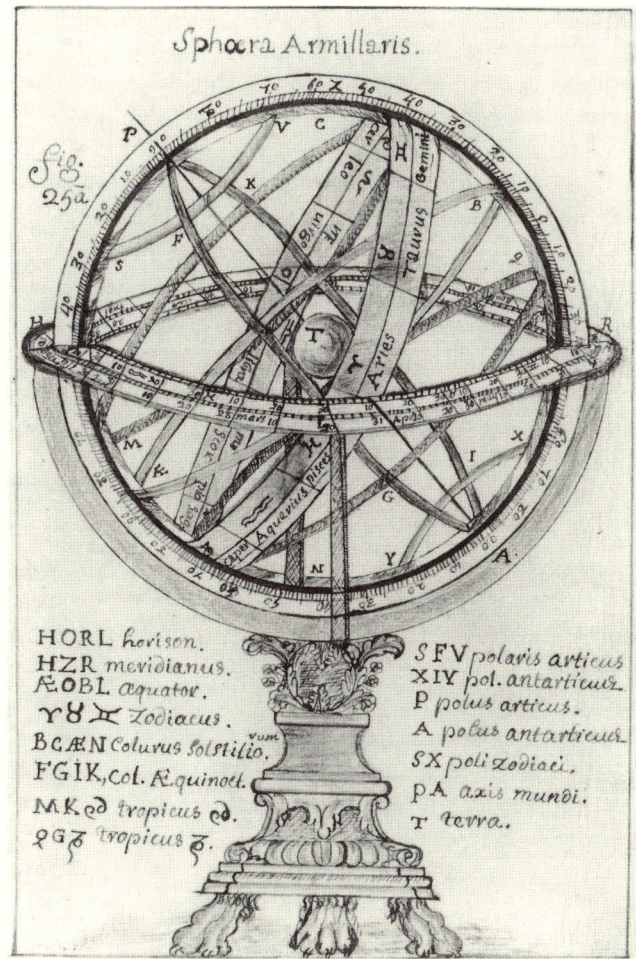

Figure 7. Armillary Sphere

Armillary spheres are metal or wooden objects composed of hinged, interlocking circles intended to represent the movement of the planets and the celestial sphere around the earth (*T*) as a function of the months of the year. Built principally during the eighteenth century, they constitute in effect the first mechanical models of the universe. This particular drawing of an armillary sphere comes from the manuscript notebook of the student G.L., drafted in 1713. (Collection of J.-P. Changeux) represent properties intrinsic to matter, without necessarily being the expression of some original mathematical law? If this were the case, the task of the scientific "naturalist" would consist in apprehending these regularities, forging the necessary tools, creating the language and the concepts—mathematical ones, for the most part—needed to describe them. In order to choose between the two points of view, these external regularities must be matched up with mathematical objects. If mathematics were really the organizing principle of matter, sooner or later we should find a *perfect* fit between the regularity of material objects and that of mathematical objects. Otherwise mathematics—as a product of the human brain—amounts to no more than an approximate language that serves to describe a material world that in large part escapes our comprehension.

Proceeding hypothetico-deductively, as physicists do, biologists build thought objects, or models, that they test against external physical reality. These models are simplified representations of an object or a process; they are coherent, noncontradictory, minimal, and subject to validation by experiment. A good model is predictive, in the sense that it leads to experiments that enrich our knowledge; and also generative, because it can suggest other theoretical models that enrich theory. Finally, unlike the entrenched beliefs that characterize a defined cultural tradition, a model is *revisable*. It seems to me necessary, in fact, to admit that the majority of the models science produces are valid only at a given moment in the history of science, and that at least some of their propositions can be revised or amended. All of this, of course, makes possible the cumulative growth of knowledge. Once we've selected the model that appears the most adequate, we use these thought objects to capture the regularities of the physical world, to describe them in physical terms. Proceeding in this way, we treat natural regularities indirectly. We try to dress them up, as it were, with a certain number of thought objects, some of which are mathematical objects. But that doesn't necessarily imply the identification of these natural objects with the mathematics we use to describe them.

THE "UNREASONABLE EFFECTIVENESS"
OF MATHEMATICS

CONNES: The idea that mathematical reality is located in the physical world is foreign to my way of thinking. Accordingly I make no attempt whatsoever to identify natural objects with mathematics. Once mathematical reality is distinguished from physical reality, however, the problem arises as to their relationship to each other. I will begin by giving an example of what Eugene Wigner memorably called "the unreasonable effectiveness of mathematics," which in general doesn't result simply from an attempt to dress up natural regularities in some appropriate way or other. When one takes a piece of string and makes a fairly complicated knot with it, the question arises whether it can be undone without resorting to the Gordian method. In many cases a magnificent mathematical theory—the theory of knots—provides the answer (figures 8 and 9). Very important progress in this theory has recently been achieved by the New Zealander Vaughn Jones, a mathematician whose initial motivation had nothing to do with knots. He'd started out working with me on functional analysis, and then became interested in a very tricky, related problem of infinite dimensional analysis that called for the classification of all the subfactors of a given factor—a problem that, a priori, couldn't be further removed from the theory of knots. For a long time he worked at this problem alone. No one could see the point of what he was doing; people wondered, frankly, why he was wasting his time on it.

A few years later, he succeeded in determining the set of values that the index of subfactors could assume. He found the union of a discrete set with a continuous one. In the course of proving his result he discovered a trace on a group, called the braid group, a clear picture of which can be formed just by looking at knotted or unknotted strands of a braid. It was a simple image to begin with. At conferences he would illustrate the group by drawing braids. It happened then that in New York he met a topologist, Joan Birman, and in the course of talking with her he realized that his

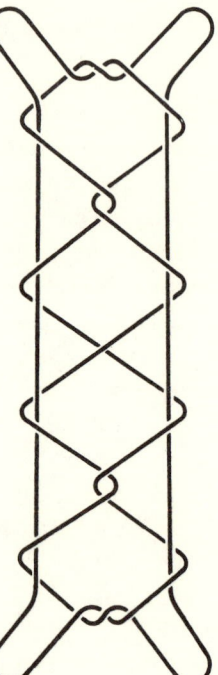

Figure 8. Jacob's Ladder
A knot familiar to children, created by passing a loop of string between four fingers and catching the free ends between the other fingers. The Jacob's ladder pictured is obviously equivalent to the trivial loop knot. The Eskimos and the Indians of North America are fond of such string games, which illustrate the infinite possibilities for generating geometric motifs from a loop, the simplest of knots.

construction, which was based on the algebra of the braid group, in fact gave a new invariant for knots. He then calculated this invariant for the simplest of all knots, the trefoil knot, and noticed that the invariant of its mirror-image wasn't the same. This was a surprise, because the classical invariants are invariant under reflection as well. Next, for a great many other knots, he made all sorts of new calculations for his invariant—which is calculated quite simply, though its purely geometric interpretation remains unknown. This is a very powerful invariant that helps distinguish knots that had been hard to distinguish before. It permits us, for example, to measure the "Gordian number" of a knot. This is a number that has an obvious interpretation: you pass one strand through another, counting the number of times you have to do this until the knot comes undone. Well, Jones's invariant makes

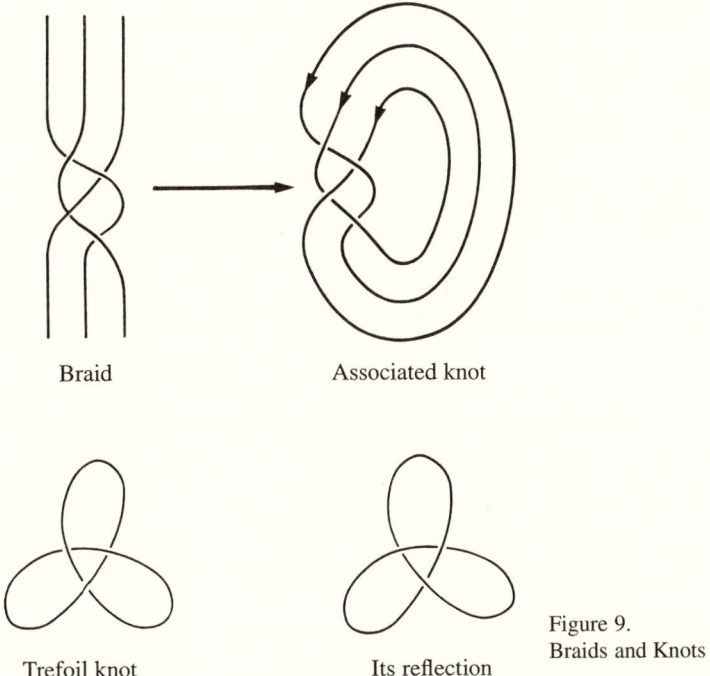

Braid   Associated knot

Trefoil knot   Its reflection

Figure 9.
Braids and Knots

it possible to measure the Gordian number of a knot—which is altogether extraordinary, because he started with a *pure* mathematical problem, a problem hidden in what was previously thought to be one of the darkest corners, one of the most desert-like regions in all of mathematical geography. But in solving this problem he was led directly to knots, which, as you know, are useful in biology, because they enter into all sorts of problems involving very complicated molecular coding, such as polymers. Right now, in fact, he's trying to apply his results to quite concrete problems—a perfect illustration of the curious power of mathematics when it's practiced for its own sake, without any prior notion of its eventual application.

CHANGEUX: The story you've just told nonetheless involves an experiment.

CONNES: It wasn't an experiment; it was more like a coincidence.

CHANGEUX: All right, but still—when he met this other topologist, this led him to apply certain types of mathematical tools to a more concrete problem. Knots can exist in nature, where most often they are the product of human creative activity. But I can't conceive of the *theory* of knots having existed in nature *before* this whole collection of diverse knot forms had been assembled. What happened was simply that a first-rate mathematician succeeded in creating a thought tool, called an invariant, and put it to use. A tool was forged in this case—just as the wheel was invented in order to travel more quickly. Instead of linking up dozens of logical steps, he devised a form of "condensed rationality" that instantly allowed him to solve the problem.

CONNES: What I find especially striking is that his research and the discovery it led to weren't motivated in the least by the problem of knots. It's a very interesting example of a discovery motivated by profound problems of pure mathematics. His research on factors led him to discover a central function of braids. As long as this function was useful solely for his work on the classification of subfactors, it obviously didn't seem to have any connection with knots. But he was fishing for a way to connect the two without knowing it. Then, talking with Birman, he learned that the braid group is also used in knot theory, and that, as a consequence of a theorem due to Markov, topologists were looking for a function on this group that satisfied a certain property. "I've got it!" he cried. "I've got it right here in my pocket!"

CHANGEUX: I understand what you're trying to say. Two paths that initially were totally independent of each other finally converged. The mathematical object created by one unlocked the door that had been closed by the other. But this doesn't mean that a lock and key already existed, waiting to be discovered!

CONNES: How can you be so sure?

CHANGEUX: Here we touch upon a fundamental problem. How can we account for the fact that certain mathematical tools, created independently of any investigation into particles, knots, or other natural objects, are so well adapted to the physical world—

CONNES: Exactly—Wigner's "unreasonable effectiveness of mathematics."

CHANGEUX: Still you need to tell me how far you think this effectiveness extends. How universal is it? Physicists and certain mathematicians, I've noticed, have a tendency to become infatuated with whatever mathematical model is in vogue. They think it applies to everything—groups of atoms, groups of neurons, groups of ants, groups of human beings. What does your own personal experience lead you to believe about the relation between mathematics and physics?

EINSTEIN AND MATHEMATICS

CONNES: First of all, in physics as in other disciplines, every model is revisable and time-dependent. We've all been forced to learn the lesson that every model of physical reality will sooner or later be supplanted by another. This is the revisable side of our perception of nature. We can go even further, and ask to what extent physical truth depends on which questions we put to nature, that is, which experiments we choose to carry out. Nonetheless, I assert that once a model has been satisfactorily worked out, the generativity of mathematics comes into play. Once this happens, it becomes possible to feel as though you're doing physics, when what you're really doing is studying the model from a strictly mathematical point of view.

Einstein's evolution as a scientist is instructive in this respect. The mathematical difficulties he encountered in trying to express the principle of general relativity caused him to alter his approach. By the 1930s he had clearly ceased to be the pure physicist he was in 1905 and had become a mathematician instead. He spent a very great part of his scientific life trying to devise a theory that would unify electromagnetism and gravity. The success of the mathematical model of general relativity was such that he came to think that the solution to his problem lay in mathematics. In 1921 he was still able to say, apropos of relativity: "I am anxious to draw attention to the fact that this theory is not speculative in origin; it owes its invention entirely to the desire to make physical theory fit observed fact as well as possible. We have here no revolutionary act. . . . The abandonment of a certain concept . . . must not be regarded as arbitrary, but only as conditioned by observed facts. . . . The justification for a physical concept lies exclusively in its clear and unambiguous relation to facts that can be experienced. . . . The general theory of relativity owes its existence . . . to the empirical fact of the numerical equality of the inertial and gravitational masses of bodies." But in 1933 we find him saying, to the contrary, "If, then, it is true that this axiomatic basis of theoretical physics cannot be extracted from experience, but must be freely invented, can we ever hope to find the right way? . . . I am convinced that we can discover by means of purely mathematical constructions the concepts and the laws connecting them with each other, which furnish the key to the understanding of natural phenomena. . . . The creative principle resides in mathematics."[1]

In theoretical physics today we're witnessing a very similar phenomenon: the theoretical physicist, having exhausted all the resources available to him, has no alternative but to become a mathematician. Let me say a word or two here about string theory. Physicists in the late 1960s were looking for a direct way, independent of any knowledge of the local mechanism of strong interactions, to find the mathematical form of a matrix known as the S-matrix. This matrix determines the probability that from two ingoing particles with given momenta p^1 and p^2, two outgoing particles emerge after strong interaction with momenta p^3 and p^4. The problem is to find the probability amplitude, a function in four variables (p^1, p^2, p^3, p^4) whose absolute square is the

---

[1] Quoted in J. Schwinger, *Einstein's Legacy* (New York: W. H. Freeman, 1986), pp. 237–38. See too Einstein's remarks on the free invention of mathematics by the mind in his essay "Remarks on Bertrand Russell's Theory of Knowledge," reproduced with facing-page translation from the German in vol. 5 of the Library of Living Philosophers, *The Philosophy of Bertrand Russell*, ed. P. A. Schilpp (Peru, Ill.: Open Court, 1944), p. 287; and the related remark contained in his "Autobiographical Notes," in vol. 7 of the same series, *Albert Einstein: Philosopher-Scientist*, ed. P. A. Schilpp (Peru, Ill.: Open Court, 1949), p. 13.

probability. Relativistic invariance allows it to be reduced to a function in two variables, and by means of a simplifying hypothesis it can then be solved, with a solution specified in integral form for processes involving even more than four particles. This is known as Veneziano's model. Theoretical physicists later were able to demonstrate that this model in fact described the interaction not of point particles but of short strings.

Interest in the theory for analyzing strong interactions was nonetheless short-lived. With the proof by t'Hooft of the possibility of renormalizing gauge theories, and the discovery of asymptotic freedom, and so on, it was rapidly supplanted by chromodynamics. Nevertheless, a bit later, around 1974, it was suggested that string theory could be used in order to reconcile gravity with quantum mechanics. Finally, in 1980 or thereabouts, string theories were resuscitated and refined considerably, this time not as models of strong interaction but as models of quantum gravity.

CHANGEUX: Is the mathematical formalism the same?

CONNES: Yes, but with a change in scale: for strong interactions, the standard scale is 10^{-13} cm, while for quantum gravity it's 10^{-33} cm. The energies required are therefore considerably greater than those we are presently capable of generating, so we know that no testable experimental result will come out of the theory any time soon. For the time being, the theory is of consequence only on a formal level, if not merely a purely philosophical one. We know that divergences in field theory can be eliminated by replacing points with strings. The advantage of doing this can be described quite simply: when one particle is created from the collision of two others, or when one particle divides in two, a singular process takes place that yields a sort of point with three branches (figure 10a). In this case there exists a singularity that is responsible for the divergences I've just mentioned, which arise from the exchange of one or more virtual particles. But if the line that the particle follows is replaced by a small cylinder, along which the string is now imagined to move, it turns out that by connecting different cylinders it becomes possible to join three of them without singularity, so that the junctures are perfectly smooth

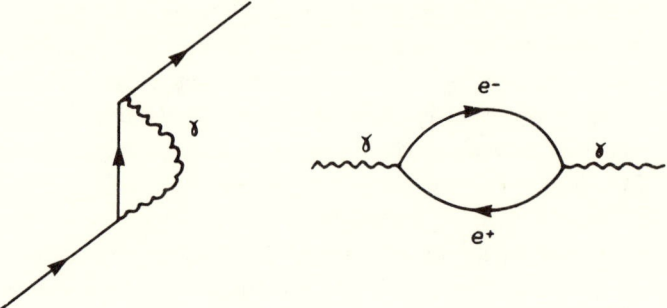

Figure 10a. Examples of Divergent Diagrams in Quantum Electro-dynamics

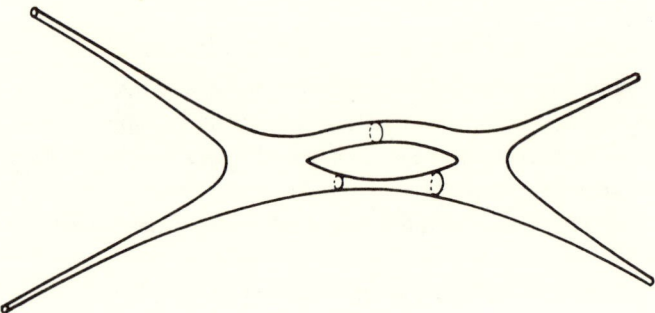

Figure 10b. Singularity-Free Diagram in String Theory

(figure 10b). What may we expect to prove by means of such a theory? That because singularity can be avoided by replacing trajectories with cylinders, the new theory is finite rather than infinite, in which case the infinities of quantum field theory are removed in a natural manner.

I should repeat that my own attitude toward physics isn't at all that of a physicist, even though I admire all discoveries—Heisenberg's, for example—that have been pragmatically derived from experiment. Quantum field theory was an extraordinary discovery. But it still doesn't square in any simple way with what has been discovered up to now about mathematical reality. Why should this be? We've got plenty of raw data—it's not a question any longer of needing *more* experimental results. The reason is that mathematics isn't as developed as it will have to be if mathematicians are going to be able to digest the advances physicists have made. We've got to get down to work. Whether or not we should try to distance ourselves from their discoveries, we must be careful to work within the framework of pure mathematics without trying to force anything that doesn't fit naturally.

CHANGEUX: The impression I get from all of this is that the work of physicists and mathematicians has a lot in common with the "intellectual tinkering" so dear to Claude Lévi-Straus and François Jacob. One takes a model here, and applies it to an experimental observation there. If string theory won't do for explaining particle diffusion, we abandon it! But then, suddenly, it turns up again—this time looking like a plausible explanation of quantum gravity. Doesn't this amount to a sort of trade in off-the-rack (as opposed to custom-made) theoretical clothing? Certainly it goes some ways to demystifying, to softening the edges of what are sometimes a bit too frivolously called the "exact sciences"!

I notice too that when you speak of the relation of mathematical objects to physical objects, you use the term "fits" or "squares with" rather than "is identical with." This framing metaphor permits you to describe physical reality in a very particular, even peculiar way. But if matter is organized according to mathematical laws—if mathematics is really to be found in nature—it seems to me that we should arrive at a perfect *identification* of mathematical objects with natural objects. And yet we don't. According to you, this means that such laws are to be located somewhere else than in the physical world. But where? In some state, in some form, that you still haven't defined. You end up with a sort of dualism—an abrupt cleavage, in fact—between matter and mathematics that reminds me of the Cartesian distinction between mind and body. This, as you're well aware, is a distinction I don't accept.

CONNES: Mind-body dualism operates on a different level. The physical world that surrounds us, while not itself the seat of mathematical reality, coheres with it in a definite way that's difficult to explain. Einstein, you will recall, said that the most incomprehensible thing about the universe is that it is comprehensible. The thing that's hard to grasp about mathematics is that it governs the organization of natural phenomena. Thanks to mathematics we are able to understand the natural world.

CHANGEUX: To the phrase "organization of natural phenomena," I would add—"in our brain."

CONNES: I don't know. I don't understand how one can say, "in our brain." One could just as well say that the perception of the outside world is located in our brain.

CHANGEUX: Well, it is!

CONNES: Okay—but are we agreed that the outside world exists independently of us?

CHANGEUX: Yes, but we apprehend it by means of our brain and sensory organs.

CONNES: Our relationship to the mathematical world is exactly the same. It exists apart from us, because, as all mathematicians agree, its structure is independent of individual perception. But on the other hand, of course, it's easy to say that the mathematical world is real only to the extent that it is apprehended by the brain, in the same way that the outside physical world is perceived only by means of the brain.

CHANGEUX: Quite right. I see your point, of course, but still I can't quite agree—especially not when you say "in the same way that . . ." I've already drawn attention to the danger of using metaphor in such cases. Analogy isn't the same thing as demonstration. Finally, when you get right down to it, biologists have a still simpler (and far less ambiguous) relationship with mathematics than physicists. Constructing models requires using a mathematical apparatus, as you point out. Our point of view is less ambitious, perhaps, but it creates a crucial distance, and for this reason I think our position is sounder than that of many physicists.

CONNES: The distance is certainly greater, I agree. It's because mathematics and physics overlap that physicists find it so hard to keep their distance.

THE USEFULNESS OF MATHEMATICAL
MODELS IN BIOLOGY

CHANGEUX: The belief in the explanatory virtues of mathematical models is less frequently encountered among biologists. For us, mathematics serves two principal functions: first, the analysis of experimental data—

CONNES: This is a question of statistics.

CHANGEUX: Yes—more generally, of extracting data. A computer can even take care of this automatically, bypassing the brain of the researcher altogether. Second, mathematics helps us to construct theoretical models, which are then elaborated on the basis of experimental data, as in physics. In the case of the propagation of the nerve impulse, for example, the premises include the degree of variation of the potential at a given point along a nerve, and the magnitude of the currents carried by sodium and potassium ions as a function of the potential. Working from these premises, Hodgkin and Huxley proposed an equation that accounts for the ionic bases of the nerve impulse. This equation permits the propagation of the nerve impulse to be described and reconstructed from elementary data (figures 11a and b).

CONNES: It's a way of coding information—

CHANGEUX: And, above all, of reconstituting its elementary unit.

CONNES: So it's a little like a language, because a language is intended to reproduce—

CHANGEUX: Yes—it's capable of reproducing, but it also has a predictive aspect. Even so, I can't imagine any biologist saying that the Hodgkin-Huxley equation is identical with the nerve impulse, or that it governs its propagation. It's not a universal mathematical law controlling the propagation of the nerve influx, as some physicists are fond of saying when speaking of their own work!

CONNES: I presume that if we push your analysis further—let's say, to include the chemical and electrical dimensions of the phenomenon—the equation in question can be derived using the laws of chemistry?

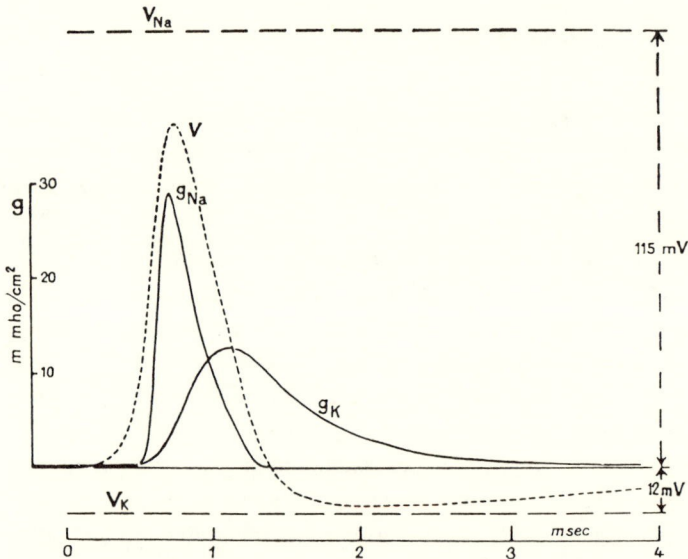

Figure 11a (*above*). Hodgkin-Huxley Model of the Nerve Impulse

The propagated wave potential is represented by a dotted line (V). This line can be broken down into the inward transport of Na+ ions and the outward flow of K+ ions, expressed here in terms of conductivities (g^{na} and g^k). (From A. Hodgkin and A. Huxley, *Quant. Biol.* 17 [Cold Spring Harbor, 1952], pp. 43–52)

Figure 11b (*opposite*). Primary Structure of the Sodium Ion-Selective Channel Involved in Propagating the Nerve Impulse. (Reprinted with permission from *Nature* 312 [1984]: 121–27, copyright © 1984 by Macmillan Magazines Limited)

The methods of molecular genetics have led to the identification of the genetic material coding for the protein responsible for transporting Na+ ions through the cell membrane during the propagation of the nerve impulse. This protein is composed of a single chain of 1,820 amino acids. The bottom line is the DNA sequence represented by a series of triplets of the four ATGC bases; the top line is the protein sequence resulting from the chain of amino acids taken from the 21 natural amino acids, denoted here by a three-letter code. (From Noda et al., "Primary Structure of *Electrophorus electricus* Sodium Channel Deduced from cDNA Sequence," in *Nature* 312 [1984]: 121–27)

```
                                    5'-----ACCGTGATGACGCTTTAGTGTGCAGTTCTGCTGGGTGTCGTATACCAGAAATCGAATCTTGTTACCTCACTGCAGTGACTCTCT  -301
AGATGCTGTTCTTAGATTAATATAATTAGAAGTAATCCTGTGTCTTTAAGCTTGAATACAAGTACTTTTCTTTATTTTATAGTGTAAATCCATTTTTTTTTACACTTTTTTAGAGGAAGCAAAAAAAACCAAAAACCCAAAAACTTAG  -151
CATTGAGTTTGCAATACTAATGCTCTCTACTGGTTGTGGAGTATTGCTATTCTATCTCTGGGCTATTGCTAGTCTGCAACATTGATCTTCTGCATCTGAGCTTCGGATAGAGATTCCACTCTGAGGTGATATCTTTCCGCGATGCGAAG  -1
1          10         20         30         40         50
MetGluArgLysPheSerSerAlaArgProGluMetPheArgArgPheThrProArgSerLeuGluGluIleGluAlaPheThrGlueuLysLysSerCysThrLeuGluLysLysProGluSerThrProArgIleAspLeuGlu
ATGGCTCGCAAGTTCTCTTCCGCACGCCCCGAAATGTTTCGCCGCTTCACCCCAGATTCACTGGAGGAGATTGAGGCGTTCACTGAGCTGAAGAAAAGTTGTACGTTAGAGAAGAAGCCGGAGTCAACACCTAGAATTGACCTGGAG  150
...
```

(Full-length nucleotide and deduced amino acid sequence, positions −301 through 6750.)

CHANGEUX: This is a very important point. The mathematical equation could ultimately be explained, at least in part, by the underlying molecular processes. The molecule containing the channel sensitive to voltage, through which the sodium ions pass, has recently been isolated, and the nucleic acid that codes it has been cloned and sequenced. So now we've got a better grip on the molecular mechanisms that determine the propagation of the nerve impulse. But what needs to be kept in mind is that the mathematical model didn't directly lead to the elementary structure that, in the last analysis, accounts for the phenomenon. Access to this structure was the result of a very different approach grounded in the methods of biochemistry and molecular biology. The mathematical equation of the propagation of the nerve impulse is based on a certain number of propositions having to do with the channels postulated by the model. It defines, of course, a certain number of elemental *ionic properties* that the molecule in question must display. But it doesn't give us the least indication if these channels are proteins or lipids. The equation requires cooperative phenomena at the level of the membrane and of ionic transport. It doesn't tell us what the *exact* number of subunits or proteins involved will be. Mathematics plays a definite predictive role for the biologist, but a limited one. It doesn't give us *direct* access to structure.

I can illustrate this point with another example, this time from the laws of heredity—one of the simplest and best known examples, in fact. Mendel showed that the hereditary transmission of color in pea blossoms follows a behavior expressed by an extremely simple mathematical equation. These laws make it possible to infer the existence of stable, hereditarily transmissible determinants, but they certainly didn't predict that chromosomes, still less DNA, are the material supports of heredity.

In the two cases I've just cited—the propagation of the nerve impulse, and Mendel's laws—the mathematical equation describes a function. It allows us to grasp a certain behavior, but not to fully *explain* the phenomenon. In biology, explanation goes hand in hand with the identification of the underlying structure that determines the function. Scientific discovery involves more than just the description of a process by a mathematical equation. The "royal way" of discovery is traveled only by relating structure to function.

CONNES: I agree. In physics, too, one often begins by writing equations for a mean field in the style of nineteenth-century physics. So long as the underlying microscopic structure is unknown, the equations can hardly be proved; but when the theory is sufficiently worked out, the generativity of mathematics comes into play. My favorite example is borrowed from Heisenberg. Guided by the results of experimental spectroscopy, such as the Ritz-Rydberg law of combination, Heisenberg realized that the algebra of observable quantities had to be a noncommutative—matrix—algebra. This single observation, and a bit of mathematics, produces Schrödinger's equation, which explains the mysterious numbers (representing the difference between the inverse squares of two integers) that govern the regularities of the spectral lines of the hydrogen atom. With Pauli's exclusion principle, and some more elaborate mathematics, we can then analyze Schrödinger's equation for an atom with n electrons. One could hardly hope for more generative power from mathematics.

CHANGEUX: And we can completely describe Mendeleev's periodic table of the elements . . .

CONNES: Which is extraordinary. We can see two stages in the modeling of a phenomenon: first, the descriptive theories of nineteenth-century physicists for macroscopic phenomena; then, as the microscopic structure of matter came to be better understood, the use of the generativity of mathematics, which made it possible to discover that the number of stable elements is limited, and even to anticipate their chemistry (with the help, for instance, of Schrödinger's equation) (figure 12).

CHANGEUX: But doesn't this generative aspect come precisely from the fact that, as you've just said, once we reach a lower level, regularities appear that can be universally applied?

Atomic Number	Element		First Ionization Potential in Volts [W_1 (ev)]	1s	2s 2p	3w 3p 3d	4s 4p 4d 4f
						Electron Configuration Shell	
						[Spectral Notation]	
1	H	Hydrogen	13.6	1			
2	He	Helium	24.6	2			
3	Li	Lithium	5.4		1		
4	Be	Beryllium	9.3		2		
5	B	Boron	8.3	full	2 1		
6	C	Carbon	11.3		2 2		
7	N	Nitrogen	14.5	(2)	2 3	Number of electrons	
8	O	Oxygen	13.6		2 4	in each state	
9	F	Flourine	17.4		2 5		
10	Ne	Neon	21.6		2 6		
11	Na	Sodium	5.1			1	
12	Mg	Magnesium	7.6			2	
13	Al	Aluminium	6.0			2 1	
14	Si	Silicon	8.1	— full —		2 2	
15	P	Phosphorus	10.5			2 3	
16	S	Sulphur	10.4	(2)	(8)	2 4	
17	Cl	Chlorine	13.0			2 5	
18	A	Argon	15.8			2 6	
19	K	Potassium	4.3				1
20	Ca	Calcium	6.1				2
21	Sc	Scandium	6.5			1	2
22	Ti	Titanium	6.8			2	2
23	V	Vanadium	6.7	— full —		3	2
24	Cr	Chromium	6.8			5	1
25	Mn	Manganese	7.4	(2)	(8)	(8) 5	2
26	Fe	Iron	7.9			6	2
27	Co	Cobalt	7.9			7	2
28	Ni	Nickel	7.6			8	2
29	Cu	Copper	7.7			10	1
30	Zn	Zinc	9.4			10	2
31	Ga	Gallium	6.0				2 1
32	Ge	Germanium	7.9	— full —			2 2
33	As	Arsenic	9.8				2 3
34	Se	Selenium	9.7	(2)	(8)	(18)	2 4
35	Br	Bromine	11.8				2 5
36	Kr	Krypton	14.0				2 6

Figure 12. Beginning of the Periodic Table of the Elements, Showing the Distribution of Electrons in the Atoms

CONNES: Of course. As long as we haven't been able to go beyond the level of the mean field to the next level, the generative aspect is limited.

CHANGEUX: It's almost the same as the example from biology. The Hodgkin-Huxley equation is generalizable and has a predictive aspect. But once we arrive at the analysis of the individual ionic channels and the molecules whose collective activity constitutes the nerve impulse, a new set of rules and predictions appears. These are expressed in a new mathematical form that can be applied to other systems: to calcium-selective channels, or to other categories of channels sensitive to neurotransmitters.

CONNES: I agree completely. At the same time, I'd like to make a general criticism of the kind of mathematics used in this sort of modeling. The mathematics involved always hinges on partial differential equations or, at best, on models of statistical mechanics. In each case, as with most models in physics, the guiding principle is the fundamental notion of local interaction. Even apparently nonlocal interactions, such as Newtonian attraction, are localized once the appropriate fields are introduced. This principle of local interaction amounts to a golden rule of modern physics, the essential tool of which is the manipulation of Lagrangian functions. And yet it's not obvious to me, at least not a priori, that this is the only useful and interesting sort of mathematics for a biologist concerned with how the brain functions. It would be good if biologists had even a rudimentary acquaintance with topology, for example, whether or not they actually used it.

CHANGEUX: We'll get around to this later in the course of our discussions.

CONNES: Fine—but keep in mind that this is one of the main reasons I was so interested in having these conversations with you. In biology, mathematics is used as a language: if, for example, you have a response curve, it's obviously easier if a simple mathematical function can be used to describe it instead of having to retrace the curve each time and isolate its parameters. This is simply a sign of the youthfulness of biology as a science. If one looks at the development of physics historically, one notices that it was possible from an early period to formalize certain phenomena, to express them in terms of mathematical functions (thus, for example, Planck's discovery of the law of black body radiation). But after a while, because it is generative, mathematics made it possible to keep adding in new elements—and not only because equations make prediction possible. The internal coherence of mathematics that manifests itself in the case of the hydrogen atom, for example, gives us a fairly good intuition—an intuition that obeys criteria of simplicity, of mathematical aesthetics—of what should be true in cases where virtually no experiments have been conducted, and then enables us to verify whether or not it's actually right. And so I'm very optimistic about the generative role mathematics could eventually play in biology. Ultimately—not just now perhaps, but once we've been able to determine which branches of mathematics are best suited to biology—I think its generativity will be extremely useful.

THE AUSCULTATION OF QUANTUM MECHANICS

CHANGEUX: I'd like to come back to quantum mechanics and what we can conclude about the admittedly crude—but, everything considered, fairly pertinent—use of mathematics by biologists. From time to time we cooperate with mathematicians, or are forced to turn ourselves into mathematicians, in order to find the mathematical clothing, so to speak, that fits the biological phenomena we're interested in. It's therefore absolutely out of the question for us to think of identifying biological reality with mathematical objects. We merely try to construct mathematical objects that are compatible with natural objects. We reason, we solve equations, we work out model after model, we consult a literature that's full of trial and error. But, in the end, what do we do? We *select* the most suitable model. Our view of mathematics is therefore extremely concrete and pragmatic. We retain only that which fits best with the real world. For us, mathematics is a creature of our own thought processes—nothing more, nothing less.

This leads me to ask you again about quantum mechanics, a

branch of physics I don't know as well as I'd like. I have the feeling that physicists working in this area have trouble modeling what happens on a scale vastly different from that on which our brain and sensory organs function. When physicists tell us that the laws of quantum physics impose a fundamental indeterminacy—I intentionally use their own terms—one wonders if they haven't committed a serious epistemological error—

CONNES: You mean a "linguistic error"—

CHANGEUX: Namely, of identifying nature with the model they build to describe it. One may ask whether they take into account not only the measuring instrument and the observer's bias (figure 13), but also the functioning of their own brain and its ability to capture phenomena on a scale where ordinary experience and common sense no longer apply. How do you view this problem?

CONNES: Having had firsthand experience of the fundamental indeterminacy you mention, I have a quite definite opinion. First, there is the problem of language, though it's not the main problem. When we speak of a particle, and picture it as a material

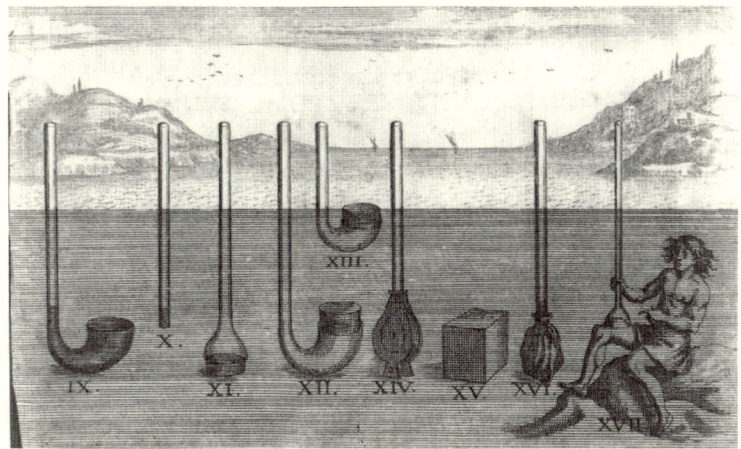

Figure 13. Observational Bias in Measurement

This engraving, taken from the second edition (1664) of Pascal's *Traité de l'équilibre des liqueurs*, illustrates the problem of physical measurement from the perspective of the experimentalist, who curiously is pictured here below water level.

point with a determinate position and velocity, we know that these aren't the right terms. If, for example, we want to imagine an electron orbiting the nucleus of a hydrogen atom, it's much better to think of the wave function determined by Schrödinger's equation and the level of energy than to think about a planetary system. Moreover, for a complex atom, such as the helium atom with two electrons around its nucleus, it's much harder to come up with a mental picture because the wave function, whose size in space can at least be visualized in the case of a single electron (figure 14), is now a function of *two* variables in space—that is, a function in six-dimensional space.

The next point to be made is that the language of particles, while it's poorly adapted to this purpose, nonetheless permits questions to be formulated to which nature provides an answer. To take a concrete example, consider a discrete source of particles—of electrons, for example—that from time to time emits an electron in the direction of a very narrow slit, thus creating a diffraction phenomenon. One can describe the system in terms of wave functions, and predict a pattern of diffraction against a screen placed behind the slit, corresponding to the path of the electron. If talk of particles were entirely useless, the proof would be that the electron becomes transformed into a cloud because of the phenomenon of diffraction. Yet this isn't the case: each time the experiment is conducted, an impact is registered at a precise spot on the screen. The electron therefore remains a particle. It's during experiments of precisely this type that the indeterminacy you mentioned appears. In fact, each time an electron is emitted by the source, an impact is measured at position x on the target screen (figure 15), but—and this is the crucial point—the experimental result "The source emits an electron that lands on the screen at point x" can't be reproduced. This has nothing to do with the precision with which x is specified. Even the experimental result "The source emits an electron that lands on the upper half of the screen" is not reproducible. It won't *ever* be possible to specify the initial experimental conditions precisely enough that we can be sure of obtaining the same final result every time.

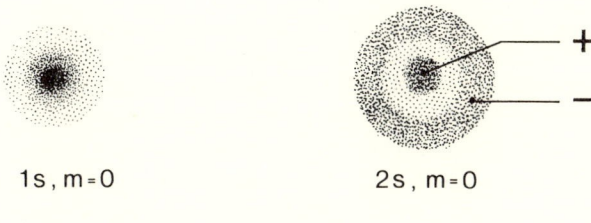

1s, m=0   2s, m=0

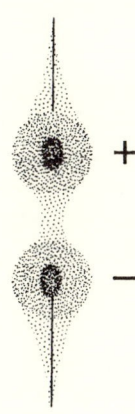

2p, m=0

Figure 14. Examples of the Wave Function of the Electron in the Hydrogen Atom

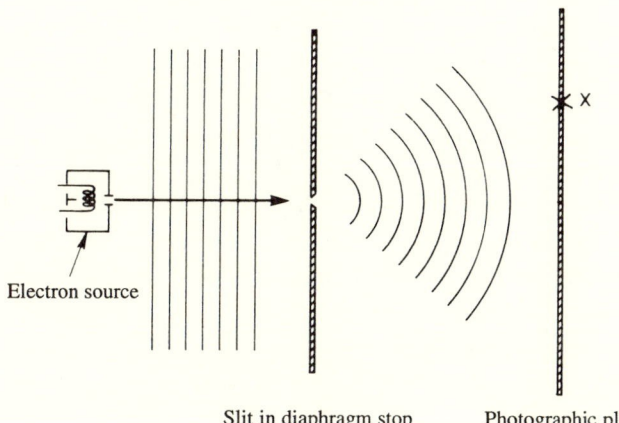

Electron source

Slit in diaphragm stop   Photographic plate

Figure 15. The Diffraction Phenomenon

On the second try, there's only one chance in two of obtaining the same final result. No matter how precise the instrument that emits the electrons, the experiment can't be repeated with the same result. The only thing that can be reproduced is a certain density, a certain frequency curve of impacts from which the probability of the electron hitting a given portion of the target screen can be derived. It will have the shape of a diffraction curve, and will allow us to say only that the electron will hit the screen at such-and-such a spot with such-and-such a probability.

CHANGEUX: That doesn't prove the existence of a fundamental indeterminacy. The same thing could occur in a more macroscopic situation, as the result, for example, of Brownian motion—

CONNES: Yes, it does. It's important to see the mistake in considering the fact that the electron goes "tick" at a certain point on the screen to be a reproducible result. No theory can predict the result of this experiment, because it isn't reproducible. When we want to do physics, we must define what counts as a physical phenomenon. As soon as we give a coherent definition, there's nothing confusing about it, there's no paradox in quantum mechanics. The theory fits perfectly with its mathematical model. What definition can we give of a physical phenomenon? We can only speak of a physical phenomenon as a reproducible experimental result. A physical phenomenon is therefore the result of an experiment whose outcome will be identical every time, assuming the initial conditions are specified (even if only for the benefit of researchers at another laboratory). If, on the other hand, we can't precisely convey the initial conditions to others in such a way that they will achieve the same experimental result, then the phenomenon we're studying is not a physical phenomenon. Accordingly, it can't be predicted by a theory.

CHANGEUX: Therefore there's no fundamental indeterminacy. The fact that an electron has one point of impact at one moment and a different one at another might one day be explained deterministically.

CONNES: No, not at all. We know that the phenomenon can't be explained by reference to "hidden variables"—

CHANGEUX: Because the hypothesis of hidden variables derives from a very particular model. But perhaps another model exists that physicists haven't yet thought of.

CONNES: No. The hidden variable hypothesis isn't compatible with the current model of quantum mechanics—a model whose only justification is its incredible success. A series of experiments could be imagined testing Bell's inequalities, which demonstrate that the interpretation of hidden variables is incompatible with the current model. My position is very simply stated: certain results belong to physics, because they are reproducible, and others don't, because they aren't reproducible.

CHANGEUX: I wonder about the use of the term "nonreproducibility." Stimulating the eye triggers a burst of neuronal impulses. But, recording the same cell, using *exactly* the same stimulus, we won't necessarily find the same number of impulses or the same firing frequency from one experiment to another.

CONNES: Of course not. But a reproducible law could be extracted from these experiments, and that's the only one that counts.

CHANGEUX: Exactly. After a certain number of experiments an average response will emerge that is far easier to reproduce. But then biologists will say that a "determinism" governs the genesis of this response, from the sensory receptor to the neuron—the intervening fluctuations notwithstanding. I use the term "fluctuations" because we're talking about a variability due to the finer modalities of the signal's transmission at the synaptic level, at the level of the geometry of the connections between nerve cells and so forth, which the researcher can't control in this sort of experiment. In fact, there are several levels of variability in the transfer of information within the nervous system, none of them in the least mysterious. If the processes that physicists study were analyzed in the same way, one might ask if they simply hadn't yet found the right model, or at least one yielding a deeper explanation. Granted, the hidden variables model doesn't work. But I hesitate, in the face of a negative result or a failed interpretation, to say that one day a more rational explanation won't be found.

CONNES: In the case of the eye, we know that if the experiment were to be repeated under the same initial conditions, we would obtain the same burst of impulses.

CHANGEUX: Theoretically, yes—but as a practical matter, no.

CONNES: Whereas in quantum mechanics, it's impossible for theoretical reasons—that's the difference.

CHANGEUX: I don't quite follow. Theoretically it appears impossible—but isn't that simply because the right theory hasn't yet been discovered?

CONNES: No. This is a subtle point that unfortunately you seem not to grasp. Certain experimental results can't be considered physical phenomena because they're not reproducible. No theory can hope to predict a phenomenon that can't be reproduced. I can't make my position any clearer than this.

CHANGEUX: But it's not out of the question that such a phenomenon might one day become reproducible. Physicists give the impression of being obsessed with theories that explain natural phenomena well enough that they don't want to try to find better ones—unless they're preoccupied by a certain problem and are willing to go to the trouble of getting to the bottom of things.

CONNES: It *is* out of the question. Theory, such as it is, shows that this fundamental indeterminacy manifests itself as soon as we take two successive measurements of observable quantities that don't commute. Heisenberg's uncertainty principle quantitatively specifies this indeterminacy. The principle therefore has experimental as well as theoretical validity. Quantum mechanics thus poses the problem of experimentation, of nonreproducible experimental results, at the experimental level. If, in the electron experiment, I were to close the slit and measure the backward movement of the screen due to the electron's impact, this phenomenon would be perfectly reproducible and perfectly explainable by physics—by the rule of conservation of momentum. If I were to say, "When a considerable number of electrons are fired, the probability of their landing at such-and-such a spot on the screen has such-and-such a value," this would be a perfectly reproducible phenomenon, perfectly explainable by the theory. But if I were to say, "The electron hit the screen at such-and-such a spot," this wouldn't be a reproducible experimental result.

CHANGEUX: By "physical phenomenon" you mean a reproducible phenomenon. Therefore the experimental conditions must be defined in such a way that the phenomenon becomes reproducible. If we knew the events that determine the movement of the electron toward the top or bottom of the screen, the phenomenon would become reproducible—

CONNES: If you knew this much, you'd be looking at a different phenomenon—a different experimental result, even at the statistical level.

CHANGEUX: I'd say then that your theory is bad.

CONNES: Fine, but it precisely explains the experimental phenomena that are reproducible. And, as I described earlier in some detail, it even predicts what is known as the anomalous magnetic moment—of an electron, for example—to a degree of accuracy equal to the thickness of a hair divided by the distance from Paris to New York. That's pretty good.

CHANGEUX: But there remains an unexplained sublevel to which theoreticians haven't yet gained mental access, as it were. The Hodgkin-Huxley model, for example, is perfectly suited to accounting for the electrical phenomena of the nerve impulse in terms of ionic transport. Nonetheless it didn't lead right away to the identification of the underlying ionic channels. This was done by molecular biologists using methods radically different from those employed by Hodgkin and Huxley in their experiments.

CONNES: Limiting the field of investigation to reproducible phenomena, one ends up with a perfectly coherent whole. But the impossibility of predicting exactly where the electron will strike the screen entails a very frustrating form of self-denial for theoretical physicists. There is a way to escape the quandary posed by the apparent indeterminacy of quantum mechanics: Everett's notion of parallel universes.[2] Everything takes place on the assumption that all possible events can occur—as if our electron could land anywhere on the screen. But each of these choices would

---

[2] Several of Everett's most important papers, along with commentary on the implications of his work, are collected in *The Many-Worlds Interpretation of Quantum Mechanics*, ed. B. S. DeWitt and N. Graham (Princeton: Princeton University Press, 1973).

signify a bifurcation from one universe to a parallel one. To simplify matters, let's suppose that we take a measurement with two possible results. The actual result then creates a bifurcation between two parallel universes: we find ourselves in one or the other depending on which one of the two possibilities actually occurs. These parallel universes are sufficiently coherent that, statistically, the average result is the same. Each experimental result depends on the particular parallel universe we branch off toward; but neither result, in and of itself, is reproducible.

CHANGEUX: That's an interesting idea, I think. But the stubborn confusion between irreproducibility and indeterminacy suggests that the majority of theoretical physicists are faced with a failure that unconsciously they refuse to admit to.

CONNES: One can't hope to predict theoretically a result that isn't reproducible. The primary characteristic of a physical experiment—everyone, I think, is in agreement on this point—is its reproducibility. If it can't be reproduced, it's not really physics. The failure isn't only theoretical; it's experimental. When we adjust the experimental equipment, we don't know how to specify the initial conditions in order to determine the electron's point of impact in advance. Heisenberg's uncertainty principle says that this can never be known, and that the same indeterminacy manifests itself when two noncommuting quantities are successively measured, as in the Stern-Gerlach experiment.

CHANGEUX: One could perhaps control for an unknown physical parameter. This is both a theoretical and an experimental question, of course. For a mathematician to suggest an experiment to physicists would be an intriguing reversal of the usual situation!

CONNES: It's nonetheless very important to see that the failure is as much an experimental failure as a theoretical one—which is why I like to use this example, of the electrons and the screen. One tends to suppose that only the theory is at stake. The experiment itself is at issue: we're faced with an experimental result that we don't know how to reproduce.

CHANGEUX: It's harder to design a good experiment than a mediocre theory. Our discussion makes it clear that the mysterious indeterminacy which some physicists talk about isn't very meaningful really. We'd all do better to face up to the fact that the state of our knowledge hasn't yet reached the point that we can usefully entertain such notions, either on the theoretical or the experimental plane. The thought of accepting ignorance as a law of nature troubles me.

CONNES: What our discussion makes clear is that you still don't understand the problem of indeterminacy. The body of current scientific doctrine is perfectly coherent, and enables us to account for exactly those experimental results that are reproducible. I hardly see how we could account for results that aren't. It's very difficult to accept that at the microscopic, quantum level there are phenomena that aren't reproducible—nevertheless, this is a fact. The philosophical implications are not easy to assess. What seems incomprehensible here is that nature, at the atomic level at least, may be unpredictable. Even physico-chemical "reality" is more subtle than it appears, threatening to undermine the foundations of materialism.

4. *The Neuronal Mathematician*

CHANGEUX: Few mathematicians today take much of an interest in the workings of the brain. I notice that Dieudonné in his *Pour l'honneur de l'esprit humain* (a title that recalls the *Ad majorem dei gloriam* of Ignatius Loyola, by the way), mentions the word "brain" only very rarely, in any case not in an explanatory way. Quite the opposite, in fact. He says, for example, that no one has succeeded in giving a rational explanation for the creative activity of the brain, whether in mathematics or in any other field. I read this book with great interest, and I like it very much, despite the fact that Dieudonné examines the evolution of mathematics as if it were wholly independent of the brain—rather like art historians who consider the evolution of painting and sculpture without taking into account the fact that we see more with the brain than with the eye! It's important to remember that one does mathematics with the brain as well. There's no other way to do it!

CONNES: I couldn't agree more. The brain is a material tool. Understanding its function in the work of the mathematician is fundamental.

CHANGEUX: Still we find certain mathematicians in the past, such as Poincaré and Hadamard, whose interests were similar to our own. Hadamard, in his excellent work *The Psychology of Invention in the Mathematical Field*, inquires into the role of the unconscious and its successive layers in mathematical creation. He cites Hippolyte Taine's *On Intelligence*, the work of a philosopher who still deigned to recognize scientific data, neuroscientific data in particular—a practice that since Sartre, Foucault and their successors has been largely neglected in contemporary philosophy (to the benefit of psychoanalysis, it needs to be said). Some notable exceptions now begin to make their voices heard, however, in France and elsewhere.

Hadamard describes his work as a mathematician in a way I find very interesting. First off he distinguishes "preparation," which involves—let's be honest about this—the trial and error that the mathematician piously omits to mention when he presents his work in polished form. (Poincaré's attempts to "govern the unconscious" is subjected to special scrutiny in this connection.) He goes on to distinguish two further stages in mathematical creation that build upon the first, "incubation" and "illumination." He also emphasizes the use of signs as well as of mental imagery, making reference to a psychologist of the period, Alfred Binet, who like Taine was much interested in mental imagery experiments, following the English associationists. It's interesting to note that this interest in mental imagery has now resurfaced in experimental psychology with the work of Kosslyn and Shepard in America and, in France, of Denis. Here again one finds psychologists and neurobiologists working on a common problem. Mental images for them aren't to be understood as being in any sense evanescent or immaterial, but rather as concrete and well-defined forms of cerebral activity. Following upon the preparatory and incubation stages, Hadamard notes, it sometimes happens that the mathematician experiences a surge of mental images accompanied by a sudden sense of *illumination* spreading throughout his brain and his entire being. This is the critical step in the work of mathematical creation. But a fourth and final stage, more conscious than the preceding two, necessarily follows. It consists in the deliberate process of verification and definition that permits an argument, a theorem or a proof, to be precisely stated and then put to use. In this last step, reasoning and judgment are called into play.

Hadamard's approach is introspective in character. Accordingly it is often criticized by psychologists, philosophers and, of course, neurobiologists, for being subjective. But it may be that the sensations he reports are common to all mathematicians. What do you make of Hadamard's account of mathematical creation?

CONNES: I myself have experienced sensations of the sort he describes—or at least I believe I have. There are several phases, corresponding more or less to the stages Hadamard mentions. The first builds on knowledge that has already been acquired. Gradually one comes to concentrate upon a very precise object of thought; one tries to focus on preparing the groundwork, on surrounding oneself with familiar things. This leads into Hadamard's second phase. At the end of the incubation period, if one is lucky, one experiences the illumination he describes. The final phase, verification, begins once illumination has taken place. The process of verification can be very painful: one's terribly *afraid* of being wrong. Of the four phases it involves the most anxiety, for one never knows if one's intuition is right—a bit as in dreams, where intuition very often proves mistaken. I remember once having taken a month to verify a result: I went over the proof down to the smallest detail, to the point of obsession—when I could have simply entrusted the task of checking the logic of the argument to an electronic calculator. But the moment illumination occurs, it engages the emotions in such a way that it's impossible to remain passive or indifferent. On those rare occasions when I've actually experienced it, I couldn't keep tears from coming to my eyes.

I've often observed too that once the first hurdle of preparation has been gotten over, one runs up against a wall. The main error to be avoided is trying to attack the problem head-on. During the incubation phase, you have to proceed indirectly, obliquely. If you think too directly about a problem, you fairly quickly exhaust the usefulness of the tools accumulated in the course of the first phase, and are apt to become discouraged. Thought needs to be liberated in such a way that subconscious work can take place. Relatively long but elementary algebraic calculations, for example, in the course of which thought is only indirectly focused, are quite favorable to subconscious intervention. Obviously one needs to dispose of a certain degree of serenity, enough anyway to enable one to achieve a state of contemplation, as it were—the opposite of the sort of concentration that a student brings to an exam. The best a student who relied on the technique of a mature mathematician could hope to say afterward would be, "Well, I blew the test, but at least I came up with an idea I'll want to work on for a long time." What's striking, when you proceed indirectly, is how far removed the initial problem appears to be from subsequent areas of investigation.

CHANGEUX: Of course. During this whole time your brain is spontaneously active, busily evolving new hypotheses, making rough sketches—

CONNES: But not of the initial problem.

CHANGEUX: How is it possible for the solution to appear so suddenly, when you've been circling round the problem for so long?

CONNES: It's rather difficult to say. Experience shows that if one attacks a problem directly, the resources of rational "straight-ahead" thought are very quickly used up. One succeeds in getting a grip on the difficulty, but if one doesn't manage to free oneself from it, one generally doesn't succeed in solving the problem— again, the opposite of what usually happens in an exam situation, where it's only a question of automatically carrying out certain operations. At this borderline stage between preparation and incubation, the mathematician is working pretty much with the knowledge he already has of a given problem. One takes in the problem easily enough, one manages to precisely identify the difficulty, but beyond this one quickly finds that a straightforward approach no longer helps. Only by coming up with an oblique strategy of some sort, one that involves thinking about related questions not known to have any direct connection with the problem itself, is it possible to make further progress.

CHANGEUX: Are these quite different questions, or are they fairly similar?

CONNES: They're apt to be quite different.

CHANGEUX: Is it a matter simply of giving working memory enough to do and giving greater rein to an unconscious process that relies more on long-term memory? Or is it, to the contrary, a kind of associational procedure that takes time because the elements that need to be put together belong to rather different contexts? I understood you to mean that circling round a problem makes it possible to bring forth new mathematical objects, which in combination with other objects more directly related to the problem lead to a solution, or which, in acting upon long-term memory, somehow obliquely conjure up a more adequate representation of the problem. Are we talking about a kind of "blackout" of rational thought, a kind of attenuated consciousness, that allows "incongruous" internal representations to reveal themselves, which in turn allow mathematical objects to become "unnaturally" associated? Are you saying that these are all elements of a parallel process of reflection, that they're incorporated in a final solution through the back door, so to speak? I'll explain my reasons for asking this question in just a moment.

CONNES: I can only speak of my own experience. I was concentrating upon something quite distinct from the problem itself, though my thoughts remained within the same general problem space. Eventually I arrived at a solution to the problem, without ever having the impression that the problem had guided me to it.

CHANGEUX: Just the same, the solution was deep inside of you somehow.

CONNES: Probably so, though I wasn't in the least conscious of it. I asked myself another question, which came to assume a different form and eventually led me to the solution of the original problem.

CHANGEUX: Let me then ask you again: when you draw upon a reservoir of knowledge to solve a problem, whether it's directly or indirectly related, does this mathematical material persist in recombinant form, as it were, in the final solution?

CONNES: Again, it's hard to say. The problem I was wrestling with essentially involved showing that a certain definable mathematical object was unique—a highly technical and arduous job that was difficult to attack directly because, as I say, I very quickly found that I'd used up all the tools at my disposal. By wandering over into an adjacent—but nonetheless distinct—field of mathematics, where objects were more numerous and easier to manipulate, I managed to develop an expertise, an intuition that could be applied to the first problem. It was a matter, therefore, of having a framework for thinking, a neighboring field for exploring the problem indirectly.

CHANGEUX: You used a framework, then, rather than thought objects.

CONNES: Exactly—a framework in which my thinking could move about and evolve, instead of being pinned with its back against the wall, as it were—when it found itself blocked by the sheer difficulty of the problem, by its excessively specific context, so to speak.

CHANGEUX: You somehow managed to enlarge the context to let *variability* appear. This is a perfect metaphor for Darwinian evolution! In effect, you defined a period in the course of which conscious or unconscious variations could emerge, thought objects could become associated, and Desanti's "subframeworks" could link up within a more general framework than that of the problem at hand.

CONNES: Let's say, to simplify matters, that mathematicians who don't succeed in solving a problem usually try to generalize it in order to be able to solve a particular case—to create an opening into which a small piece of the puzzle can be made to fit. The hope, of course, is that by solving this particular case of the generalized problem, which has little to do with the initial problem, it will become possible to generate an idea that can then be adapted to help solve it. One tries, therefore, to generalize in order to discover several different aspects of the problem; and then, proceeding by relatively small steps, to arrive at a solution.

CHANGEUX: One tries, therefore, to combine previously unrelated elements by bringing them together within a larger framework. It's been suggested that a similar process takes place when a subject is faced with the problem of "understanding" a given task needing to be carried out.

CONNES: The distinction between the subconscious process of Hadamard's second stage and the type of procedure I've just mentioned, which is explicit and forms part of the common cultural heritage of mathematics, shouldn't be obscured. The latter isn't at all an unconscious strategy: all mathematicians are familiar with it. Nonetheless I've often had the impression that the brain operates in ways that can't be directly perceived but that are based upon quite analogous mechanisms.

CHANGEUX: It may very well be that there exists a step whereby memory objects are collected in the brain, making them accessible to what might be called *consciousness*. A sort of division of mental labor results, without the conscious will having to perfectly master all of the operations involved. This is true for mathematics, as for thought in general. Thought without language is, in fact, possible. The experience of the working mathematician that you describe suggests an incubation phase does actually occur, marked by transitory mental variations that recombine over time. When one of them is found to suit the initial problem, a solution emerges within the enlarged framework you mention: thus illumination!

But now we come to an important point: under what conditions is this attempt to fit things together likely to be successful? A great many transient mathematical objects are summoned up, consciously or unconsciously, and then, all of a sudden, everything clicks—the key fits the lock and opens the door. In terms of a "mental Darwinism" schema, selection processes come into play once a diversity generator produces a certain range of mental variations that Stanislas Dehaene and I have also referred to as "pre-representations."

CONNES: It's difficult to know whether a diversity generator plays such a role during the incubation phase. Your model is appropriate to the behavior of a computer programmed to play chess, which is relatively Darwinian. The computer is capable of processing a very large number of possible moves. This would come to nothing in the absence of a selection function that measures both the advantage obtained after several moves and the strength of the resulting position. It's therefore necessary to introduce a quantity that expresses the gain and the positional strength, which the computer itself must be able to optimize. To posit a Darwinian mechanism that governs the functioning of the "mathematical brain," it would be necessary first to identify and locate the analogue to this selection function.

Mathematicians know very well that understanding a theorem doesn't mean understanding, step by step, a proof that can take several hours just to read. It's a matter instead of taking in the whole thing in an extremely short time. The brain must be capable somehow of "verifying" this proof in the space of a second or two. One is certain of having understood a theorem if one has this feeling—not if one is able to run through the proof without finding anything wrong, which yields only a sort of local comprehension. At the moment of illumination some mechanism comes into play that I can't really describe, except to say it ensures that the key will indeed open the lock. To establish the existence of a Darwinian mechanism in the brain, it would be necessary to understand what type of evaluation function is at work during the incubation period for selecting the solution to the problem. One could then very roughly say that the first stage—preparation—consists in consciously constructing an evaluation function connected with affectivity, which could be crudely expressed by the formula: "*That's* the problem I want to solve." The Darwinian mechanism would correspond then to the second stage—incubation—with illumination occurring only when the value of the evaluation function is large enough to trigger the affective reaction.

CHANGEUX: A kind of "pleasure alarm" goes off, in other words, rather than a danger alarm, signaling—

CONNES: That what's been found works, is coherent and, one might even say, aesthetically pleasing. I'm certain that this pleasure is analogous to that experienced by painters the moment that they find a solution, the moment they see that a canvas is perfectly coherent and harmonious. The mathematical brain must function in the same way. But the word "Darwinian" seems to suggest that there is something hidden that controls the selection function, that determines the quantity to be optimized.

CHANGEUX: Of course. But nothing's hidden. Selection is built into the mechanism. Darwinian-style analysis is concerned mainly with distinguishing stages of evolution that are mistakenly run together or otherwise remain unclear. A model is of interest to the extent it helps us make progress, at least in analyzing a phenomenon if not also in understanding it.

THE BRAIN AND ITS MULTIPLE LEVELS OF ORGANIZATION

CHANGEUX: Now we are ready to go on to another question: what role does neuroscience have to play in understanding the mechanisms responsible for producing and processing mathematical objects? Recall Desanti's argument against a strong materialist epistemology. Such an epistemology must include a description of the knowledge acquisition apparatus and its function—that is to say, of our brain and the manner in which it produces mathematical objects. The attempt to understand the neural basis of mathematics therefore assumes a fundamental scientific importance. This approach is rejected as useless by philosophers and psychologists of the "functionalist" school, such as Fodor, Pylyshyn, or Johnson-Laird. For them it's enough to give an algorithmic description of thought processes. They distinguish the neural organization of the brain from what Anglo-Saxon authors call "mind" (the English term carries none of the metaphysical connotation associated with the French *esprit*)—that is to say, they distinguish the brain's neural organization from its *functions*. On this view, structure and function are to be sharply separated; even so distinguished a philosopher as Fodor claims, for instance, that the attempt to pair neurological structures with psychological functions can expect only limited success. Functionalists believe that a mathematical description of cerebral functions has explanatory value, and suffices for understanding cognition in general. For Johnson-Laird, for example, the physical nature of the neurophysiological substrate places no constraints whatsoever on the pattern of thought. As a neurobiologist, I've always been opposed to this attitude. I'm convinced, to the contrary, that the attempt to describe the neural basis of brain function, and in particular the neural basis of mathematical activity, will improve both our knowledge of the brain and of mathematics.

CONNES: Absolutely.

CHANGEUX: Before we get to the neural basis of mathematics, we should perhaps define the notion of *level of organization*. The biologist's work consists generally in matching a function and a defined structural organization, which means establishing a causal relation between structure and function. Before even tackling a problem, if one doesn't stop to ask how structure and function go together, there's a great risk of making huge errors. You're familiar with some of them. One of the most celebrated was the belief of certain nineteenth-century "physicalist" biologists, such as Buchner, in spontaneous generation. Initially the debate turned upon whether the presence of yeast is necessary for fermentation to take place. Fermentation seemed to be a process of "chemical decomposition" that could be produced wholly *in vitro*—as, in fact, Buchner showed it could be. But from this it was deduced that a living cell could be reconstituted from a population of molecules in solution, thereby demonstrating the possibility of spontaneous generation—which Pasteur denied at the time, and rightly so as it turned out. Where did the error come from? Certainly not because "vital forces" irreducible to the laws of physics and chemistry were operating to prevent the reconstitution from taking place! The difficulty arose from the fact that the extreme complexity of cellular organization, which we have still not been able to satisfactorily model even for organisms as simple as yeast or bacteria, was not properly appreciated. True, a cell is composed only of molecules. But these molecules form a highly organized whole that divides and multiplies as a result of very specialized, very intricate mutual interactions that we're still quite a long way from fully understanding. Researchers at the time didn't get the relation between structure and function right—the correspondence they hypothesized between the two, depending on different levels of organization, proved to be wrong.

This trap must be avoided in examining the relationship of mathematics to the brain. I'm aware that my simply raising the problem irritates you. The idea is so fixed in your mind that mathematics constitutes a distinct world from the neurons and synapses and all the rest of the machinery that makes up the brain, I wonder if it isn't a waste of my time trying to challenge it. You're utterly opposed to thinking of mathematics as a product of the brain. But for it to make any sense to talk of a static structure bearing causal relation to a naturally dynamic function, it has to be assumed that this relation exists at some appropriate level of organization. At the very outset, then, the biologist must define the appropriate hierarchical levels on the functional plane, before even embarking upon experimental research.

Now philosophers of mind, the greatest ones in particular, have long been interested in this question. Thus Kant, for example, distinguishes three levels, which seem to me worthwhile recalling: first, *sensibility*, which is defined by the capacity of sense organs to receive "impressions"; second, *understanding*, or the conceptual faculty that permits the synthesis of sensible elements; third, *reason*, which contains the principles governing the use of the concepts spontaneously produced by understanding. These distinctions lead us to picture three levels of abstraction: the generation of representations based on the objects of the external world; their abstraction as concepts; and the organization of these concepts at higher orders of abstraction—all this, of course, *in* the brain. Having defined these levels, one can then begin to think about trying to establish some relationship with the organization of connectivity in the brain (figure 16). Computer scientists such as Newell and Simon, it is interesting to note by the way, have long been concerned with the problem of hierarchical levels in computers.

CONNES: The question of hierarchical organization is crucial. Even if we confine our attention to mathematics, I'm convinced that the

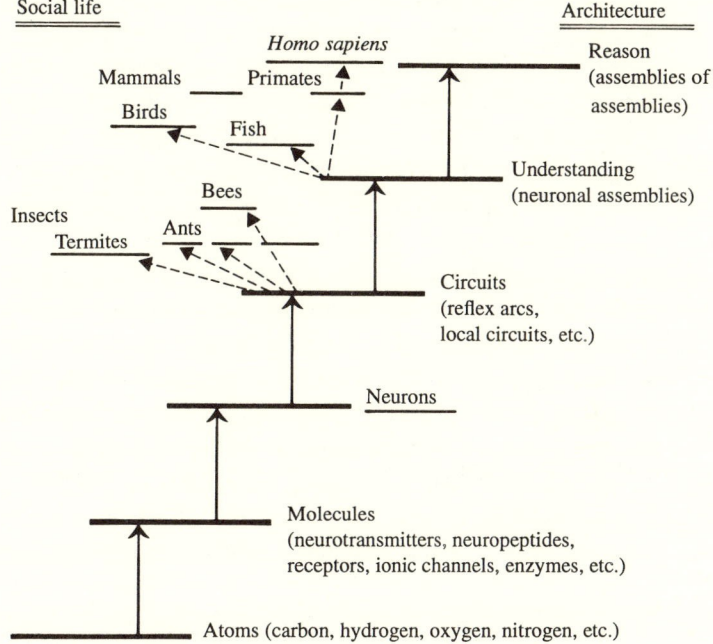

Figure 16. Levels of Organization in the Nervous System

comparison with computers can help us to sharpen the definition of different levels of activity of the brain.

CHANGEUX: Newell and Simon define what they call a *knowledge level*, which they imagine to be located in a theoretically feasible, but as yet unbuilt, machine equipped with a symbol-processing capacity well beyond that of existing computers. They conceive of the knowledge level as being permanently enriched by new experience in accordance with a "principle of rationality" that runs as follows: "If an agent knows that a certain action will lead to a certain goal or aim, then the agent will select that action."

CONNES: I'd have to amend that statement a bit.

CHANGEUX: You can rewrite it altogether if you like! The basic question is this: do you agree that there exists a cleavage between at least two levels, one roughly corresponding to understanding (the symbolic level), and the other to reason (the knowledge level)?

CONNES: It would be simple enough to more or less precisely define three levels of mathematical activity, but I'm not sure how these would relate or not relate to Kant's three levels. I'd rather we used a different terminology.

CHANGEUX: Be my guest! And then I'll see if I can make your three levels square with the neurological evidence.

CONNES: The first level, at least as far as mathematical activity is concerned, corresponds to present-day computers. Built-in mechanisms make it possible to arrive at precise answers to problems of a given (generally computational) type. It's possible, for example, to do division without understanding why it works—today, of course, computers do this much better than we can. But even in the case of very sophisticated operations, such as calculating integrals or tracing the graph of a function, the mechanism is always given in advance.

CHANGEUX: We're talking about the level of elementary operations, I take it.

CONNES: The level of calculation anyway, if not always of elementary operations. Operations can be more complicated, but no matter—the main thing is that being able to carry out these operations doesn't have any practical effect on how they're actually carried out. Once one's learned to do addition, well enough at least to pass on to the next level, one doesn't change the way one does it—one goes on applying the same method without wondering why. A lot of people can do division, can go on dividing for a long time in fact, without having any understanding of the mechanism involved. They do it automatically. Computers today haven't gone beyond simple calculation, since they have no understanding of the mechanism they apply. The algorithms they employ produce results, and much faster than the human brain does, it's true; but for all of that they remain algorithms. I've never been impressed by the human prodigies who rely on well-worn calculating tricks, or by people who think perfectly rationally—people who never miss an opportunity to point out faults of spelling or of syntax in others, for example. Why? Because they remain at the first level—the level of calculation, which doesn't require any global comprehension of the system. There isn't any interaction in this case between the system and the calculations carried out within it. The second level, on the other hand, is harder to define—

CHANGEUX: Two levels aren't enough?

CONNES: No. Mathematical activity really involves three levels. I make no claim whatsoever that they correspond to Kant's levels. What I *would* like to emphasize is the richness of the first level. It encompasses, for example, everything that one does in upper level math during the last year at *lycée* in France, tracing graphs of curves and doing kinematic calculations.

CHANGEUX: The most idiotic kind of math!

CONNES: I remember having a math teacher who liked to say, "I want you to learn to do the easy things quickly and well." One only learned to apply rules. The second level begins when the actual method of calculation is adapted to, and criticized in the context of, a particular problem. Let's suppose, for example, that there are two different methods for doing a calculation and that they yield different results. Here one finds oneself at the second level. One has to ask whether the method employed in each case is valid, whether errors were made in the course of calculating, and whether the calculations themselves lead to a meaningful result. In testing the method, one comes to understand both its aim and its mechanism. It's perfectly obvious that, for the time being at least, computers can't do this . . .

CHANGEUX: But one can ask a computer to check its own method.

CONNES: It's true that if several different computers carry out the same calculation, as is the case with a space shuttle, for example, it's possible by comparing the results to eliminate errors due to the misfunction of any single one. But this is still very far from a computer being able to reflect upon the point of the calculation, or upon the possibility of changing strategy.

CHANGEUX: It's clearly not reached the level of reason then.

CONNES: I don't claim it has. It's what I call "second-level." When a calculation doesn't work out, when for example one arrives at two different results, instead of simply applying a rule and seeing if one has made a mistake, one adapts by changing strategy. Imagine someone who, in doing multiplication, found a simpler method for obtaining a certain result; or a chess-playing computer that succeeded in understanding its errors in order not to repeat them, or that invented a new strategy—invented a new opening, for example, instead of relying on a list of openings stored in memory.

CHANGEUX: A computer able to detect errors and propose alternative strategies would begin to approach the knowledge level.

CONNES: Here again we run into that frustration I was talking about: the computer would have to have this same feeling whenever it makes an error and loses at chess, or when its strategy is suboptimal. It would have to experience stress—or, inversely, pleasure at having found a faster, more efficient method. This would require a subtle mechanism, but not an impossibly difficult one to devise, it seems to me—not if much greater speeds of computation were assumed, for example. The computer would have to be able to invent and improve the mechanisms of calculation. Perhaps in certain cases this is now possible, but on the whole it's still a matter of speculation.

CHANGEUX: There would have to be some sort of feedback mechanism—what Edelman calls a "reentry" mechanism.

CONNES: Exactly. The computer itself would have to be able to improve its own program. The brain, quite obviously, is capable of improving its own performance. But right now computers are some ways away from being able to do this, because it's hard to independently define the parameters that would produce frustration or pleasure in a computer, and that would allow it to straighten things out by itself—so hard, in fact, that computer programmers must look with a certain envy upon whatever it is in the brain that makes it possible for us to have feelings, since these play an essential role in the transition to the second level. It must be analogous to the ability to construct value hierarchies, and then to use and modify them. But let's move on to the third level: discovery. At this level it isn't only a matter of solving a given problem; it's also possible to discover—I don't say "invent," since that wouldn't fit with my philosophy of a preexisting mathematical world that is logically prior to any human intervention— it's possible to *discover* a part of mathematics to which the existing corpus gives no direct access. By posing new problems, one succeeds in opening up paths that previously were closed, in unveiling a still unexplored area of mathematical geography. Two types of mathematical activity can be distinguished: the one consists in solving problems that have already been set; the other, prompted either by a familiar problem or by pure reflection, consists in creating thought tools not found in the established corpus that will allow a new, unexplored part of mathematical reality to be revealed.

CHANGEUX: To come back to Kant—

CONNES: I don't say my levels are analogous to his. I haven't thought about that.

CHANGEUX: We'll never manage to make yours match up exactly with Kant's categories as he defined them—that's not important. The important thing is that we define levels of function. The first level, I think, is roughly that of understanding. The two others I would identify with reason, while ranking one above the other. Granger has distinguished two aspects of reason: on the one hand, a *tactical* aspect involving an observed relation between cause and consequence, formalizable by a propositional or logical calculus; and, on the other, a *strategic* aspect that gives free rein to logic and concerns itself with the plausibility of aims or ends. Tactical reason consists not merely in carrying out operations, but also in testing a logical calculus, in testing the validity of a logical proposition.

CONNES: Establishing the validity of the reasoning in a theorem belongs, as far as I'm concerned, to the first level. I continue to hope that computers may soon be able to do this.

CHANGEUX: If I've rightly understood Granger, tactical reason includes the possibility of changing tactics. This isn't only a question of testing a given tactic, but also of coming up with new ones—otherwise the word *reason* wouldn't be justified. Tactical reason seems close, then, to what you consider second level. From my point of view, however, developing a new *strategy* amounts to something more like pure creation, the opening of a new field of knowledge and investigation, the definition of a new category of problems.

CONNES: Yes and no. It seems to me that what I call second level takes in both Granger's tactical and strategic reason. It really doesn't matter that his divisions and mine don't coincide exactly, though, because I'm speaking as a mathematician rather than as a philosopher.

THE CELLULAR LEVEL

CHANGEUX: I'm not saying we've got to make all these definitions square precisely with each other. As a matter of fact, I reject this way of thinking—it's too reductive, too intransigent. What's more, it would be absurd to think that the brain is strictly compartmentalized. While the classification of mathematical activity by levels seems to accord fairly well with empirical reality, bear in mind that the classification is itself an operation that we carry out as scientists using our *brains*!

We're ready now to tackle neuroscience. Certain levels are very easy to distinguish, others more difficult. The simplest is that of the nerve cell, or neuron. The neuron consists of a cell body surrounded by a treelike structure of dendrites along which nerve impulses travel toward the cell body, and a single axon along which the propagated nerve impulse travels upon leaving the cell body (figure 17). As you know, our brain as a whole is composed of about one hundred billion neurons—a pretty huge figure any way you look at it! These neurons are linked to each other by areas of discontinuous contact called synapses. On average there are about ten thousand of these per nerve cell. The total number of synapses in our brain then is astronomically large,

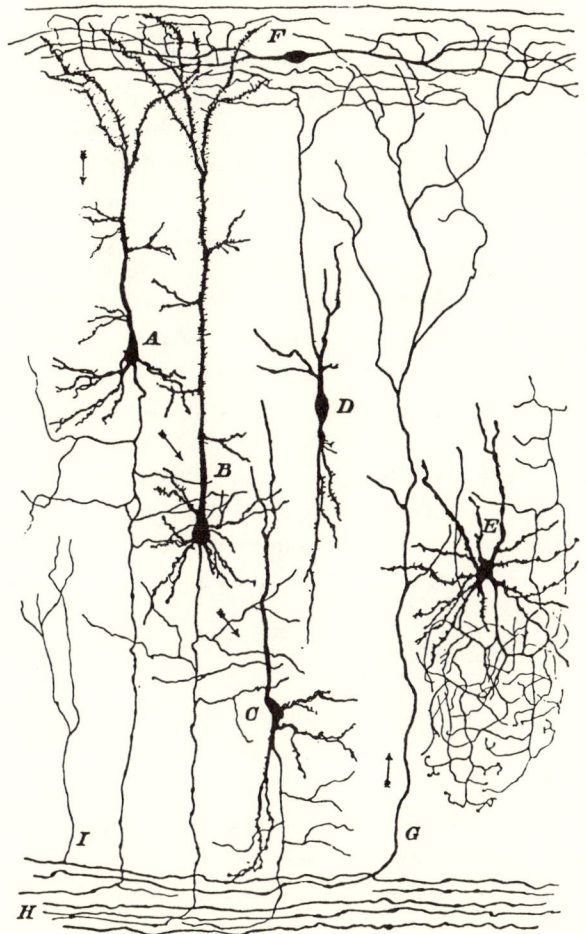

Figure 17. Principal Types of Neurons in the Mammalian Cerebral Cortex

The cells have been stained in black by the Golgi method. The dendritic branchings, which collect nerve signals, are connected by slender spines; a unique axon displays collateral ramifications often perpendicular to it. The arrows indicate the direction in which nerve signals are propagated. Three types of cells are shown: pyramidal cells (*A, B, C*); ascending axonal cells (*D*); and granule cells (*E*). (After S. Ramón y Cajal, in J. de Felipe and E. G. Jones, *Cajal on the Cerebral Cortex* [Oxford: Oxford University Press, 1988]) roughly on the order of 10^{15}–10^{16}. Where else in nature does one encounter this order of complexity?

CONNES: It's really colossal. At the atomic level one thinks of Avogadro's number, which isn't too far off at 10^{23}.

CHANGEUX: The neuron is the elementary building block—the tessera, to use a term from mosaics—of cerebral activity. Its function is relatively easily defined: to generate nerve impulses having an amplitude of roughly one hundred millivolts with a duration on the order of a millisecond. They propagate from one neuron to another along the axon at speeds less than the speed of sound, traveling anywhere from several meters to several dozens of meters per second, sometimes over considerable distances. In the brain, axons can reach a centimeter, even a dozen centimeters, in length; in the organism itself, they can be up to a full meter long, since the motor neurons of the spinal cord control the movement of the toes. Nerve impulses are discrete on-off signals; they propagate in the same way as solitons, and convey most of the information that can be processed within the central nervous system. They are discrete, universal, elementary units of activity.

CONNES: Can't you build in the chemical and hormonal component as well?

CHANGEUX: Of course—it's along this line that we've been working for the last twenty-five years. The chemical component is essential to the transmission of signals across synapses and to the regulation of synaptic efficacy, or strength. To think of the nervous system as a network of cables throughout which only electrical signals circulate would be too rigid—

CONNES: A bit too reductive . . .

CHANGEUX: The electrical pulses that circulate through our nervous system are all the same. They're identical in squid, flies, and human beings. They can be described by a single equation—Hodgkin's and Huxley's. And they can be produced autonomously and spontaneously by the nerve cell in the absence of any interaction with the outside world. But nerve impulses can also be evoked by contact with the environment. The visual system gives a good illustration of these two kinds of impulse-generating activity. Light impinging upon the receptor cells of the retina triggers after a few steps electrical activity in the ganglion cells, the axons of which form the optic nerve. The electrical pulses proceed along the optic nerve and reach the lateral geniculate body, where they stimulate relay neurons that send signals to the cerebral cortex at the level of the visual area. This, then, is externally generated activity. But our visual system is equally capable of spontaneous activity, for instance in the case of the fetus retina, where it can plausibly be interpreted as regulating the system's epigenetic maturation process. Nerve impulses therefore can be both spontaneously and externally generated, though of course once produced they are indistinguishable.

At the systemic level, the signaling "code" associated with these propagated waves is extremely simple. In addition to solitary waves, we note trains of impulses that are either regular or else spaced in time in a definite manner (exponentially, for example). Periodic pulse bursts can occur, with clocklike regularity in fact, but not as a sort of shorthand, or Morse code, for a language. (The "semantics" of the system is primarily located at the level of connective anatomy.) The state of neuronal activation throughout the network dictates the selection of a particular set of neurons, with a sort of "contrast" appearing between active and inactive neurons, or between neurons that are more active than others, or between neurons according to whether or not their states of activation are correlated (i.e., coherent). I should make clear that all of this takes place at the cellular level.

CONNES: Before going any further, a general question: looking at the electrical connections alone, I'm struck by the fact that the voltage propagates rather like a soliton, but at a speed far slower than that of light—on the order of sound, in fact!

CHANGEUX: Rather slower than sound actually.

CONNES: This is a great mystery to me. I really hope that one day it will be possible to explain how the extraordinarily slow rate at which information is propagated in the brain can have a positive rather than a negative effect. Present-day computers currently process information at a much higher rate of speed; and with the discovery of superconductivity at relatively high temperatures there is a good chance of being able fairly soon to build computers a thousand times faster than the ones we have today, thanks to dramatically reduced resistivity. How is it that the brain can function as effectively as it does with such a vastly inferior propagation system?

CHANGEUX: The rate of speed can't be said to play either a positive or negative role—it's simply a fact. You've got to think about the problem in another way, again adopting an evolutionary point of view. Cellular organization developed over the course of evolution in bacteria, then evolved further in the so-called higher organisms with true nuclei on the basis of a restricted number of existing elements—which is why François Jacob speaks of "tinkering." On the basis of these elements, an impermeable lipid membrane containing ion-selective transport systems (channel proteins selective for Na+, K+, Ca++ ions and the like) resulted in the generation of an electrochemical gradient and, in consequence of this, a membrane potential. This electrical potential was then "exploited" by the cell to produce a self-propagating signal. This mechanism of signal generation and propagation has been conserved and utilized in far more complex systems.

The nerve impulse, or action potential, probably first appeared in very primitive unicellular organisms. Propagated electrical signals are recorded, in fact, in paramecia and unicellular algae. In more complex multicellular organisms of the "animal" type, certain cells are differentiated by their capacity to produce fibers, or cables, that serve to communicate, to transmit orders to other cells. The nervous system develops as a control center for the organism. The specialized cells constituting it make use of existing electrical properties to propagate signals, to give and receive signals from the other cells of the organism. The relatively slow rate at which signals pass through the nervous system is the result of its evolutionary history: primitive living organisms didn't generate components capable of exploiting the superconductive properties of matter that could have produced faster signaling systems.

To come back now to your point about the importance of chemistry in neuronal signaling, we mustn't think of the nervous system as a "rigid," purely electric machine. The transfer of information within the nervous system may be modulated by specialized chemical mechanisms. Learning became possible not only at the level of the neuron itself, where nerve impulses originate, but also at the synaptic level, where nerve cells come into contact. At the synaptic level, the cell membranes are juxtaposed rather than fused. The resulting gap poses an obstacle to intercellular communication. Two solutions exist. In the electrical synapse, the cell membranes are sufficiently close to each other that electrical impulses can pass directly from one cell to another; more frequently, the signal is relayed by a chemical substance—a neurotransmitter, such as acetylcholine. About forty such substances have been identified in the nervous system. Generally speaking, the neurotransmitter is synthesized by the nerve cell, accumulates in the nerve ending and, with the arrival of the nerve impulse, is released into the synaptic cleft where it rapidly diffuses. Upon reaching the adjacent cell, it binds to specific receptors and at this point provokes an electrical response due to the opening of the associated ionic channel.

The acetylcholine receptor has been intensively studied in my laboratory. It's found at the junction between the motor nerve and the skeletal muscle, where various substances (such as curare, used by Amazonian Indians to make poison arrows), can block its action. In the brain, acetylcholine receptors are also the target of a well-known drug: nicotine. They consist of large integral membrane proteins (having a molecular weight of about 300,000) that traverse the lipid film of the cell membrane. The molecule carries the binding sites for the neurotransmitter, being exposed to the synaptic cleft, and also contains an axial channel that, in the case of an excitatory neurotransmitter such as acetylcholine, is selective for Na+, K+, Ca++ ions. The binding of acetylcholine to its site causes the opening of this channel through a discrete change of the conformational state of the receptor molecule, with the result that the ions flow through the channel along their electro-

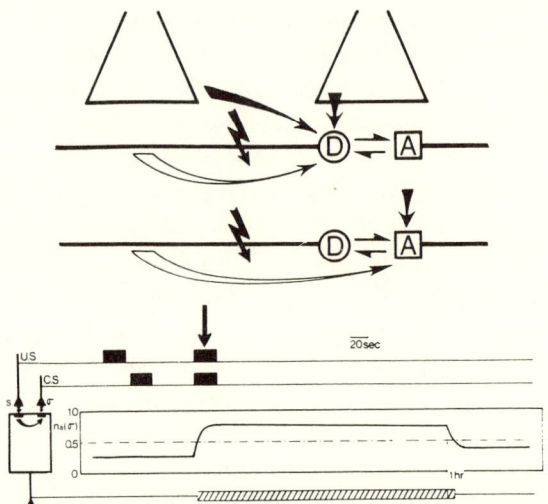

Figure 18. Molecular Model for the Regulation of Synaptic Efficacy Based upon Conformational Transitions of the Postsynaptic Receptor

The diagram above represents two nerve endings (*triangles*) in contact with the surface of a single neuron (*horizontal line*) containing molecules of the receptor that recognize the neurotransmitter. The receptor can exist in two mutually convertible conformational states, one (*A*) more efficient for the transfer of information than the other (*D*). Chemical signals (e.g., neurotransmitters, neuropeptides) and/or electrical signals (*arrows*) produced by the left synapse control the efficiency of the right synapse when they jointly affect one of the two states of the postsynaptic receptor. Their relative effect on *A* or *D* increases (*lower line*) or diminishes (*upper line*) the efficiency of the synapse.

The diagram below shows the evolution over time of the efficiency of a conditional regulatory synapse, *CS* (designated by σ) when stimulated simultaneously with the nonconditional regulatory synapse, *US* (designated *s*). The simultaneous stimulations (*arrows*) leads to an increase in efficiency ($\eta_a(\sigma)$) that persists for several minutes (*hatched area*). (After J.-P. Changeux and T. Heidmann, "Un modèle moléculaire de régulation d'éfficacité au niveau post-synaptique d'une synapse chimique," *C. R. Acad. Sci., Paris* 295 [1982]: 605–70; and T. Heidmann and J.-P. Changeux, "Allosteric Receptors and Models of Learning," in G. M. Edelman, W. E. Gall, and W. M. Cowan, eds., *Synaptic Function* [New York: John Wiley, 1987], pp. 549–601) chemical gradient, producing an electrical response. This, then, is the basic mechanism of chemo-electrical transduction at the synapse. The resulting elementary synaptic signals are summed up by the nerve cell, which may or may not generate an action potential.

The position of these receptors vis-à-vis the cell membrane is such that they can integrate signals from both outside and inside the cell. Most often they're located in the postsynaptic membrane, a critical point in the transfer of information between cells. In addition to the signal transduction mechanism I've just described, receptors can assume several mutually convertible conformations having different response efficacies. Electrical and chemical signals may shift the equilibrium response from one state to another by means of relatively slow molecular transitions, in particular when "convergence" occurs among a series of signals within a given "time-window." Thierry Heidmann and I have proposed an elementary learning mechanism on this basis that can implement the so-called Hebb rules for changes in synaptic efficacy resulting from the coincidence of pre- and postsynaptic activity (figure 18). Postsynaptic receptors are therefore capable of integrating several elementary signals simultaneously in space and time—so successfully, in fact, that chemical engineers are now looking for a way to introduce molecules of this sort into the design of computers. Their research has actually given birth to a new discipline, called bionics. It doesn't yet have much to show in the way of results, but there's reason to think that one day it may be possible to equip computers with ultrathin transistors—integrated microcircuits—made out of receptor molecules only billionths of a meter in thickness!

FROM ELEMENTARY CIRCUITS TO MENTAL OBJECTS

CHANGEUX: Let's now move on to the next highest level of organization: neuronal circuits. It's clear that neurons are organized into elementary networks specialized to handle specific functions such as reflex action—walking, the first stages of vision, and so forth. The retina, for example, is an extremely complex system that constructs a first-stage representation of the outside world out of the photons it captures by means of specialized photoreceptors. A second level of neuronal organization, fully realized in invertebrates such as the earthworm or the sea slug *Aplysia*, is responsible for what ethologists call "fixed actions": foraging, flying, mating, preying, and so forth.

CONNES: In other words, without knowing whether a given behavior is innate or acquired, it's nonetheless said to represent a second level of organization.

CHANGEUX: Right—the level of the *elementary circuits* of the spinal cord, of the brain stem, even of the cerebral cortex. In invertebrates, small clusters of neurons are grouped in ganglions. An additional level is found in certain particularly evolved invertebrates such as the octopus, which behaves rather similarly to vertebrates, but more commonly it's found in the higher vertebrates and human beings, all of whom construct "representations." Their nervous system is sufficiently developed that assemblies of neurons are capable of encoding fairly complex motor functions, such as hand pointing in a defined direction. But they also display a capacity for more "abstract" representations, which depend on being able to graft *hierarchical* organization upon a *parallel* organization in multiple neural maps—the "perceptual maps" you mentioned at the beginning of our first conversation.

The neural bases of the coding involved in such motor representations in the case of hand pointing in the monkey have been carefully studied by Georgopoulos. He recorded the individual activity of several hundreds of neurons in the motor cortex while the monkey pointed its hand in a given direction, and tried to define how this motor program was encoded, or "represented," at the neuronal level. He was able to show that each cell of this population displays a maximal activity when the monkey points in a specifically preferred direction (figure 19a). For each neuron a vector is defined whose orientation corresponds to this optimal direction, and whose length corresponds to the activity of the neuron when the monkey points its hand in a defined direction. This length varies when the direction of the hand changes. It corresponds to the "vote" of this particular neuron, as part of the overall "ballot" encoding the hand's direction by the whole population. The direction in which the monkey points its hand is in fact represented, with a margin of error less than 10 percent, by the vector sum of these elementary neuronal vectors. The direction vector for hand pointing coincides with the vector sum of the elementary contribution of the individual neurons (figure 19b).

CONNES: You get this result just by adding up the vectors? That's extraordinary—a Cartesian representation, as it were, by means of coordinates!

CHANGEUX: Corresponding to the activity of the individual neurons, yes. The vector sum of these elementary "microscopic" activities corresponds very closely to the "macroscopic" direction of hand pointing in the monkey. The encoding is carried out, as I say, at the level of the neuronal assembly. A model of this sort, based on animal behavior in one of the higher vertebrates, is generalizable I think. Once the central nervous system of an organism exhibits a certain level of complexity, "representations" or "mental objects" emerge that are definable with reference both to the state of neuronal activity over the entire population and to the behavior of individual neurons. Each neuron in the population differs from its neighbor. Each possesses a functional specificity within this whole, an individuality, a "singularity."

CONNES: In the octopus, for example, is this specificity an acquired trait, or is it innate?

CHANGEUX: For the moment at least, until I've finished defining levels of organization, I'd like to try to keep the question of neural encoding separate from the issue of innateness. For the moment we find ourselves at what may be called the *symbolic* level, or, to use Kant's term, the level of *understanding*. Let's now consider the possibility of defining mental representations in physical terms. At a higher level, what I call the level of *reason*, chains of representations are formed. Over time, neuronal assemblies aggregate on a larger scale, forming "assemblies of assemblies,"

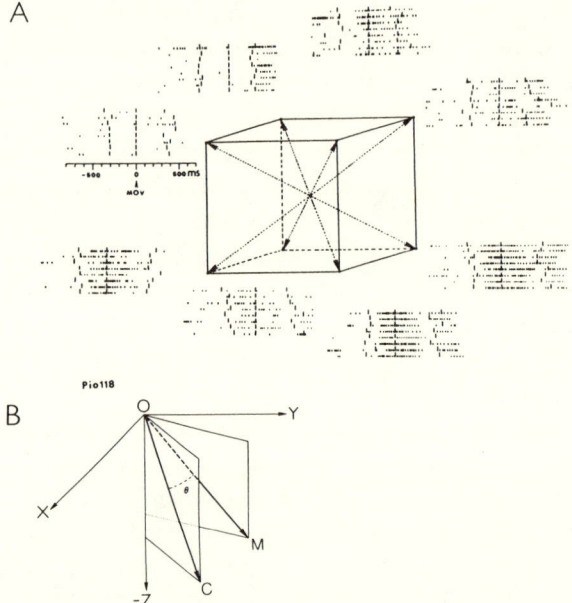

Figure 19a. Finger Pointing in the Alert Monkey: Impulse Activity of a Motor Cortical Cell

States of impulse activity in an individual neuron of the motor cortex of a monkey trying to reach for a target successively located in eight directions in three-dimensional space, represented here by arrows.

A. The recorded electrical activity of the motor cortical cell is indicated by small vertical bars, each corresponding to a nerve impulse; each superimposed line corresponds to a different trial. The vertical line common to all the recordings (*Mov*) indicates the onset of movement. Examination of the set of movements shows that this neuron responds optimally when the monkey points its hand in a privileged direction—at what would be about 4:30 in the above figure, where the small bars are closest together.

B. The amplitude of the response (the predicted frequency of cell discharge) when the monkey points its hand in a given direction (*M*) is a linear function of the cosine of the angle formed between the direction of movement and the preferred direction (*C*) of the neuron. This amplitude constitutes the "tax" paid by the neuron for coding movement over the whole of the population. (After A. Georgopoulos et al., "Neural Interpretation of Movement: Role of Motor Cortex in Reaching," in *FASEB J.* 13 [1988]: 2849–57. Reproduced from *Science* 233 [1986]: 1417 [copyright © by the American Association for the Advancement of Science])

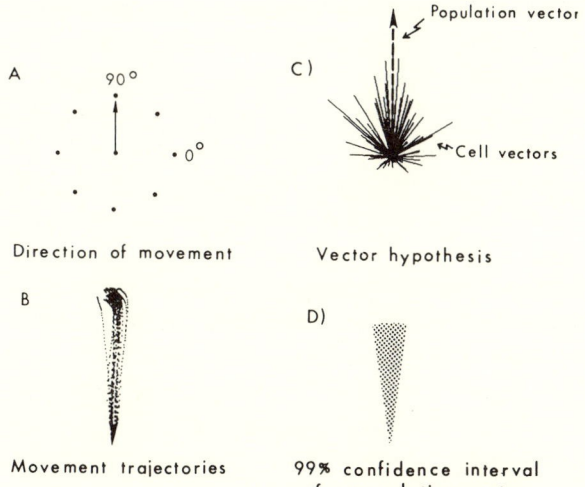

Direction of movement

Vector hypothesis

Movement trajectories

99% confidence interval
for population vector

Figure 19b. Finger Pointing in the Alert Monkey: Neural Population Coding of Movement Direction

Coding of the direction of movement over a population of neurons in the motor cortex of the direction of movement, represented here as a median position (ninety degrees) on a two-dimensional work surface. A well-trained monkey produces a fairly tight family of movement trajectories. The sum of the "votes" of each of 241 neurons—or cell vectors (*continuous lines*)—yields an overall "ballot" or population vector (*dotted line*) oriented in the direction of movement predicted by the vector hypothesis with a confidence interval of 99 percent. (After A. Georgopoulos et al., 1988 [copyright © 1984 by the Neurosciences Institute]) so to speak. At all levels, by the way, temporality is extremely important—we haven't talked enough about this.

The most anterior part of our brain, the prefrontal cortex, seems definitely to be involved in these higher-level functions, at the "reason" level (figure 20). By way of illustration, let me cite an example drawn from clinical research into patients suffering from lesions of the frontal lobe: the response to the classic Milner-Pétridès ("Wisconsin card-sorting") test. The test requires subjects to determine the principle according to which a deck of cards is to be sorted. The standard material consists of cards bearing figures that vary in color (red, green, blue, or yellow), shape (triangle, star, cross, or circle), and number (one, two, three, or four items). Four "reference cards" are lined up in front of the subject throughout the test. The subject is given a deck of "response cards" and instructed to place each response card in front of *one* of the four reference cards. Let's suppose the deck is to be sorted according to color—say, red. After each response the subject is told whether the response is "right" or "wrong," but not in front of which reference card it should have been placed in the case of a wrong response. The goal of the subject is to get as many right responses as possible, gradually improving her performance until the sorting principle has been discovered. Suddenly, however, without warning the subject, the examiner may change the rule: the cards must now all display the same shape, for example—triangle, say. Initially the subject will make mistakes, which the examiner will point out to her, in continuing to select red cards. After a certain number of mistakes, the normal subject figures out the change in the rule, whereas the patient who suffers from a lesion of the frontal cortex doesn't—she persists in her error. According to Milner and Pétridès, the abnormal subject fails to formulate the hypotheses that would enable her to correct her mistakes. She has lost a very elementary, but characteristic, rational function.

CONNES: Which therefore is traceable to a precise spot.

CHANGEUX: Right. The subject initially exhibits neurological troubles, due to a vascular injury, say. A neurologist performs

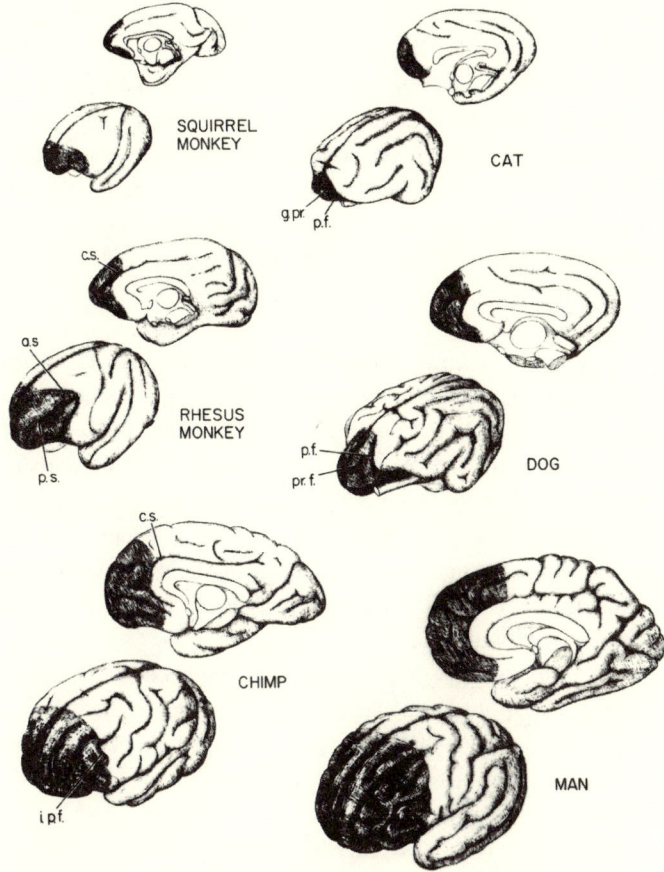

Figure 20. Evolution of Relative Surface Area of the Prefrontal Cortex in Mammals

From primitive mammals to *Homo sapiens*, the relative surface area of the prefrontal cortex (*shaded*) increases by 3.5 percent in the cat, 7 percent in the dog, 8.5 percent in the lemur, 11 percent in the macaque, 17 percent in the chimpanzee, and 29 percent in *Homo sapiens*. Sulci and fissures serve as reference marks to delimit the prefrontal cortex in different species. (After J. M. Fuster, *The Prefrontal Cortex* [New York: Raven Press, 1980]) tests, finds abnormal responses in a particular case, and diagnoses a frontal lesion that can subsequently be confirmed or disconfirmed by brain scanning. A correlation can then be established between a functional deficit and the lesion of a defined domain in the brain. Many such observations support the notion that the frontal lobe contributes in some way to what one might call *the neural architectures of reason*. The English neuropsychologist Shallice has nicely distinguished what he calls "contention scheduling" from "attentive supervision," arguing that the latter function is involved in error recognition, the formulation of new hypotheses, the invention of new strategies. Stanislas Dehaene and I have designed a formal neuronal architecture capable of satisfying the Milner-Pétridès test that includes two distinct levels of organization. It's reasonable to suppose that definite parts of the brain contribute to the process of rational thought. The remarkable fact that the surface area of the frontal lobe increases relative to the rest of the neocortex in the course of evolution, undergoing considerable expansion from rat to monkey and from monkey to man, supports this view.

CONNES: This function of attentive supervision corresponds exactly to my description of the second level.

CHANGEUX: In this particular case, yes—and perhaps of the third as well, although the tests I've just mentioned don't suffice to decide the point.

CONNES: I'm convinced from what you say about the frontal lobe that its functions correspond to the functions of the second level—and that the second and third levels should be kept separate. I'm not sure what goes on at the third level.

CHANGEUX: The frontal lobe plays an important role in generating hypotheses. The hypotheses acted upon by the subject in Milner's and Pétridès's card-sorting tests are quite rudimentary. Much more complex hypotheses are likely to be generated at this level, but discovering them is going to be very difficult—in effect, you'd need to be able to do a PET scan of Archimedes' brain just a few fractions of a second before he cries, "Eureka!"

THE NEUROPSYCHOLOGY OF MATHEMATICS

CHANGEUX: Localized encephalic lesions make it possible to "dissect" mathematical faculties with reference to distinct levels of organization in brain function. You may be familiar with the work of the great French neuropsychologist Hécaen, who distinguished several categories of deficits:

- In the case of numerical alexia, or agraphia, the subject can no longer read or write numbers, but retains the use of letters. Hécaen was able to demonstrate the involvement of the left hemisphere—more specifically, the parietal lobe of the left hemisphere—in the reading and writing of numbers.
- Patients subject to spatial acalculia have trouble ordering numbers. It appears that this deficit has to do with a system of visual-motor numbering that allows numbers to be simultaneously read and ordered. In this case it's the right hemisphere that's involved in controlling eye movement in particular.
- A third deficit is one of calculation proper, called anarithmetic. The patient can no longer perform calculations, in spite of the fact that he or she can read them, write them, and put them in correct sequence.

In all these cases the deficits are connected with the first level we've been discussing. Luria has made a further interesting subdivision. He maintains that these deficits occur in the parieto-occipital area of the cortex, and distinguishes them from deficits affecting the temporal lobe that lead to problems of memory. Lesions of the latter type have the effect that the subject can no longer keep track of what he's doing; he's no longer able to follow the thread of his calculations.

Frontal patients present difficulties of another kind. They have trouble grasping the problem to be solved. In fact, they're no longer capable of connected reasoning: they respond impulsively, almost randomly, and fail to learn from their errors. A series of successive mental subtractions is used as one of a number of tests to detect frontal lesions. It's therefore plausible to assume that the frontal lobe is involved in linking up mathematical operations, in solving problems perhaps, even in posing them. Accordingly it would seem to correspond to both the second and third levels.

CONNES: Not to the third, really.

CHANGEUX: The tests employed are inevitably elementary.

CONNES: But tests can't be devised for the third level.

CHANGEUX: Why not? You'd simply have to come up with a test that cognitive psychologists and neurobiologists could work with. One test given to frontal patients consists in reading them a story—*Little Red Riding Hood* in Lhermitte's case, *The Golden Cock* in Luria's—and then asking them to retell the story.

CONNES: We're still at the second level in this case.

CHANGEUX: No—they put the elements of the story back together, but the result is incoherent: the end comes before the beginning, and the episodes are mixed up—

CONNES: This occurs at the level of organization, not imagination.

CHANGEUX: Fair enough. But find me then an objective test of imagination—neuropsychologists would be delighted!

CONNES: I don't know that I can. But I've got a question for you. It's often said that mathematicians lose their creativity as they grow older. The phenomenon is fairly familiar, in fact. Do you think they really do?

CHANGEUX: The cerebral cortex—the frontal one in particular—is subject to relatively rapid aging, particularly in the case of Alzheimer's disease, whose victims are liable to lose their faculties of calculation and memory very quickly; they probably also lose their scientific creativity as well—

CONNES: But surely it must be possible to distinguish the third level from the second more precisely—

CHANGEUX: It's particularly difficult in the context of everyday activities. The frontal patient described by Lhermitte, for example, displays what he calls "utilization behavior." The patient is perfectly well adjusted to his surroundings. Presented with an object, he utilizes it appropriately and without hesitation: given a pen, he writes with it; a pair of glasses, he puts them on his nose; a hammer, he drives a nail with it—but he does these things automatically, indiscriminately as it were, without exhibiting any identifiable sense of purpose or goal. Though he does retain the use of language, he's the slave of his immediate environment. He can carry out routine activities, but he doesn't succeed in solving the minor problems presented by new situations and the attempt to achieve long-term goals. The unforeseen is a real obstacle for the patient suffering from certain frontal lesions.

TRANSITION AMONG LEVELS BY VARIATION-SELECTION

CHANGEUX: A new question will help us sharpen the distinction between second and third levels, I think: how do we pass from the one level to the other? The thesis I've been developing for a number of years (and that has been argued by other authors as well, Edelman in particular) consists in applying a sort of generalized Darwinism (figure 21) to the transition between any two levels.

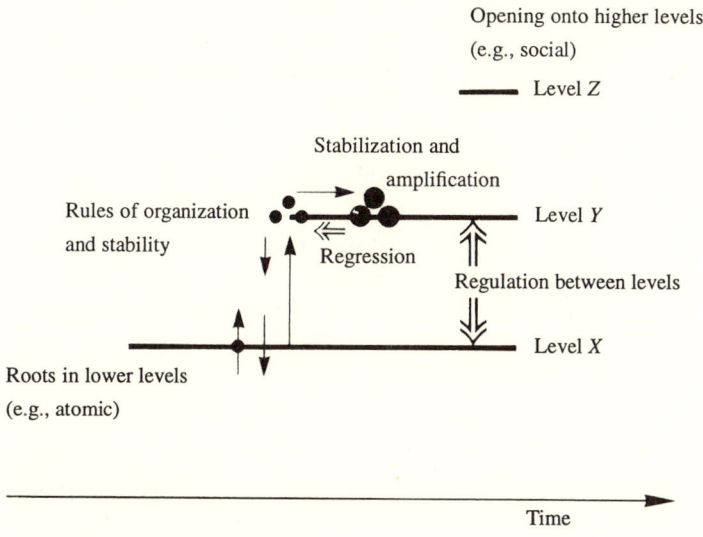

Figure 21. Generalized Darwinism

The idea—not dissimilar to what Karl Popper called "evolutionary epistemology"—is that the transition from a given level to the next requires two fundamental components: a diversity generator and a mechanism of selection, in addition to a process of amplification or propagation. At a given level, elementary units or building blocks are recombined among themselves in "blind," random variation, thereby assuming transitional "forms" that depend upon the immediately higher level of organization. These forms emerge from already structured elements—not necessarily, then, from atoms! In this way Darwinian variations appear that lead by stages to a higher level of organization. A selection mechanism acts to stabilize certain of these transition states, thus creating the next higher level.

CONNES: How does the selection mechanism operate?

CHANGEUX: The general model is of the type:

$$\text{matter} \rightarrow \underset{\displaystyle \big\uparrow\underline{}\big|}{\text{variation} \rightarrow \text{form}} \rightarrow \text{function}$$

The function feeds back into the variation → form transition. The criterion of selection is therefore related to the "new" function determined by a transitional form produced by the diversity generator. If this new function corresponds to an activity in the outside world that favors the survival of the organism, it may be selected.

CONNES: Inside the brain or outside it?

CHANGEUX: I'm coming to that in a moment. I wanted first to give you a very general and, I trust, adequate formal model that holds for any initially assumed level of organization. Now let's try to apply it. The simplest and best known case is the evolution of species. The diversity generator is located at the level of the genome, that is to say of chromosomal DNA. The usual Darwinian variations—genetic mutations, recombinations, duplications, transfers of chromosomal material, and so on—are random but relatively rare events that lead only *secondarily* to modifications of the phenotype of the organism, accompanied occasionally by adaptation to particular environmental conditions. Segregation of particular genetic combinations can also occur, without any intervening selection, as a result of geographic isolation—what is called "non-Darwinian evolution," though I don't much like this term. Under these conditions so-called neutral variations persist while others disappear.

The nervous system is just one organ among others, of course, but it enjoys a special status. Connections among nerve cells—synapses—aren't formed at once, but only as the result of a long and complex process of development lasting until puberty in humans. This development is subject therefore to multiple epigenetic evolutions nested within the organism. In fact, at least two categories of internal evolution can be distinguished: growth in the *number* of neuronal connections during the course of development, and in the *efficacy*, or strength, of these connections (and therefore of their state of activation). Let's begin with the first type of evolution, *epigenesis by selective synaptic stabilization*, which occurs during embryonic and postnatal development. Due to the very profound genetic determinism that controls cerebral organization, the human brain is assured from the outset of remaining distinctively human, clearly distinguished from that of the monkey. The genes responsible for cerebral development in vertebrates are now the object of important research. The *Drosophila*, or fruit fly, supplies a suggestive basis for analysis because it possesses a head, thorax, abdomen, and legs, just as we do. Some of the genes that fix the "Cartesian coordinates" of the embryo (e.g., head-tail, back-stomach) have recently been identified, along with others that determine the segmentation of the body—which is formed of successive segments, a bit like a small worm—and the identity of each segment—the cephalic segment with its antennae and mandibles; the thoracic with its wings and legs; the abdominal with its genital organs, and so forth.

These three sets of genes are differentially and sequentially expressed in the course of embryonic and postnatal development. And from these overlapping genetic expressions emerges an organism having an overall architecture, a plan of organization, that's the same from one individual to another within a given species. Homologues of these genes have been identified in vertebrates as playing a decisive role in determining the plan of cerebral organization. We may reasonably suppose that the expansion of the frontal cortex in mammals, from mice to humans, is subject to the control of at least some of these genes, though probably not a very high number of them. Given that the DNA of chimpanzees is 99 percent identical to human DNA, is the far superior cerebral capacity of human beings to be explained by the 1 percent that isn't shared? It's conceivable that the regulatory genes are shared, but that they remain active a little longer in the anterior region of the embryonic framework of the human brain, producing a further differential increase in the surface area of the frontal cortex. In either case the evidence suggests that the overall design of the brain, the core of our cerebral architecture, is genetically determined.

Genetic influence nonetheless has its limits. These can be illustrated, first, by comparing the connectivity of a single neuron identified with respect to form and position in two genetically identical individuals—*genuine* twins. The relevant experiment was done by the Levinthals with a parthenogenetic crustacean—the daphnid, a water flea possessing a simplified nervous system composed of a fixed number of neurons, all arranged in space in the same, or almost the same, way. By parthenogenesis it's easy to obtain several genetically identical, or isogenic, individuals. Nerve tissue taken from them is then cut into thin slices and examined under an electron microscope in order to compare the complete pattern of axonal branching of a given neuron in each individual. While the broad lines of connectivity are preserved, variation appears in the precise spatial distribution of synaptic contacts. A second proof is furnished by the study of the evolution of cerebral connectivity as a function of experience. Hubel and Wiesel have shown, in a classic series of experiments, that if a kitten or newborn monkey is exposed during the critical period immediately following birth to artificial visual environments different from those in which they ordinarily develop—if, for instance, the eyelids are sutured on one side—the functional specialization of individual neurons in the visual cortex of the adult animal (specificity of orientation, binocularity, and so on) is greatly disturbed, very often irreversibly. In humans, the equivalent of such an experiment occurs spontaneously when, for example, a child is born with a cataract. The opacity of the eye's crystalline lens in the early stages of development causes a visual deficit—blindness, in fact—that persists in the aftermath of an operation on the cataract done *following* the critical period. This deficit is located, therefore, in the brain—more precisely, in the cerebral visual cortex.

These experiments, among many others, suggest that the actual pattern of *activity* in the nervous system over the course of development controls the "fine tuning" of connectivity in the adult. Here the structure of the genetic material is unchanged—hence the evolution is "epigenetic" rather than genetic, proceeding in this case by the selective stabilization of synaptic contacts. In 1973 Philippe Courrèges, Antoine Danchin, and I proposed a formal model of the evolution of neuronal connectivity based on a variation-selection framework. The basic idea is that the genetic determinants of surface recognition among individual neurons— neurons belonging to two main classes of cellular "partners"— are the same, or very similar. Only a few genes are necessary, then, to encode this property of recognition. At a certain critical point, these two sets of neurons come into contact. It's not a matter of neuron x of the first group coming into precise contact with neuron y of the second, but rather of an exuberant branching of axonal and dendritic trees, a sudden arborization producing diffuse, multiple, and overlapping connections. At this critical stage there is redundancy, but also maximal diversity in the connections of the network: the Darwinian diversity generator at work! A pruning process now takes place, establishing adult patterns of connectivity by the stabilization of certain connections and the elimination of others. This model makes it possible to simulate simple learning situations, as well as some of the more complex situations that appear in the course of development—particularly in human development, which is marked by successive waves of synaptic formation and selection that wash through each other in a continual process of ebb and flow lasting long after birth. Obviously the biological constraints leading to the selection of one connection rather than another need to be specified. Specifying these selection rules will require us to take into account, sooner or later, the interaction of the organism as a whole with the outside world.

CONNES: But because all these connections exist, why aren't they used? They should be. What explains the selection?

CHANGEUX: The modeling of the network's final state depends upon the distribution of neuronal activity throughout the entire system. No two neurons behave *exactly* alike. In our model, *local* rules of evolution determine the evolution of a given synapse as a function of its own state of activity and that of the cell on which it terminates. For example, as I've already mentioned, a coincidence in the activity of two cells in synaptic communication with each other can bring about the stabilization of this contact. Learning establishes new input-output relationships. After learning takes place the same input systematically leads to the same output, whereas beforehand a given input can produce any one of several outputs.

This formal model possesses an interesting mathematical property that is formulated as a *theorem of variability*. It states that the same input-output relationship can be established after learning even if different connectivities have been retained through selection—which corroborates the point I made a little while ago about variations in connectivity. It's also known that language centers are distributed over the left hemisphere of the brain in a majority of people; in a minority, over the right hemisphere; and, in a very few, over both. But no one's been able to distinguish them on the basis of the particular language they use. The neural phenotype, despite a remarkable similarity in function, therefore exhibits considerable variation. And so we arrive at a rather useful conclusion for our purposes: mathematicians, despite important differences of detail in their cerebral organization—as opposed to that of nonmathematicians—recognize identities among different mathematical objects by means of their brains.

Now that we've looked at the role of "neural Darwinism" in the evolution of connectivity, let's take up the second category of internal evolution I mentioned earlier, a higher-level phenomenon that might be called "mental Darwinism" or "psychological Darwinism." Neural Darwinism manifests itself principally in the course of development from early childhood—or even from the embryonic stage, since the embryo displays spontaneous activity related to the "internal" selection of those synapses that serve, in particular, to coordinate different neural centers. Mental Darwinism, by contrast, principally concerns the adult brain, at the level of "understanding" as much as the level of "reason." On the scale of psychological time, it produces changes in *synaptic efficacy* rather than in the *number* of neuronal connections. The units of selection are no longer individual synapses, or elementary circuits, but assemblies of neurons that are capable of coordinated activation. These assemblies are made up of elements already selected in the course of previous development under the influence of neural Darwinism. The diversity generator no longer operates as a function of the evolved variability of neuronal connections, but as a function of the spontaneous and transitory activation of groups of neuronal connections—of what might be called "pre-representations." A sort of spontaneous combinatorial activity develops that *anticipates* interaction with the outside world, as it were. Where there is a "congruence," or "resonance"—or, more generally, a definite relationship—between the internal state of the system and the external world, the prerepresentation is stabilized and stored in the network; in the absence of such a fit between the system and the world, no such storage in memory takes place. The act of memorization alters the efficacy, or strength, of synaptic connections involved in storing a given configuration of the network.

The sequence of mental representations summoned up by reason in the working compartment of short-term memory proceeds by a similar sort of mental Darwinism. Is this a model, I wonder, that can be applied to the work of mathematicians? During the incubation period, various representations of mathematical objects can be imagined to follow upon one another in a transitory way, linked together almost at random. It may be that a sort of *internal* selection by resonance then takes place among representations or prerepresentations, yielding a result that suits the prob-

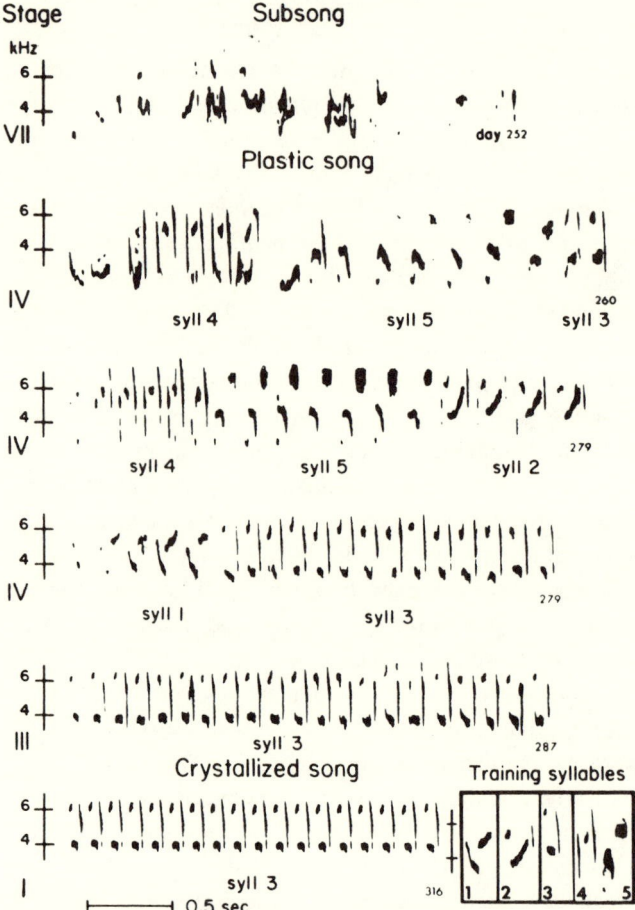

Figure 22a. Song Learning in the Swamp Sparrow

These diagrams represent sound production as a function of time. The training syllables are shown at bottom right. The young bird hears and memorizes them between twenty-two and sixty-two days after being hatched. Some two hundred days later, the fledgling produces its first vocalizations. These are regrouped into syllables that reproduce the training syllables heard seven months earlier. Only syllable number three survives in the song of the adult. The crystallization of song is accompanied by a loss of syllables (or syllabic attrition) that testifies to the "selectionist" character of learning. (After P. Marler and S. Peters, "Subsong and Plastic Song: Their Role in the Vocal Learning Process," in D. E. Kroodsma and E. H. Miller, eds., *Acoustic Communication in Birds*, vol. 2: *Song Learning and Its Consequences* [San Diego: Academic Press, 1983], pp. 25–50)

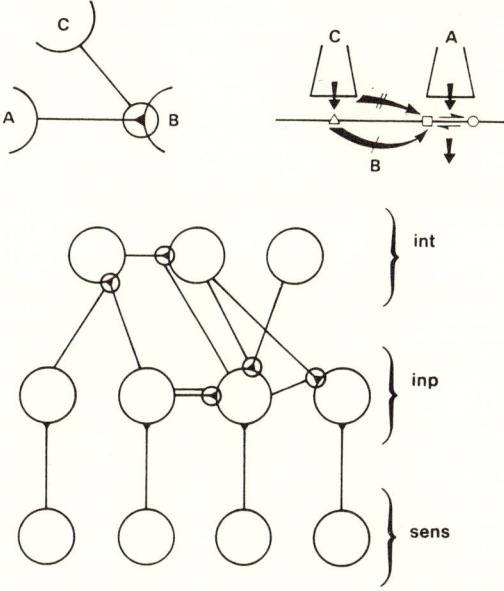

Figure 22b. Neural Network Model of Song-Learning Behavior
A neural network formally capable of recognizing, producing, and selectively storing in memory temporal sequences of "representations." The architecture is very simple, consisting of three layers of neurons (sensory, input, and internal) that are subdivided into groups of auto-excitatory neurons (*circled*) that encode representations and are connected by synaptic triads (*ABC*) whose efficiency is chemically modifiable. (After S. Dehaene, J.-P. Changeux, and J.-P. Nadal, "Neural Networks that Learn Temporal Sequences by Selection," *Proc. Nat. Acad. Sci. (U.S.A.)* 84 [1987]: 2727–31)

lem at hand, the "intention" needing to be satisfied. For the moment I doubt whether any more precise form can be given to this notion, which I admit is merely suggestive, nothing more. Stanislas Dehaene, Jean-Pierre Nadal and I have sketched out a model—albeit a still very elementary one—of a neural network arranged in successive layers that is capable of recognizing sequences and melodies, holding them in memory, and later reproducing them. This model accounts fairly well for song learning in certain birds (figures 22a and b). It provided the basis, by the way, for the formal model I mentioned earlier that Dehaene and I developed to satisfy the Milner-Pétridès test. We're far from done, but I think one day it will be possible to model in detail the various stages involved in the unfolding of thought.

MENTAL DARWINISM AND MATHEMATICAL CREATION

CHANGEUX: What I'm asking, then, is that you entertain the possibility at least that some aspects of a mathematician's mental activity follow a sort of Darwinian evolution, as thought in general seems to.

CONNES: One could equally advance the hypothesis that random Darwinian process and elemental mathematical reality—a reality that I believe exists independently of our Darwinian world, whose coherence and harmony are the very opposite of randomness—together constitute a sort of dualism. That several more-or-less unconnected arguments tend to converge seems to indicate that we're on the right track. At the third level of mathematical creation, it's precisely the inexplicable coherence of mathematical reality, it seems to me, that permits neuronal assemblies to achieve collective resonance and harmony—they come together at just the moment that they match up with the structure of external mathematical reality.

CHANGEUX: As a function of the combinatorics of the prerepresentations—right.

CONNES: This would mean having to postulate a world that exists independently of the brain, the coherence of which can be glimpsed through the resonance of random mechanisms.

CHANGEUX: I was going to suggest something of this sort. What if we were to go beyond the definition of mathematical objects as mental objects, and consider them, first, as private mental representations—as physical states observable by means of a PET scan or an MRI?

CONNES: In and of itself, a mental representation signifies nothing—

CHANGEUX: But it acquires an explicit "sense" the moment it is communicated. Mental objects are, in fact, mental representations: they possess the essential property of being able to be communicated from one individual to another—unlike the ineffable states of the great mystics. They become public representations. Mathematical objects can be transmitted in a rigorously exact way from one brain to another, and manipulated with comparable rigor by genetically, and epigenetically, distinct individuals.

Certain anthropologists distinguish several types of social representations. In Sperber's classification, *first-order representations* refer to propositions of the type: "bread is edible," "lions are dangerous," "plants are green." They're stored in long-term memory and exclude any empirical inconsistency or contradiction in terms. Despite their contingent character, they come to acquire universal validity because they go uncontradicted by experience. *Second-order representations* are representations of representations—of relations among facts and mental states, or among intersubjective mental states. To these I would add a third order: artistic representations.

Beliefs, by definition, vary from one culture to another. They are *authoritatively* transmissible as "truths," despite the fact that they often constitute a "permanent provocation against common sense" (in Sperber's phrase). Developing alongside beliefs are hypotheses, scientific models, and mathematical objects, all of which are defined by their coherent, unambiguous, noncontradictory, predictive and generative character. Because they fit with reality, on account of the fact that they're falsifiable and ultimately revisable, they stand opposed to beliefs. Beliefs, by contrast, are untouchable, insulated from experimental test by the particular body of doctrine—chiefly, theological doctrine—in which they're expressed! (Beliefs plainly display an evolutionary pattern of their own, by the way, that can be interpreted in Darwinian terms, but naturally it's distinct from that of the scientific representation of mathematical objects.) These are the features peculiar to mathematical objects as second-order public representations, the purest, most "distilled" scientific objects there are.

The emotional component seems much more important than

the rational component in the selection and propagation of beliefs. How far does it matter in the selection of mathematical objects? Among the different stages of a mathematician's work, you singled out the moment of illumination that occurs following a period of incubation. This would seem to be the period when the Darwinian combinatorial process takes place. Perhaps illumination can be thought of, then, as coinciding with the mutual resonance of mental representations. Now we know that the frontal cortex, where this resonance presumably takes place, is richly connected with the limbic system, which in turn is involved in the production of emotional states (figure 23). Our frontal cortex is not only responsible for cognitive functions; it is also capable, by virtue of these very rich connections with the limbic system (figure 24), of influencing their emotional quality—their "tone"—as well. I should imagine that the mathematician develops emotional as well as rational strategies for problem solving. Since resonances overflow the frontal cortex into the limbic system in the course of illumination, one could even go so far as to say that emotional states contribute to cognitive evaluation—

CONNES: Exactly. This is very important.

CHANGEUX: This *evaluation function*, which helps us recognize a sort of harmony between ourselves and our environment—an inner adequacy or fit among different representations, in effect—can be interpreted either as a pleasure trigger or as a warning signal. The conditions under which illumination occurs need to be distinguished, finally, from those under which its results are transmitted from one mathematician to another. These are two different processes. Nonetheless, even though creation is distinct from the transfer of knowledge, the receiving brain must possess a particular faculty in order for communication to take place—

CONNES: Of course.

CHANGEUX: A certain level of competence is required for the receiver to accept or reject a mathematical object or demonstration. This competence must therefore be taken into account as a function of the existing mathematical corpus. The acceptance of a new proposition by the mathematical community as a whole signifies,

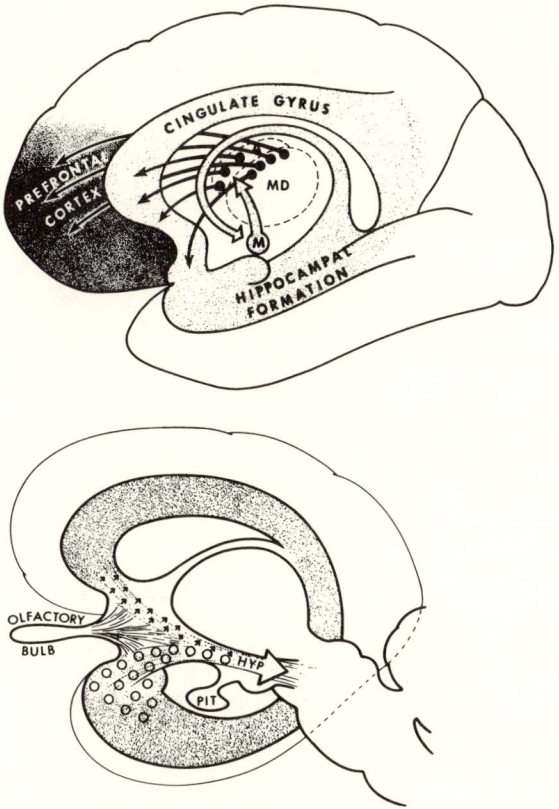

Figure 23. The Limbic System and Pleasure
A highly schematic representation of the limbic system and its inner organization, first described by Papez. The basic elements include the hippocampus, which receives information from the neocortex; the hypothalamus (*hyp*), with its mamillary bodies (*M*); and the anterior and posterior nuclei of the thalamus (*MD*). These are projected respectively upon the prefrontal cortex and the cingulate gyrus, whose circular form resembles a "limb"—whence the name coined by Broca, "great limbic lobe." Electrical stimulation of specific points in the limbic system triggers autostimulation behavior and thus produces a sensation of "pleasure." The oblique arrows indicate a response manifested by an erection of the penis in the male. (After P. MacLean, *A Triune Concept of the Brain and Behavior* [copyright © 1973 by the University of Toronto Press])

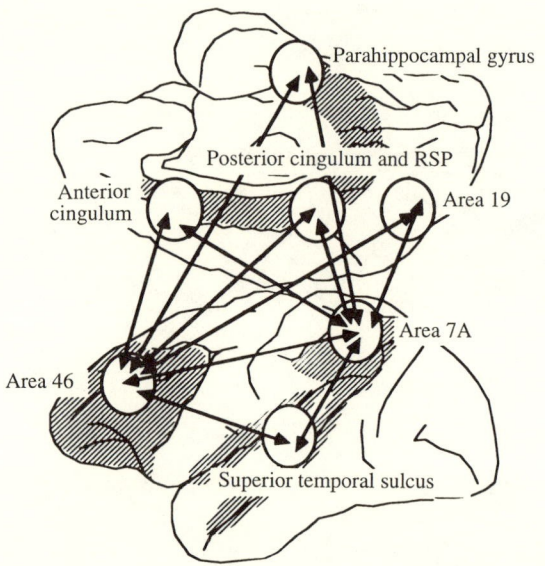

Figure 24. Anatomy of the Neocortex and Limbic System in the Monkey

Network of anatomical connections established in the monkey between the frontal lobe (area 46), the temporal lobe (superior temporal sulcus), and the parietal lobe (area 7A), with the limbic system (anterior and posterior cingulum and parahippocampal gyrus). The lower part of the diagram represents the lateral view of the left hemisphere, and the upper part the medial view. The central part of the limbic system is found on the medial surface of the cerebral hemispheres in the midbrain. The reciprocal connections of the neocortex and limbic system link cognition with emotion. (After P. Goldman-Rakic, "Topography of Cognition: Parallel Distributed Networks in Primate Association Cortex." Reproduced with permission from the *Annual Review of Neuroscience*, vol. 11 [copyright © 1988 by Annual Reviews, Inc.])

in particular, its coherence and its integration with this corpus. The internal coherence of mathematical objects that you find so astonishing is therefore something that's gradually built up, you see.

CONNES: No doubt we gradually create a copy of the corpus in our brain by a process of mental imagery—but that doesn't cast doubt upon the existence of mathematical reality itself.

CHANGEUX: To the contrary: mathematical reality is constructed in stages by this susceptibility to variation and the integration of new mathematical objects with the rest of this corpus. That's why I deny the existence of a mathematical reality prior to our experience of it. The coherence of mathematics seems to me a posteriori, rather than a priori, the result quite simply of its noncontradiction—which, by the way, is why Morris Kline titled his recent history of mathematics *The Loss of Certainty*!

CONNES: We're back to our original point of disagreement. I think it's time we got beyond this.

5. *Darwin among the Mathematicians*

CHANGEUX: The notion that mathematical creativity may be to some degree a Darwinian phenomenon seems to me worth pursuing. Poincaré actually suggested as much almost a century ago, in *Science and Method*. Before developing the idea further, it may be useful to begin by summarizing what we mean by the different levels we've been discussing, in the hope of being able then to define more precisely the sort of evolution by variation-selection peculiar to each one.

CONNES: I don't have much to add. In a fairly formal way, for purposes of discussion, three levels can be distinguished. I don't pretend for a moment that they have any absolute meaning. The first is defined by the faculty of calculation—being able to apply a given algorithm rapidly and reliably. Present-day computers can do this.

CHANGEUX: We're talking about the level of symbolic operations.

CONNES: Yes, but the operations can be very complicated. Nonetheless, no matter what the degree of complexity may be, the rule is always given in advance—without its having to be in any sense understood. Therefore no variation or change of strategy is possible.

CHANGEUX: The symbolic level is the level of understanding, which, in Kant's scheme, is situated between sensibility and reason.

CONNES: At the second level, by contrast, for a given purpose—in order to solve a problem, for example—it's possible to choose a strategy and then change it depending on the result. If an error is made, it's possible to compare different calculations. This level therefore presupposes an understanding of the mechanism employed. Doing division, for example, one understands why one carries out such-and-such an operation rather than another; or—to exaggerate slightly—in the case of addition, when one carries over a number one is aware of using a 2 co-cycle in a group. It's therefore necessary to have formalized the operations in question, to have ordered them in a hierarchical relation as a function of the goal that the strategy's been chosen to achieve—and, to do this, to really stick to what one's doing. In mathematics this is what often makes it possible to solve problems that aren't too difficult or that don't require any new ideas (on the condition, of course, that they don't depend on the first level—that it's not a question of a simple calculation or the simple application of a rule).

CHANGEUX: This is a form of reason, though possibly an inferior one similar to Granger's "tactical reason." It involves putting a strategy into effect, and later searching for new tactics if the ones originally chosen for carrying out the strategy fail.

CONNES: The thread of the thought is never lost at the second level, which is what seems to me to clearly distinguish it from the third. At no moment is the functioning of the brain separate from the object to which it applies itself.

CHANGEUX: That's the definition Granger gives to *tactical* reason, it seems to me. One changes tactics, one changes the means, the method, but keeps the same mathematical intention. The third level, by contrast, permits a complete change of strategy, even of the end that's being sought.

CONNES: Just a moment—that's not the distinction I wanted to make. The third level, as far as I'm concerned, is to be defined as the level at which the mind, or rather conscious thought, is occupied with another task while the problem in question is being solved internally—that is, subconsciously. The essential thing is exactly this dissociation between present, active thought and the capacity of the brain to function in a way that isn't apparent . . .

CHANGEUX: I don't think one's being conscious of an operation or not depends on a particular level. Consciousness has to do instead with a mode of *inner perception*, of perceiving both what's going on inside the brain and what's going on in the outside world. What seems to characterize the third level is the possibility of sneaking up upon and capturing, as it were, a moment of illumination that will permit a wholesale change of strategy—of creating a new framework for thought in which new tactics can then be applied. Do you agree?

CONNES: Yes.

CHANGEUX: Now that we're finally in agreement about the three levels of mathematical creativity, let me ask if the Darwinian variation-selection schema seems useful to you.

CONNES: To judge its effectiveness, I'd need to be able to define an evaluation function with some degree of precision. At the second level, for example, a function of this sort would make it possible to intuit that one strategy is better than another and to choose between them. For what we've been calling mental Darwinism to work, the brain must be able to select from among different possibilities—which is to say: among different aggregates of neurons—the ones that are most successful. To do this, it must be able to choose as a function of the end in view. But if we try to take Darwinism a step further, imagining a sort of *conceptual* Darwinism that governs mathematical creativity, it's difficult to form even a vague, imprecise idea of what a roughly analogous evaluation function for judging between strategies would look like. Might an evaluation function of this sort be formalizable as part of a computer program?

CHANGEUX: The ball's in your court.

CONNES: Well, if one assumes as a principle the one I've adopted since the beginning to demonstrate the independent existence of mathematical reality, then a certain number of ideas can be proposed—at least as crude hypotheses needing to be tested against experience, against physical reality. Taking the internal coherence of mathematics as a guide, in the sense of structure as opposed to randomness, one can entertain the possibility that when the brain tries to construct an imaged representation of a part of mathematical reality, its coherence is what acts as a selection mechanism.

CHANGEUX: That would in no way imply the preexistence of mathematics. You talk of mathematics as a guide to thought. The evaluation function is a function that verifies integration with a coherent, noncontradictory structure. This verification takes place in our brain, where a certain number of mathematical representations are found stored in long-term memory. With the appearance of a new object they all somehow fall into harmonious relation with each other. In other words, a process of global activation occurs.

CONNES: The coherence I was thinking of is internal to mathematical reality.

CHANGEUX: The coherence is internal both to the brain and to mathematics because mathematics exists *in* the brain of the mathematician—more precisely, in the mathematician's long-term memory. Mathematical reality is represented by a set of indices, all of which suddenly become connected with the appearance of a new mathematical object—that is, they all become activated in a coordinated way. Almost all the elements of the puzzle are present, only one missing piece needs to be found for the whole thing to be put together. With the fitting in of the final piece, the entire picture can at last be seen.

CONNES: But let's come back to the opposition between disorder, on the one hand, and organization on the other. Mathematical reality, by its very structure, its internal harmony, is an inexhaustible source of organization. In choosing at random among formulas, the mathematician will have the sensation of resonance only if, taken together, they exhibit a certain coherence. The point of mathematics is to show that this coherence exists. It's perfectly plausible to suppose that different assemblies of activated neurons resonate with each other only when such coherence obtains. For the moment this is a rather vague notion, I grant you. It deserves to be made more precise.

CHANGEUX: Apprehending this coherence requires the mathematician to estimate degrees of variability during the incubation period. In this respect the brain doesn't function like a chess-playing computer—not all possibilities are taken into consideration and evaluated. To the contrary: combinatorial activity, if it occurs at all, seems to bear upon a relatively small number of thought objects.

CONNES: Once a minimal structure is established in the brain, even a very primitive model yielding a mental image of a small part of mathematical reality, it's tempting to posit the existence of an evolutionary circuitry mechanism inside the brain that permits more elaborate structures to be created. Take reasoning by analogy, for example. This type of reasoning, based on a simple syntactic structure, amounts to creating a similar model whose elements have a different semantic interpretation. Testing the compatibility of this new structure with mathematical reality, we can modify it in order to improve its usefulness. Solving a problem doesn't therefore necessarily occur as a result of a series of random attempts. One can very well have direct access to a smaller number of possible solutions, thanks to an analogy constructed on the basis of an existing model. In the case of chess, which we talked about a while ago, I believe this form of intuition is what enables the great masters to succeed in drastically reducing the number of moves they need to consider, whereas computers have to go through millions of them.

CHANGEUX: Psychologists have studied the great chess masters and analyzed the strategies they employ. Chess masters can be thought of as having in some sense learned a new language, which expresses a series of possibilities. If we think of each possible move as corresponding to a word, their language consists of about seven to ten thousand words all told—far fewer than the lexicon of a natural language such as French, which contains about eighty thousand words. Instead of systematically and combinatorily analyzing the distribution of pawns on the chess board, the grandmaster relies on this special "linguistic" memory to work out the right strategy. Rather than continually invent new strategies, therefore, he reasons preferentially, on the basis of previously stored images and strategies.

CONNES: The notion of stability in configurations and forms seems to me very important here. The brain perceives as similar certain forms that, strictly speaking, are different. In chess, for example, this allows a grandmaster to discover and classify a small number of "attractors" from among a great number of configurations that *in his mind* occupy neighboring positions, though on the chess board they're far apart. This specifically mental mechanism, which for the moment computers are unable to imitate, therefore permits him to limit his problem to a small number of possible solutions. AI researchers are hoping to find a way to mimic this process by means of topological dynamics.

CODING STABLE FORMS

CHANGEUX: Long-term memory is therefore hierarchical. It has nothing in common with a dictionary arranged in alphabetical order. To the contrary—

CONNES: Its hierarchical ordering, it seems to me, is the result of topological mechanisms.

CHANGEUX: The organization of long-term memory is a fundamental theoretical problem for neurobiologists, who are accustomed to talking of semantic trees, hierarchical classifications, and so forth. What can topology teach us?

CONNES: Before answering this question, I feel obliged to interject a word of caution. A colleague of mine, an excellent mathematician, became interested a few years ago in psychoanalysis for some reason—maybe because he thought topology might be a useful tool for psychoanalytic investigation, I'm not sure. Apparently Lacan had recently heard about compact spaces, and one day tried to impress his class, claiming that Don Juan is compact in the mathematical sense. Certain members of Lacan's circle subsequently came to adopt the habit of employing the language of topology, without having the least idea what it referred to, in order to gain a psychological advantage over certain of their rivals who knew no more about mathematics than they did. Lacan and his disciples succeeded only in creating a chimerical picture of the world that corresponded to no reality whatsoever. We need to take care to avoid all pretension to false knowledge of this sort in our discussions.

For my part, I don't claim to have any new insight into the function of the brain. I simply think it would be a good thing if certain elementary notions of topology, which I'm going to try to explain in some detail, were better understood by you and your fellow neurobiologists. Why topology? The structure of the brain, as you've pointed out, isn't identical from one person to another, any more than our perception of external objects is uniform. But the properties we're in agreement about are invariant in character. They exhibit the property of "structural stability," in Thom's phrase, which a theoretical framework such as topology accounts for fairly well.

CHANGEUX: Mental representations—memory objects—are coded in the brain as forms in the Gestalt sense, and stored in the neurons and synapses, despite significant variability in synaptic efficacy. There are two problems here that need to be kept separate. The first is how perceptual invariants are represented by the nervous system. The second concerns the way in which these representations are filed away in memory. Let's start with the representation of perceptual invariants.

CONNES: First off, I want to try to explain the rudiments of simplicial topology. The simplest case involves a notion you've already mentioned in connection with dendritic arborizations: a tree. Simplicial topology examines topological invariants of objects known as *simplicial complexes*. A simplicial complex is a finite set of points that I'll call vertices. Just so you can have some mental picture of what these are like, think of a vertex as corresponding to a single neuron, and of a simplicial complex as resembling a fairly complex aggregate of neurons. The structure of this object is given by a subset—which I'll call "Δ^1"—of the set of vertex pairs. Let's call these elements "edges." Continuing the analogy with neurons, you can think of an edge as a connection between two neurons. But unless the simplicial complex is one-dimensional, the structure doesn't end there. In general, for every integer n smaller than a given dimension, one must give a subset Δ^n of the set of n-tuples of vertices. For example, if the simplicial complex is of dimension 2, it will be necessary to give not only edges but also triangles. The only rule of compatibility is that the sides bordering a triangle have to be edges. This means that a triangle ABC belongs to Δ^2 only if its three edges belong to the complex: $AB \in \Delta^1$, $BC \in \Delta^1$, $AC \in \Delta^1$. But the converse is not true: even if A and B are two vertices, the edge joining them doesn't necessarily belong to the complex. Given this much, we can begin to exploit the considerable potential of simplicial topology.

Simplicial complexes of dimension 1 aren't very interesting. The fundamental group of the associated topological space is always a free group. I'm going to take several examples of simplicial complexes of higher dimension, without trying—at least not for the moment—to assign any meaning to them. But in order for you to be able to picture them more easily, I'll use the term "neurons" for the vertices of my simplicial complex, "simple connections" for the edges that connect one neuron to another, and "multiple connections" when speaking of an n-tuple of neurons.

As a first example, let's consider a simplicial complex having the topology of a two-dimensional sphere. It's formed by four neurons A, B, C, D. All pairs (AB, AC, BD, etc.) are connected by edges, and all triples by a triangle. The dimension being equal to 2, however, no higher connections are possible. Now let's look at another simplicial complex that's equivalent to the preceding one—that is, a complex that defines the same topological object—only with a different number of vertices. Adding a fifth vertex E, the edges are the same ones as before plus three new ones joining E to vertices A, B, and C. Note that E and D are not joined. The triangles are all the possible ones that can be formed by connecting edges to vertices, except for the triangle ABC (figure 25) Thus AEB is a triangle, for example, but AED is not because ED isn't an edge. The resulting simplicial complex is of dimension 2, and the associated topological space is homeo-

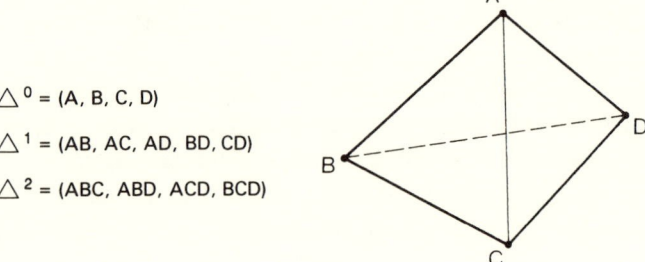

$\triangle^0$ = (A, B, C, D)

$\triangle^1$ = (AB, AC, AD, BD, CD)

$\triangle^2$ = (ABC, ABD, ACD, BCD)

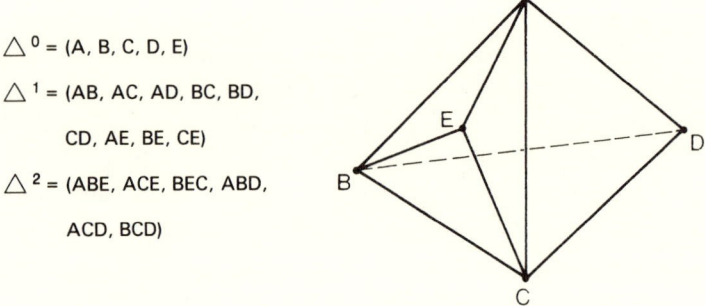

$\triangle^0$ = (A, B, C, D, E)

$\triangle^1$ = (AB, AC, AD, BC, BD,

CD, AE, BE, CE)

$\triangle^2$ = (ABE, ACE, BEC, ABD,

ACD, BCD)

Simplicial complex   Geometrical realization

Figure 25. Geometrical Realization of a Simplicial Complex of Dimension 2

morphic with the topological space associated with the first simplicial complex. Both spaces, therefore, are homeomorphic with the two-dimensional sphere. Passing from the first simplicial complex to the second amounts to making what is called a *subdivision*.

The first obstacle to comparing simplicial complexes and neuronal assemblies is determining whether neuronal assemblies of dimension greater than 1 exist. This in turn requires that the triple connections, or triangles, in a simplicial complex be correctly defined, which can only be done experimentally—more precisely, by building a machine that instead of relying solely on a mechanism based on tree-branching would be capable of exploiting the much richer resources of higher-dimension topology.

CHANGEUX: That's an interesting suggestion. It's known that each neuron possesses tens of thousands of connections, all of which can, in fact, figure in different representations. The schema you describe would exploit this possibility. Let's consider, for example, how my brain goes about encoding a particular shape—your face, let's say. The critical factor is the size of the neuronal ensemble involved. We've both referred already to mental representations, understanding them as physical states defined in time and space by the activity of particular populations of neurons. But not everyone shares this point of view. Barlow has defended an alternative theory (sometimes called the "grandmother cell theory") according to which each neuron in the brain possesses a functional specificity such that it's capable of encoding representations as singular as one's grandmother—hence the name—or a yellow Volkswagen. Some experimental data may seem at first glance to point in this direction. In the parietotemporal cortex of the monkey, individual neurons have been recorded that serve to encode the recognition of faces, even certain facial features (figures 26a and b). Certain neurons respond to a face in front view *or* in profile, others to a face in front view *and* in profile; still others to a face *with* eyes, but not *without* eyes, or to the face of one experimenter but not of another; some are even sensitive to the orientation of the eyes of the experimenter—all of which gives you some idea of how extremely fine the functional specificity of certain neurons can be. But this point can't be pushed too far. For if there were really only a single neuron in the temporal cortex that encodes each one of these features, the chance of recording it would be very small. The fact that reproducible recordings can be made proves beyond a reasonable doubt, I think, that whole populations of neurons possessing these specificities exist. Facial recognition very likely involves highly differentiated *ensembles* of neurons: ensembles of neurons that individually

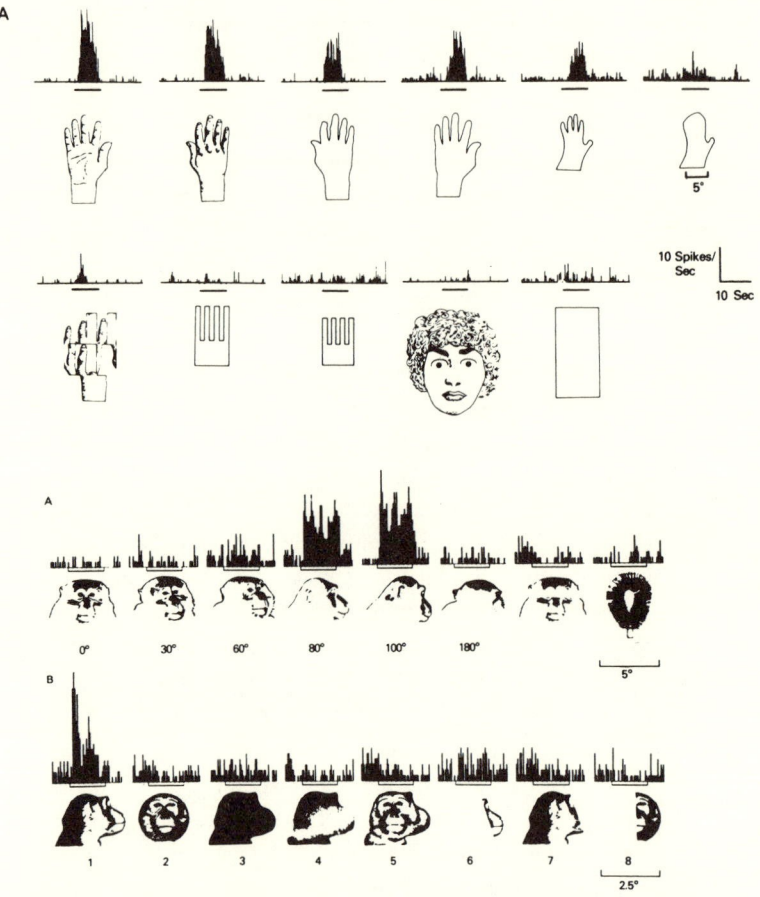

Figures 26a and b. Response-Specificity of Individual Neurons in the Temporal Cortex of the Macaque to Highly Complex Objects

The response of individual neurons is recorded with the aid of a microelectrode in the macaque. Nerve impulses are indicated by a vertical bar of constant length (*a*). The frequency of these impulses for a finite space of time is represented by a mark of variable length (*b*). The neuronal specificities recorded at three different points in the temporal cortex represent, respectively, response to a face in front view; to a face in profile; and to a hand. Note that the presence of eyes is necessary for the response to a face, like that of fingers in the case of a hand. (After C. G. Gross, C. J. Bruce, R. Desimone, J. Fleming, and R. Gattas, "Critical Visual Areas of the Temporal Lobe," in C. Woolsey, ed., *Cortical Sensory Organization*, vol. 2 [Clifton, N.J.: Humana Press, 1981], pp. 187–216; and R. Desimone, T. Albright, C. Gross, and C. Bruce, "Stimulus-Selective Properties of Inferior Temporal Neurons in the Macaque," *Journal of Neuroscience* 4 [1984]: 2051–62)

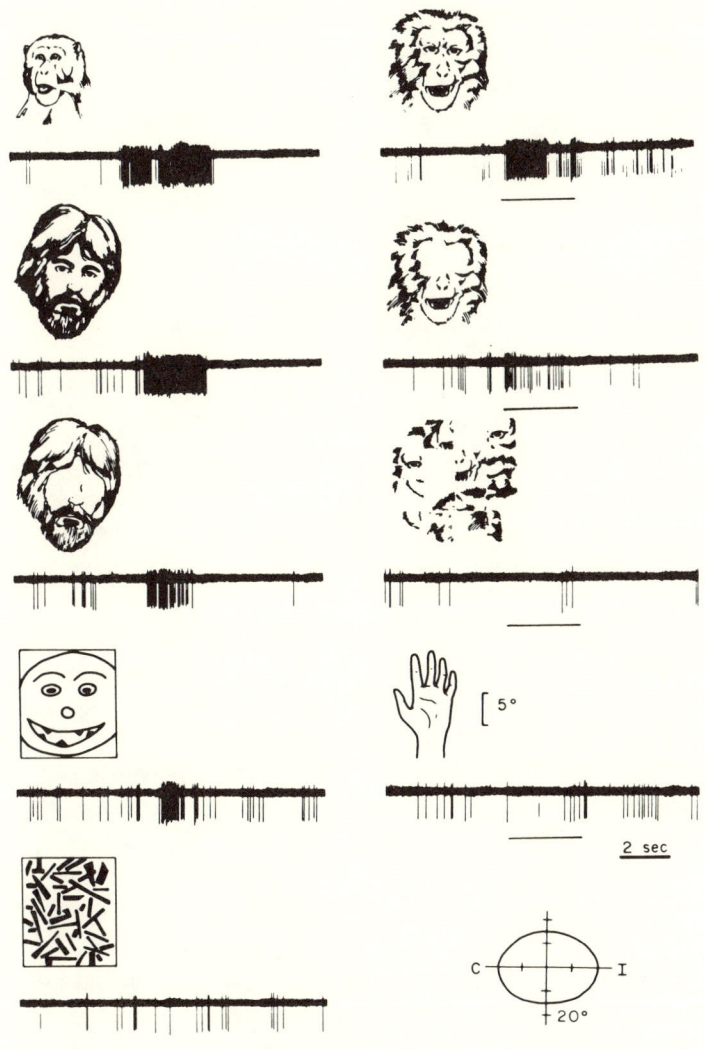

respond to such specific features are, in fact, connected to other ensembles of neurons located in the secondary and primary visual areas, which themselves are activated in turn by ensembles of retinal neurons. In the case of the brain, then, we're dealing with systems that are both highly hierarchical and highly parallel. For this reason I'm not sure that the analogy you suggest with simplicial topology applies in this particular case.

CONNES: I'm not sure that what I've been saying really has much to do with memorization.

CHANGEUX: It isn't a question just of memorization, but also of the way in which information is stored and processed in the nervous system. How the brain *encodes* mental representations may well be a problem for topology.

CONNES: Yes, but I wanted to introduce topology in our discussions for a rather different reason. We've been supposing that the structure and function of brain is characterized by a large degree of diversity, but also by a certain invariance, across individuals. Topology is just the right framework for understanding this kind of phenomenon, because the same topological object can assume many different realizations. Many different simplicial complexes can have the same topological properties. Simplicial topology provides the ideal means for encoding the notion of form, for example, so long as the quantitative part of its geometry is no longer insisted upon. To take the simplest example of an invariant that doesn't change when one replaces a simplicial complex, let's say of dimension 2, by another that describes the same topological object, I need to explain the Euler-Poincaré characteristic to you. This involves a number that is simply the number of vertices less the number of edges, plus the number of triangles, and so on. It isn't difficult to verify that when one carries out the subdivision I explained a moment ago (i.e., passing from a simplicial complex with four vertices to another with five that nonetheless describes the same topological object [figure 25]), one doesn't change the number that I've just defined: calculating the Euler-Poincaré characteristic for a two-dimensional sphere with four vertices, six edges, and four triangles, this turns out to be 2—the same as in the case of five vertices, nine edges, and six triangles. One could easily enough imagine an electrical system that would generate this number for any given simplicial complex.

In addition to subdivisions, topology involves a certain number of more complicated transformations that modify the topological object—that is, they yield a nonhomeomorphic object—without, however, altering what is called its *homotopy type*. An essential invariant of a topological space up to homotopy is called its *fundamental group*. It is trivial—that is, reducible to one element—in the case of a sphere, but it's not trivial for general simplicial complexes of dimension 2. Topology, then, is to be understood as the study of the invariants of topological spaces, up to homeomorphism or up to homotopy. It seems to me not improbable that the brain applies topology at least in an elementary form, possibly in an extremely rich form, thanks to the combinatorics of simplicial complexes. The combinatorics of simplicial complexes can be incredibly elaborate. In developing mechanical models of memory, for instance, it would be a shame to restrict oneself to trees—which is to say, to simplicial complexes of dimension 1 whose fundamental group is trivial—rather than take advantage of advances in topological theory.

The definition of fundamental groups is easy to grasp. Once a base point is chosen for purposes of reference—a vertex, in other words—one considers all the paths (or sequences of consecutive edges) along which one can travel from that point throughout the network and return to the same point. Paths can be "composed" by first tracing one and then another. The sole subtlety involves deciding when two paths define the same element of the fundamental group. I could try to explain this in combinatorial terms, but it would be a lot of work. Let me suggest a visual image instead. Despite the fact that it's a combinatorial object, a simplicial complex has a geometrical realization (as we've already seen). One places the vertices of the simplicial complex in a space of sufficiently large dimension, connects the vertices at the extremities of an edge by a true line segment, connects the triples made up of the vertices of a triangle by a true triangle whose sides are limited by the preceding segments, and so forth (figure 27). In general, it's difficult to supply an image for a simplicial complex because usually it's embedded in a space of quite large dimension, in which case the visual geometric image must be replaced by combinatorics. But for a small-dimensional space, it's easy to explain what it means to say that two paths define the same element of the fundamental group, or, equivalently, that one path defines the identity element of the fundamental group. This occurs if a path can be deformed—but not torn apart, mind you—in such a way that it becomes trivial (figure 28). Using this construction alone it's possible to obtain every interesting group, which shows the incredible richness of the combinatorics for simplicial complexes of two dimensions and higher. The stunning thing is that the brain disposes of a potentially huge number of ways for realizing this same combinatorics, and so of generating a truly unbelievable number of possibilities. Counting the number of holes in a surface, for example, is the same thing as calculating its Euler-Poincaré characteristic.

CHANGEUX: Could a machine be built that could do this? That would really be the best proof.

CONNES: Counting the number of holes in a surface is very easily done. To extract the invariant, the machine would simply have to count the number of vertices, subtract the number of edges, and add back in the number of triangles. An electrical system could do this.

CHANGEUX: As far as I can tell, the brain doesn't seem to work this way.

CONNES: But an electrical system does. Imagine a system in which each vertex possesses an equal and positive electrical charge, and each edge a negative charge, with each triangle adding a positive charge. If you looked at the total charge of the system, you'd obtain a topological invariant.

CHANGEUX: You'd have to be able to actually build such a system.

CONNES: Of course—but it's not impossible. And besides, the machine could handle chemical as well as electrical phenomena.

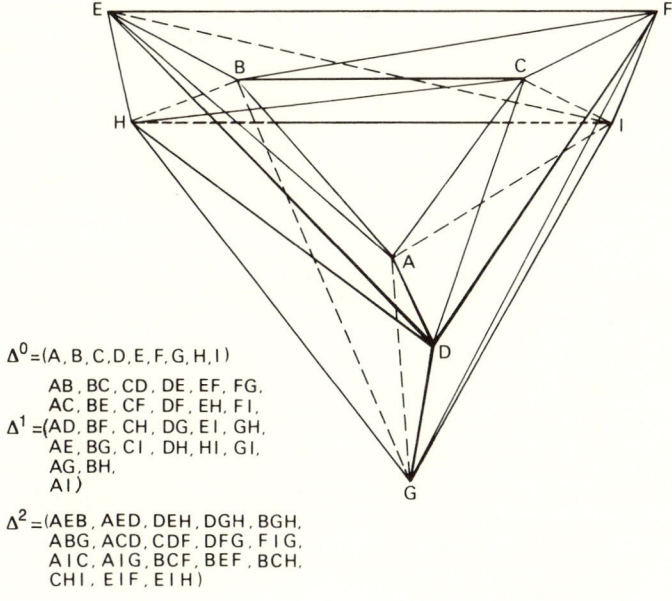

$\Delta^0 = (A, B, C, D, E, F, G, H, I)$

$\quad AB, BC, CD, DE, EF, FG,$
$\quad AC, BE, CF, DF, EH, FI,$
$\Delta^1 = (AD, BF, CH, DG, EI, GH,$
$\quad AE, BG, CI, DH, HI, GI,$
$\quad AG, BH,$
$\quad AI)$

$\Delta^2 = (AEB, AED, DEH, DGH, BGH,$
$\quad ABG, ACD, CDF, DFG, FIG,$
$\quad AIC, AIG, BCF, BEF, BCH,$
$\quad CHI, EIF, EIH)$

Simplicial complex   Geometrical realization

Figure 27. Geometrical Realization of a Simplicial Complex of Dimension 2

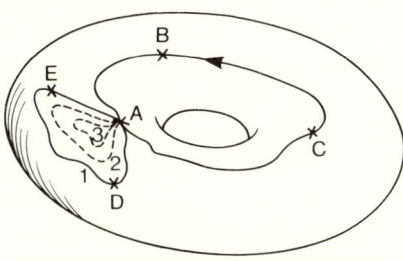

Figure 28. Deformation of a Loop

The loop *ACB* represents a nontrivial element of the fundamental group of the simplicial complex in figure 29. The loop *AED* represents the trivial element because it can be deformed as indicated in this figure by steps 1, 2, and 3.

CHANGEUX: Of course. I've confined my attention so far to electrical phenomena because they're more directly measurable. Measuring the release of chemical transmitters is more difficult, but in principle it can be done, at least indirectly. We're still a long way from actually being able to do it, however. Another difficulty in the case of the central nervous system is how to interpret the activity of small ensembles of neurons in the context of higher-level organization. It's not easy, but it's possible—as, for example, in the case of face recognition at the level of the temporal cortex.

CONNES: It's conceivable, for example, that the recognition of forms having not more than topological dimension 2 might be carried out by a system formed solely of points (i.e., neurons), edges and triangles; in other words, a system in which it would only be necessary to systematically excite neuronal triples. But obviously all this is pure speculation.

CHANGEUX: No—it's a simple prediction for physiologists to decide! Measuring correlations of neuronal activity has already been done in several laboratories. But now that we've addressed the question of perceptual invariants and representations, let's turn to the second question we've set for ourselves regarding long-term memory. Long-term memory is typically represented as a tree structure. If representations are considered in terms of this new topology instead, how do you explain the organization of memory and our access to it? Also: how does reasoning by analogy work? It could, after all, be pictured simply as a relation between two distinct trees.

THE ORGANIZATION OF LONG-TERM MEMORY

CONNES: I realize that where problems of memory are concerned, the familiar model is the tree model you've just mentioned. Short of actually proposing a real model of my own, I can't avoid introducing a more general notion, more refined than that of a tree: a *hyperbolic simplicial complex*, or a simplicial complex of negative curvature. I haven't any very precise idea how this notion might be applied to the processes of memory; but it's clear that trees are much too restrictive, because correcting an error requires going back along exactly the same path that led to it. Hyperbolic simplicial complexes are far more flexible, yet they retain the properties of trees that are useful in current models of memory. Whereas trees are one-dimensional and organize the information of memory in a "linear" way, hyperbolic simplicial complexes organize it in a more subtle fashion.

What is a hyperbolic simplicial complex? We can define its distinctive property in a purely combinatorial way by saying, for example, that a simplicial complex of dimension 2 is hyperbolic if every vertex of a triangle is common to at least seven other triangles. But it's much easier to understand what this means in terms of geometry and geodesics, which requires looking again for a moment at non-Euclidean geometries. In Poincaré's model of hyperbolic geometry, where the space is the interior of a disc in a plane, the geodesics are the arcs of the circles perpendicular to the edge of the disc. Taking such a geodesic, and a point P external to it, it's easy to construct an infinity of other geodesics that pass through P without intersecting with it (figure 29). In hyperbolic geometry, the Euclidean axiom of unique parallel lines doesn't hold. In this model, the angle between two geodesics is the angle between the corresponding circles. It can be shown very easily that the sum of the angles of a triangle is always less than 180 degrees, the characteristic property of a space of negative curvature.

One can also specify how to measure the distance between two points in Poincaré's geometry. The shortest path between two points A and B is the geodesic, that is to say the portion of the circle perpendicular to the edge of the disc that passes through the two points. This geometry possesses a property, similar to that of a tree, which Euclidean geometry doesn't have at all: hyperbolicity. It can be simply expressed. Let BC be a segment (i.e., a portion of the geodesic) and A a point outside this segment. Then the distance from A to B differs only by a bounded amount from the length of the broken path, which consists, first, in going from

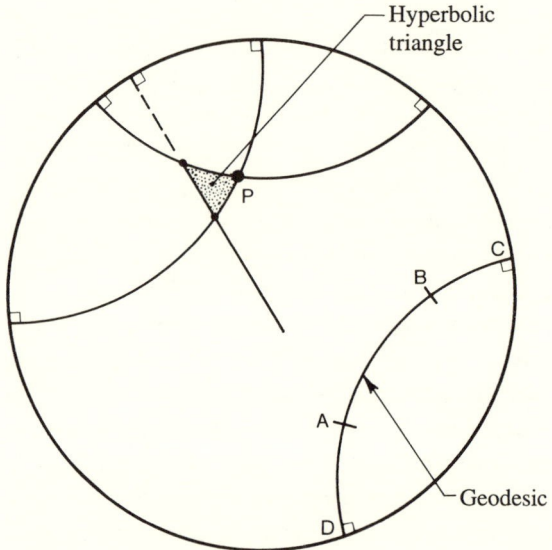

Figure 29. Hyperbolic Geometry
In this geometry, points are points of the disk above, and straight lines are arcs of a circle perpendicular to the edge of the disc. The distance between A and B is the logarithm of the cross-ratio of (A, B; C, D) on the circle ABCD.

A to the closest point *P* of *BC*, and then from *P* to *B* along the segment *BC*. This property, while evidently true for trees, is false for Euclidean space; but it's true for hyperbolic Poincaré space (figure 29). What's more—and this is the point I want to emphasize—it's true for a very large class of simplicial complexes, namely the hyperbolic simplicial complexes.

Returning now to the problem of how memory is organized, a model in which the objects of memory were located in a hyperbolic space would imply the following: to move conscious attention *A* toward an object of memory *X* located on a finite convex portion *P* of the hyperbolic space in question, it isn't necessary to know in advance the precise position of *X* in *P*, even if *P* is relatively large. It suffices, first, to move in the direction of *P*, and then, once in *P*, to move in the direction of *X*. Like trees, a hyperbolic space has precisely the property of coherence that's needed,

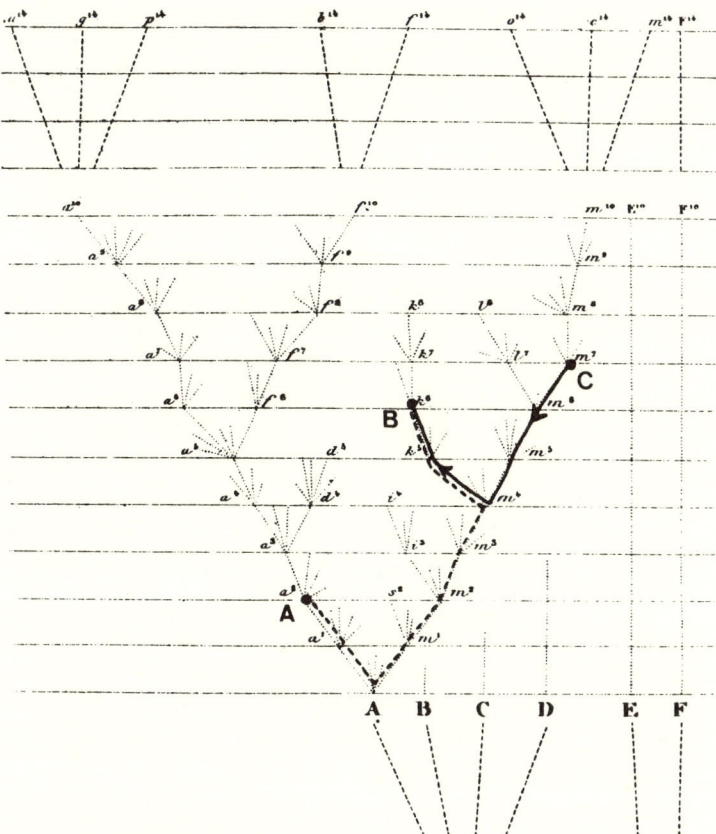

Figure 30. Tree and Geodesic
The solid line indicates the geodesic from C to B, and the dotted line the geodesic from A to B.

without however being a one-dimensional structure, with all the disadvantages that implies.

CHANGEUX: True—but there's a big difference between having a good understanding of such a model and being able to use it. Having a quite general formal theoretical model at hand isn't by itself enough. What you need to do next is make sure that these propositions can be converted into feasible laboratory experiments.

CONNES: As a matter of fact, the American mathematician William Thurston has been working for several years now on ways that hyperbolic geometry can be used to improve computer performance.

REASONING BY ANALOGY

CONNES: You also asked my opinion on reasoning by analogy. My guess is that reasoning by analogy involves two stages. The first consists in detecting the existence of an analogical relation in the first place, which is probably the harder of the two to do, and which is probably related to shape recognition. The second consists of a three-step process I'll call *replication-translation-amelioration*. Here the first step involves being able to reproduce a given configuration of neurons or, in mathematical terms, a simplicial complex obeying a certain function. Assuming an analogous neuronal system can be constructed, then the second step involves exploiting the analogy between the two to connect the elements of the replica by replacing the words associated together in the first neuronal system by their translations in the second system. Once this is done, the third phase involves testing how the new neuronal system functions in order to improve its structure. I wonder, though, if the brain is capable of making such a replica? What do you think?

CHANGEUX: Don't forget that the two hemispheres of the brain are interconnected. It's by no means impossible that certain representations are present simultaneously in each of the two hemispheres, or are capable of being transferred from one hemisphere to the other—

CONNES: Or that a representation could be constructed for a specific purpose and then made to pass over from one side to the other.

CHANGEUX: Considerable transfers of information do take place from one hemisphere to another, but it's still difficult to say that such transfers are involved in reasoning by analogy. The two hemispheres, as you know, aren't perfectly symmetrical. It's conceivable that a representation produced by one hemisphere might be modified, amplified, or attenuated by the other. Understanding the relationship between the left and right hemispheres is very important. Among lower mammals lacking a command of language there is much less lateralization: hemispheric specialization seems to appear with the development of language. Lateralization also makes it possible for the two hemispheres to function independently, leading to an explosive increase in the surface area of the cortex that subsequently becomes usable in a nonredundant way. Owing to epigenesis, minor genetic changes creating a mild asymmetry in the surface of the cortex have the effect of sharply reducing the incidence of redundant function, enabling each hemisphere to take advantage of the possibilities of the other. This is perhaps one of the origins of what is sometimes called the "human phenomenon": at a certain evolutionary moment, a small number of modified genes and, everything considered, a relatively small increase in brain size combined to achieve an altogether new level of performance.

LINKING REPRESENTATIONS WITHIN FRAMEWORKS OF THOUGHT

CHANGEUX: Perhaps we're now in a position to come back to our opening theme: the operation of what might be called *mathematical Darwinism*, linking representations—in the sense of constructing a coherent proposition out of them—and so making possible the sort of rumination about mathematical objects that occurs prior to "illumination" within the framework of a defined problem. To simplify matters, let's distinguish two questions: first, under what circumstances the linking of mental representations over time leads to a falsifiable proposition capable of expressing a "truth"; and, second, the question of how intentions are to be defined in mathematics—that is, how to define the frameworks of thought in which reflection, and perhaps even mathematical creation, take place.

CONNES: The concept of *conditioning*, an important concept in the theory of probability, may be applicable in this context. To define an intention—the intention of winning a game of chess, for example—I think one has to identify it with an evaluation function that serves to estimate at any given moment how far one stands from the goal one wishes to reach. How the brain actually constructs this evaluation function remains to be understood, however—I'll come back to this. For the moment, let's suppose that we have this function at our disposal. Let's use it, then, as in probability theory, to condition systems. I'd like therefore to suggest the following image, which corresponds to the type of Darwinism you propose: assuming mechanisms of internal evolution, such as analogy, let's suppose that the brain has elaborated an ensemble consisting of a thousand neuronal assemblies—a thousand simplicial complexes of neurons, if you will, all of them activated and conditioned by the evaluation function. Each neuronal system produces a result. From among these thousand results the brain must be able to select the one that optimizes the evaluation function. Physicists have come up with a very good idea, I think—not a solution for this exact problem perhaps, but at least it involves an interesting mechanism by which functions may actually be optimized—the *stationary phase principle*. Let's suppose that each neuronal system produces an electrical current whose phase is proportional to the value of the evaluation function for this system. In the case of systems that don't maximize this function, the existence of lower and higher neighboring values of the function for other systems means that the sum of the resulting currents is canceled by the mechanism of *destructive interference*. In those systems where the evaluation function is maximized, this canceling doesn't occur, and so they alone contribute to the current resulting from all the partial currents—here the mechanism is one of *constructive interference*. This kind of system certainly isn't economical—much simpler ones can be imagined in the case of computers that play chess, for example, where the evaluation function is specified once and for all. Just the same, it has great flexibility, which physicists exploit all the time using Feynman's path integral.

CHANGEUX: It amounts almost to a selection mechanism, then, doesn't it?

CONNES: Yes, but unfortunately only on the assumption that the evaluation function has already been constructed. I confess I haven't the vaguest idea how this might be done.

CHANGEUX: It *would* have to be constructed.

CONNES: All I know is that this function must be tied to the limbic system, or to some other part of the brain. It can't be disconnected from the external world.

CHANGEUX: But that's already a start—the notion that there might be such a loop.

CONNES: A correlation must exist, it seems to me, between the evaluation function and the frustration, or pleasure, that one feels when one gets nearer to solving a problem. But I don't know exactly how to define it. How can the specific goal, which belongs to active, present thought, be manifested through a mechanism of destructive or constructive interference?

CHANGEUX: It's possible that when the goal is attained, at that very moment—

CONNES: I know—but that won't do, because in probability theory the probability is completely conditioned in advance by the end to be reached, prior to any destructive or constructive interference.

CHANGEUX: That's it! The calculation is carried out within a framework! This is very important. If you were to distinguish, as I do, logical reasoning from—

CONNES: I'm not talking about creation; I'm still at the second level.

CHANGEUX: Even there the end to be reached plays a role: it's fixed. One could even consider it as a sort of internal "obsession," meaning that a persisting state of neuronal activity—

CONNES: Should engender a kind of frustration or discomfort.

CHANGEUX: Hold on. It's also possible to imagine a circuit, looped back on itself, that involves the limbic system as a function of desire. Imagine the brain generates a hypothesis that has "pleasure" written all over it, and that this serves as a guide and shows the way to a solution—which, however, may or may not turn out to be as pleasurable as anticipated—

CONNES: Or, inversely, as a function of frustration—which is very often experienced in mathematics. Whenever there's a hitch, it's frustration, not desire, that intervenes—

CHANGEUX: On account of the anxiety that comes from not having attained the desired goal. The limbic system keeps one representation "switched on," creating a context in which other mental representations are produced and eventually aligned with the end one has in mind. In this way the other representations come to share in the feeling of pleasure, in the achievement of the initial representation, as it were—a metaphorical way of speaking, I know, but it's consistent with the promising delayed-response task-learning model recently devised by Stanislas Dehaene and myself that I described earlier.

CONNES: I agree, but this image doesn't really take into account the possibility of measuring how far away the goal lies at any given moment. So long as it hasn't been reached, its *proximity* has to be judged in order for conditioning to occur. While obviously it's possible to recognize that a goal has been achieved, it seems to me more difficult to say how far away a goal lies—that is, to be able to condition it in the probabilistic sense.

CHANGEUX: Perhaps the nearer one comes to realizing one's intention, the more likely the realization itself actually becomes.

CONNES: Here we touch upon a point of great importance for the practice of mathematics. It often happens, when one is working on a problem, that being able to estimate how far away the solution lies actually makes it easier to find. It's precisely this crude intuition of the length of the path remaining to be traveled that helps solve the problem.

THE NATURAL SELECTION OF MATHEMATICAL OBJECTS

CHANGEUX: Do you have anything else to add with regard to Darwinian phenomena in mathematics?

CONNES: I suspect that if Darwinism plays a role in cerebral function, it rests on the mechanisms of constructive and destructive interference I've described, and resonance among neuronal clusters, rather than on some phenomenon of natural selection or elimination.

CHANGEUX: I think that it's a form of natural selection—interpreting "natural selection" in a way that's consistent, of course, with what's known about the structure and development of the brain. Even in the theory of population dynamics, this is often a difficult notion to pin down. It's usually defined in terms of populations that reproduce themselves according to a definite geographical distribution. Darwinism, as traditionally applied to the evolution of species, involves the notions of temporal dynamics, population growth, and geographical distribution. In the case of the nervous system, the proliferation component doesn't come into play because neurons don't increase in number; only the differential "competitive" occupation of certain territories counts. Your formulation leads exactly in this direction. It may be that the destabilization of prerepresentations and the selective resonance of neuronal clusters are mechanisms of selection peculiar to the brain. Additionally, of course, once stored in long-term memory, a representation can be re-utilized throughout the whole life of the individual: the *amplification* of the selection is gigantic. Let's move on, then, to the third level. What exactly is going on here?

CONNES: Certainly the most distinctive phenomenon at this level is illumination. Illumination is not only marked by the pleasure—the exhilaration!—one inevitably experiences at the moment it strikes, but also by the relief one suddenly feels at seeing a fog abruptly lift, and disappear. The conscious part of thought now has direct access to a world that's no longer at all strange, where laborious verification is no longer necessary. No doubt it's this sensation, so characteristic of the third level, that excites the limbic system.

CHANGEUX: You make me think of the mystical ecstasy of Saint Teresa of Avila.

CONNES: Mystical ecstasy must certainly excite the same regions of the brain—aesthetic harmony as well—but for other reasons I should think.

CHANGEUX: Here we come to a question very dear to my heart, having to do with the relation between science and art. What difference is there between a mathematical object and a work of art?

CONNES: I was talking about the harmony one experiences, perhaps only once in a lifetime, at the moment of illumination. I feel sure that a work of art, or a piece of music, can excite the limbic system in just the same way. The difference between a work of art and a great piece of mathematics is that, for the mathematician, exciting the imagination or painting a beautiful, heuristic picture isn't enough: one actually has to check all the details to know whether one is right or wrong. Since the only way we can transmit a result is by means of a logical chain of reasoning, this means returning straight away from the third to the first level. The mathematician has to get on at once, as Hadamard noted, with the tedious business of writing out and verifying the proof of which illumination permitted him to catch a mere glimpse. The state of excitement is therefore relatively brief. The proof, once broken down into its parts, can be laboriously verified, step by step. But the purely "mystical" phase has already long vanished by this point.

CHANGEUX: How does Darwinism enter in then?

CONNES: I think that "preparation," the first of the three steps mentioned by Hadamard, is what makes it possible to precisely define the evaluation function that must in principle condition any Darwinian intervention in mathematical creativity.

CHANGEUX: The fascinating thing about Darwinian evolution is that it begins with the amoeba and runs up all the way through mankind. For me, the most interesting application of evolutionary epistemology to mathematics is the "creation" of a new mathematical object by the combination of elements already belonging to established mathematics: the birth of a beautiful "monster," as it were—a chimera with a brilliant future! Despite its novelty, this particular object has nonetheless been selected by virtue of its compatibility with a preexisting corpus.

CONNES: That may very well be the case.

CHANGEUX: I recall you saying with reference to mathematical creativity that the first step in tackling a problem is "enlarging" it. Now what exactly does this involve? It must involve introducing mathematical objects that have no direct relationship to the problem at hand into the working compartment of short-term memory. The intrusion of these "outsiders" gives birth to a new mathematical object. It permits the mathematician to break out of the framework in which he found himself previously, and gives him access to a new level of knowledge. It is the result of combining different mathematical objects, sometimes over a long incubation period. Darwinism seems to account for mathematical creation in an especially satisfactory way then. The ball is now back in your court. What conditions of selection produce illumination? Does illumination really amount to anything more than incorporation of a new object with the sum of previously existing objects?

CONNES: Illumination means that the new object has considerable coherence not only with nearby objects (with which the brain is already familiar) but also with very remote ones. It is as though the correlation length of the new object were much larger than expected, a bit as in a phase transition.

CHANGEUX: And the differences? What's different at the third level, it seems to me, is that we're no longer dealing with a familiar structure, because the object is new. It's new, and yet it somehow manages to fit in with everything that's already known. Therefore it's not a question of simple conformity.

CONNES: I don't know what to say. We no longer need an evaluation mechanism as a function of a specified goal, but an immediate measure of this compatibility, even before reflective thought comes into play. Some quite obscure mechanism makes it possible, without recourse to reasoned thought, to sense the resonance between the new thought object and the old ones we are so used to manipulating. All this, I confess, is very difficult to understand . . .

CHANGEUX: Yes, but a mathematically creative machine has to have such mechanisms. The human brain is no exception.

CONNES: Quite right—otherwise it would be an ordinary computer. What's remarkable is that the brain can perceive coherence not only among a number of different objects with which it's already familiar, but also coherence between such objects and a new object previously unknown to it. This is what the coherence of the mathematical world is all about, if you ask me.

CHANGEUX: But this is only a matter of congruence with other mathematical objects found in long-term memory.

CONNES: It simply seems to me that this is proof of the coherence of the mathematical world, independent of any individual mind—

CHANGEUX: Which is just the point I wanted to lead you back to: this coherence operates initially as part of the selection process on the basis of noncontradiction, and a new coherence results from it.

CONNES: That I'm not sure of. I'd rather say that coherence *manifests itself through* this process of selection—

CHANGEUX: Let's not go through all that again! My point is that incorporation of a new object into a set of existing objects opens up a new knowledge space. Illumination somehow puts several levels of organization in the brain into coherent relation with each other—as when we contemplate a work of art. But how are we to define the particular form of aesthetic joy that certain paintings give us? It seems to be explained by multiple resonances among different levels simultaneously linked to rationality, to understanding and the limbic system. Resonance occurs when viewers find themselves faced with a "singular" structure. One can think of illumination, then, as resulting from the production of some kind of mental object, new by comparison with everything that has gone before, which introduces links among previously disjoint objects, which reveals relationships between mental representations and bridges them.

CONNES: I'm wholly in agreement with your interpretation on this point, only I wish you would elaborate a bit further.

CHANGEUX: This metaphor applies as much—or nearly as much—

to works of art as to mathematical illumination. The more radically different the object that suddenly appears, encroaching upon a landscape already crowded with latent structures, as it were, the more powerful the illumination. What you are claiming is that these latent structures are there *in order* for the new object to appear—

CONNES: Yes, but they aren't internal to the brain; they're part of the mathematical world.

CHANGEUX: No matter whether mathematics exists in the outside world or not, it exists in the brain at the moment illumination occurs.

CONNES: Absolutely. I meant only—to come back to our opening discussion—that it's difficult not to believe in the existence of a harmony independent of the brain, which owes nothing to human creation.

CHANGEUX: That's a subjective judgment. How can one can say that the *Pietà* of Michelangelo existed before Michelangelo made it? Consider another artistic metaphor: one experiences an illumination when one sees *The Last Judgment* in the Sistine Chapel for the first time, but it would be absurd to say that this painting existed before Michelangelo painted it. The same goes for mathematics . . .

CONNES: There's certainly some truth in what you say. Just the same I think that there exists a fundamental difference between the harmony one experiences in looking at the *Pietà* of Michelangelo and the harmony one experiences one fine summer's night in verifying, with the aid of a telescope and a laptop computer, that Jupiter's four satellites orbit the planet in accordance with Kepler's laws. It seems to me very hard to conceive of this kind of cosmic harmony as the product of the human brain. To the contrary, I would even go so far as to say it was through the poet's "mysterious depth of starry nights" that this preestablished harmony—established certainly prior to the appearance of the human species—came to arouse metaphysical curiosity. But to return to the question of illumination—

CHANGEUX: Let's not once again confuse the existence of regularities in the material world with their approximate expression by mathematical equations, which are products of the human brain. We stand to make progress on the theoretical plane, I think, only by defining the properties of the diversity generator, its role in producing intentions and storing thought objects in the long-term compartment of memory, and, above all, its *selection criteria.* One of the greatest advantages of the Darwinian model, by the way, may consist in its suggesting these very concepts. I must press you to say how you picture this selection function operating. If it's not an evaluation function, what is it? At the least it would have to verify, to validate the estimated degree of coherence. Doesn't this amount to judging the plausibility of a hypothesis?

CONNES: Perhaps. The striking thing is that mathematical coherence can be evaluated *instantaneously.* In a fraction of a second one is convinced not only that it's plausible, but that it's *certain* that what one's found matches what one was looking for. This isn't a reflex phenomenon, but it occurs with the same speed.

CHANGEUX: It's akin to the phenomenon of face recognition. The brain can instantly distinguish between faces it knows and faces it has never seen before.

CONNES: This is precisely, I think, what distinguishes the second from the third level: at the second level one is capable of recognizing what it takes to solve a given problem by means of a detailed strategy. At the third, one is able to instantly comprehend the harmony and the power of a new object independently of any specific problem.

6. *Thinking Machines*

CHANGEUX: Our discussions up to this point now prepare us to ask what relation, if any, the brain can be imagined to bear to a machine. More generally, what relation do the exact sciences bear to the brain and how it operates? With regard to the problem of building machines that in some sense think, at least three approaches can be distinguished. The first, *Artificial Intelligence*, attempts to *simulate* the higher functions of the brain, of human intelligence, with the aid of the computer. It aims, in effect, to replace the human brain by a machine. Artificial Intelligence has had many successes: robots that paint cars, computers that guide the voyages of space shuttles to Mars and beyond, expert systems that provide information about the most recent developments in medicine, and so forth. Just the same, AI (as it's commonly abbreviated) doesn't aspire to understand how the human brain works, only how to mimic, or even improve upon, certain of its functions. This approach is therefore quite limited from the very start.

The *neurocognitive approach*, by contrast, seeks to *model* the human brain and its functions. This calls for a more profound method of inquiry, requiring the collaboration of experts in a number of disciplines: mathematics, physics, neurobiology, and psychology. This kind of modeling draws upon anatomical and physiological data, results from molecular biology, and, of course, a great many of the observations about human and animal behavior yielded by psychology and ethology. Despite the youthfulness of the enterprise, fairly good models have already been developed not only for certain elementary mechanisms such as the propagation of nerve impulses (the Hodgkin-Huxley model), or allosteric transitions in postsynaptic receptors, but also for a variety of more complex systems relying only on a small number of nerve cells—neuronal networks responsible for swimming behavior in the lamprey, for example, or the registering of visual information by an artificial retina, or song learning in birds. This approach seems to me by far the most important. In fact, if there's any point in our discussing matters of human intelligence at all, perhaps it's because it's in precisely *this* area that together we may be able to make a contribution.

And then there's a third approach, *neuromimetics*. The aim here is to construct machines capable of authentically intelligent behavior on the basis of real neural architectures—assuming, of course, that the theoretical models of cerebral function (models that refer explicitly to the natural object constituted by the brain and its neurons) aimed at by the neurocognitive approach can in fact be developed. Three approaches, then, but so far relatively little in the way of results. The architectures employed remain very simplistic: several layers of nerve cells, some rudimentary elementary mechanisms, and so on.

CONNES: The second seems to imply the third.

CHANGEUX: Yes. The third approach is in some sense complementary to the second—a verification of it, really, since demonstrating the adequacy of any theoretical model of the human brain will require it to be tested by constructing a machine whose performance resembles that of the real thing. This third approach can be said, then, to effectively complete the second. I'd like us now, then, to take up three questions: Gödel's theorem, the Turing machine, and, lastly, the differences or similarities between the human brain and the machines that it's succeeded in devising so far.

GÖDEL'S THEOREM

CHANGEUX: In works dealing with biology, Gödel's theorem is frequently invoked to moderate the ambitions of neurobiologists, or even to call their approach into question. It serves then to justify the idea that the "human mind" will be forever resistant to science. François Jacob writes, for example: "We can be sure that to the biochemist the characteristic reactions of brain activity will appear as ordinary as digestive reactions. But it is quite another matter to describe a feeling, a decision, a memory, a guilty conscience, in terms of physical chemistry. There is nothing to show that it will ever become possible, not only because of the complexity, but also because since Gödel we know that a logical system is not sufficient for its own description."[1] As against this, there is Cabanis's celebrated aphorism, "The brain secretes thought as the liver does bile." For my part, I share François Jacob's view regarding the biochemistry of the brain and the relatively banal character of the molecules that contribute to its structure and elementary functions (the data that have been obtained since 1970 show it is correct, though they exhibit some novel features of their own); but I don't endorse the way he applies Gödel's theorem to the neurosciences.

Obviously an interesting methodological problem could be posed if the neurobiologist examined his own brain while it was in the process of examining itself. Nonetheless, given the present state of science, I don't see any fundamental obstacle to studying another person's cerebral function—yours, for example!—using techniques of noninvasive imaging; or, even better, to studying cerebral function in an animal species closely related to ours, such as the monkey, using the methods of experimental neurophysiology—for the perfectly good reason that the method of reduction (and also of "reconstruction") which we employ in the experimental sciences consists in seeking an explanation at a level below the one we want to explain. One builds, that is, on the organization, on the rules of interaction and the properties of the elements that compose the lower level in order to explain the properties of the higher level. Thus the neurobiologist examines the neural basis of higher-level brain function, working from the bottom up as it were. And at this stage, in my view, no theoretical

[1] F. Jacob, *La Logique du vivant* (Paris: Editions Gallimard, 1970), p. 337. The passage quoted here is from the American edition, *The Logic of Life*, trans. Betty E. Spillmann (New York: Pantheon, 1974), p. 316, now available in paperback as a volume of the Princeton Science Library.

obstacle stands in the way. The major obstacles seem to me to have much more to do with the complexity of cerebral organization of the brain, its variability from one individual to another, and the possible interference of the means of observation with the functioning of the brain itself—a problem also encountered in physics, where the methods of observation are also liable to interfere with the objects observed.

Let's come back, though, to Gödel's theorem. Its mathematical translation can be thought of as being already contained in the famous philosophical paradox of Epimenides the Cretan, who said, "All Cretans are liars." Since it's impossible to say whether or not Epimenides is telling the truth (his assertion, if false, is true—and vice versa), one is faced with the problem of undecidability. Can you give a rigorous definition of Gödel's theorem? How, properly speaking, does it apply (if at all) to the neurosciences? More particularly, how does it apply to the modeling of cerebral function in mathematicians—that is, in the mathematics-producing brain?

CONNES: To my knowledge there exist two fundamental results due to Gödel concerning the impossibility mentioned by Jacob of a logical system's being sufficient to describe itself. The first shows that it's impossible, owing to a special mechanism of self-reference, to demonstrate that set theory is not contradictory. (Note, by the way, that this is true for every theory, even the most rudimentary, provided that it contains certain very simple axioms.) Then there is the incompleteness theorem. To explain this second result, I have to make clear first of all what it means for a proposition to be undecidable in an axiomatic system such as set theory.

Let me tell you a little story. For a number of years I went every Thursday to visit a mathematician friend who thought he had proved a theorem. He was working on a problem, which bears the name of a prewar Polish mathematician, Suslin, having to do with whether or not the ordered set of real numbers is characterized by a certain property. This problem had occupied my friend for almost thirty years. Every Thursday when I went to see him, he had a new solution to propose. Invariably he thought he had come up with a proof. Every Thursday we proceeded in the same manner: he proposed his solution, often in written form, and I looked for the mistake. Sometimes I found it right away, sometimes we had to go over the whole thing again the following week. Each time the mistake was found he started over, modifying his proof, over and over again. In fact, I knew from the beginning that no proof was possible. But I also knew that I couldn't convince him that the existence of a proof was illusory by coming up with counterexamples. Why? Because it had been demonstrated some years earlier, in the 1960s, that the Suslin problem was independent of the axioms of set theory. One occasionally encounters such situations in mathematics. In this particular case, it was shown that if one introduces another axiom in addition to the axioms of set theory—the continuum hypothesis, for example—the answer to the problem is yes; but if one adds some other suitable axiom, the answer is no. In other words, the situation is such that it's impossible to prove either result without adding additional axioms to those of set theory. But for just this reason it was equally impossible for me to give my friend a counterexample without using an additional axiom to which he could easily object. It's important that we be very clear about what axiom-independence implies and what it doesn't imply. Undecidability only has a meaning—

CHANGEUX: Within a given axiomatic system.

CONNES: Exactly. A statement is undecidable if one can assert either its truth or its falsehood without contradicting the axioms of the system one's working with.

CHANGEUX: The axioms internal to the system therefore don't suffice to decide the truth or falsity of a statement asserted within it.

CONNES: Right. We're now in a position to state Gödel's incompleteness theorem. This says that no matter which axioms one takes as given, assuming they're finite in number, there will always be questions to which no answer can be given by deductive proofs from the axioms—that is, which will remain undecidable. Put another way, Gödel's theorem shows that it's impossible to specify a finite number of axioms such that every question will be decidable. That doesn't mean that one can't analyze a question based on what one knows, but it does mean that the number of new and interesting questions that can't be answered is infinite. It's in this sense that Gödel's theorem is to be understood. In my view it would be a mistake to take it to mean that the power of the human brain is limited. The theorem says only that with a finite number of axioms one can't come up with an answer for everything. But even if a certain question lacks an answer, so long as it's been proved to be undecidable then one can nonetheless arbitrarily assign an answer to it and move on.

In that case every new undecidable question gives rise to a bifurcation that offers a choice between a positive or negative answer—which means that the world we explore admits of many possible bifurcations. And that's absolutely *all* it means. Once an answer has been assigned to a question, one can go on to pose new questions. In this way questions that previously hadn't been decidable become decidable. Each undecidable question creates a bifurcation and imposes a choice. Paul Cohen's theorem on the continuum hypothesis, for example, yields the following bifurcation: one can choose whether there are to be no cardinalities between the countable and the continuum, or whether there are to be several of them. The first answer is recommended by its simplicity. But it's very important that the preferred answer bear upon the most primitive possible questions. In fact, there do exist more primitive questions than that of the continuum.

CHANGEUX: You see no fundamental theoretical obstacle—

CONNES: I'm speaking for the moment only about the problem of undecidability. Undecidable questions such as that of the continuum require us first to come up with a new axiom that renders them decidable, and then to test the consequences of this new axiom and its capacity to throw light on other questions. For example, if one uses the continuum hypothesis, one can show (as Mokobodski has done) that it's possible to assign in a linear way a limit $\mathrm{Lim}_w\,(a_n)$ to every bounded sequence of real numbers such that $\lim \inf (a_n) < \mathrm{Lim}_w\,(a_n)$, and that Lim_w measurably depends on (a_n) and commutes with integration. This is a very useful result in the mathematics that I use. When one introduces a new axiom such as that of the continuum, it's obviously necessary to assure oneself of its undecidability, which is to say, to assure oneself of two things: on the one hand, that it doesn't result from prior axioms (Cohen's theorem establishes this for the continuum hypothesis), and, on the other hand, that its negation doesn't result from prior axioms (which one of Gödel's results establishes for the continuum hypothesis). But I don't think it makes any sense to interpret the incompleteness theorem as limiting our understanding. One simply has to accept that there will always be choices to make, and that it won't be possible to give a recursive procedure for making them once and for all. That's what this theorem means.

CHANGEUX: To answer is to choose. Gödel's theorem bears upon the process of knowledge acquisition rather than on a logical or epistemological impossibility. We neurobiologists can therefore take heart: sooner or later we'll understand how the brain works!

CONNES: The theorem defines a sort of horizon of understanding determined by the finite number of choices already made. The larger this number, the further the horizon is extended. We mustn't accept the static picture of a world in which there exists a fixed, finite number of axioms supplying an answer for everything. Human understanding, by contrast, is dynamic: each time it increases, we can answer more and more questions, and make choices at each new bifurcation, with the result that our horizon is pushed back still further. Obviously it's an illusion to think that one day we'll understand everything. We won't—this is the predicament of human science in general. But we shouldn't limit ourselves on this account, or feel discouraged by the statement of this theorem.

In fact, in its most profound formulation, Gödel's incompleteness theorem shows that mathematics can't be reduced to a formal language. At the beginning of the century mathematicians were intent on clarifying the nature of proof in mathematics. Hilbert constructed an artificial language built upon a finite alphabet, a finite number of grammatical rules permitting the unambiguous specification of the set of coherent propositions, and a finite number of rules of logical inference and of supposed primitive (or axiomatic) propositions. On the basis of such a system, or formal language, a universal algorithm permitted the validity of any proof formulated in the language to be decided. Thus it was at least theoretically possible to establish the list of all provable theorems in this formal language. Hilbert hoped to be able to reduce the set of mathematical theorems to those that are provable in a suitable formal language. Gödel's theorem shows that this is impossible: no matter the complexity of a formal system, there will always be one statement about the positive integers that will be both true and unprovable within the formal system. (One is assuming here that the axioms are self-consistent.) This negative aspect of the theorem—the impossibility of giving a clear definition of what counts as a proof—has been much insisted upon. But if we consider it from a different angle—namely, as asserting that true propositions about positive integers can't be reduced, by means of logical inference, to a finite number of axioms—it can be seen to imply that the quantity of information contained in the set of all such true propositions about positive integers is infinite. I ask you: isn't *that* the distinguishing characteristic of a reality independent of all human creation?

But let's move on to the problem of introspection. With the development of set theory, paradoxes due to errors of syntax were detected. For example, if the set of all sets is admitted to be itself a set, it would seem legitimate to consider as a part of this set *the set of all those sets that contain themselves as elements*. This would therefore have as its complement *the set of all those sets that do not contain themselves as elements*. The paradox identified by Russell arises when one asks whether or not this latter set contains itself as an element: either answer, yes or no, yields a contradiction. To avoid this contradiction it suffices, as Russell proposed, to establish a hierarchy of logical propositions according to *type*. One begins with elements (type 0), and next sharply distinguishes these from sets (type 1), and so on. The point of making a distinction between echelons, or types, is to make sure that they don't get mixed up. The very expression "a set that belongs to itself" betrays a fault of syntax. Once the logic is organized hierarchically, then, the paradox disappears.

CHANGEUX: It's a question, in effect, of introducing order.

CONNES: Yes, the succession of types makes it possible to order the mechanisms of thought hierarchically: elements are taken to be simpler, less elevated, than sets.

CHANGEUX: One can't treat them as interchangeable.

CONNES: One can't put an element and a set on the same level. In particular, one can't pose the question of the set of sets that contain themselves as elements. Surely an analogous syntactic distinction can be applied to the problem of introspection to eliminate an apparent paradox.

CHANGEUX: Therefore it isn't undecidable.

CONNES: It isn't a question of undecidability. The paradox results from a fault of syntax. Russell saw that the logic of set theory could be reformulated in such a way as to eliminate the paradox. Once logical questions were recast in terms of this hierarchy, the paradox vanished.

CHANGEUX: In other words the paradox was rendered decidable by the addition of hypotheses.

CONNES: No, the paradox simply exposed the need for a more refined conception of logical objects, which called for them to be arranged hierarchically.

CHANGEUX: Let's go on to the second question.

CONNES: The question is to what extent Gödel's theorem limits the possibility of the brain's understanding itself. Gödel's theorem has a natural interpretation in the context of the theory of computational complexity, particularly in connection with random sequences. The notion of the complexity of a sequence is simple to grasp. Let us compare, for instance, the sequence of times of sunrise in Paris over the last ten years with the sequence of lottery results during the same period. Obviously a very simple program can be devised—essentially a trigonometric function—to give the first sequence, while the second one can only be generated by a program of scarcely shorter length than the sequence itself. Roughly speaking, it can be said that the complexity of a sequence is the length of the shortest program required to generate it. The implication of Gödel's theorem in this context, then, is that in order to decide that a sequence has at least a certain degree of complexity, a considerably *larger* degree of complexity is required.

It seems to me that this could have implications for our ability to understand how the brain functions. It might imply that the degree of complexity of cerebral activity can't be decided without having at our disposal a tool of considerably greater complexity than the brain itself. Such a tool could perhaps in principle be constructed by the parallel operation of a large number of computers—the conjunction of multiple "brains," in effect—which after all is what computational neurobiology hopes to be able to do. Even so, I don't see why it shouldn't be possible for the *result* of such an investigation to be understood by a single human brain.

TURING'S THINKING MACHINE

CHANGEUX: Let's go on then to Turing machines.
CONNES: Perhaps it would be useful if first we were to describe them in some detail.
CHANGEUX: Turing was an exceptional mathematician. His work still inspires many biologists, which makes him one of the few creative mathematical minds to have proposed theories whose application has made a difference in the development of biology. This is the case, for example, with his theory of morphogenesis through symmetry breaking. He succeeded in showing how, by a system of paired chemical reactions, form could be spontaneously created from an isotropic system. What's more, he conceived the problem in an amusing way, in seeking to explain how a hydra with six tentacles wrapped around its mouth could be

formed from a spherical egg—proof that biological problems that are concrete and precisely formulated can inspire original mathematical theories! But Turing was also one of the first to formulate the theory of information-processing machines, or computers, such as we use today. This theory has always been the object of intense debate among psychologists and neurobiologists. It poses the problem whether a Turing machine could ever be built to the same standard of performance as the human brain, and whether the brain itself is a Turing machine. Turing's famous paper of 1936 begins with the words "I propose to consider the question: can machines think?"[2] This is precisely the question before us at the moment.

First then: what is a Turing machine? The one described in Turing's paper reads and writes discrete symbols—squares—on a tape that serves as an input device, storing the symbols and therefore functioning as memory. But it also serves as an output device. The machine carries out three operations: it reads the symbols, changes state, and writes them out. The tape is, in theory, unlimited in length, and in some sense defines the program. Turing immediately distinguishes the *program*, or "software"—

CONNES: Does it read back what it's recorded?

CHANGEUX: It can, yes.

CONNES: Does the tape go by just once, or can it be rewound?

CHANGEUX: It's possible to rerun the tape indefinitely. It contains the program, or "software," while the rest of the machine—the solid part—constitutes the "hardware." With Turing we're already looking at a computer very much like the ones we know today.

CONNES: But is the mechanism by which the machine operates specified?

---

[2] A. M. Turing, "On Computable Numbers, with an Application to the *Entscheidungsproblem*," *Proc. Lond. Math. Soc.* 2, no. 42 (1937). Though the article is commonly associated with the year of its completion, 1936, it did not actually appear until January 1937 owing to delays in publication; for an account of this episode, see A. Hodges, *Alan Turing: The Enigma* (New York: Simon and Schuster/Touchstone Books, 1984), pp. 111–25.

CHANGEUX: That's the problem. Turing's machine is a *digital* calculator built to handle discontinuous quantities. It's to be distinguished from *analog* calculators that measure physical quantities. A digital calculator—and this is a very important point in Turing's theory—is capable of imitating any machine that operates on discontinuous quantities. It's therefore a *universal* machine, since any process can be represented in the form of a series of instructions permitting the manipulation of discontinuous elements. Any process of this kind can therefore in principle be reproduced by a Turing machine—even an analog calculator can be simulated by a digital calculator.

A question now arises regarding the validity of the Church-Turing thesis, which asserts that whatever can be calculated by a human being can be calculated by a machine; that whatever can be calculated by a machine can also be calculated by a general or partial recursive program; and, finally, that whatever can be calculated by a human being can be calculated by this program. This amounts to saying that the brain and its function must be identical to a Turing machine—exactly the functionalist doctrine championed by cognitive psychologists such as Johnson-Laird who, as I mentioned earlier, maintain that because psychology reduces to the study of programs it's independent of neurophysiology, which restricts itself to the study of the machine and its code. On this view, everything of a mental character belongs to the software, while the brain itself, with its neurons and synapses, constitutes the hardware. The brain therefore holds little interest for the functionalists, who go even so far as to claim that the physical nature of the brain exercises few, if any, constraints on the organization of thought. According to this doctrine, fashionable until recently in cognitive science, it matters little or not at all whether the brain is made of proteins or silicon, or how many neurons it has or what they are like. The only things that matter are the algorithms with which cerebral functions are identified. For functionalists, to take an interest in the neurobiological substrate is a waste of time!

THE THEORY OF THE *S*-MATRIX IN PHYSICS AS
ANALOGUE TO FUNCTIONALISM IN PSYCHOLOGY

CONNES: A parallel can be drawn between the two positions you've just contrasted and their analogues in field theory. Field theory seeks to understand the mechanism of interaction between elementary particles. Here too there are two opposing tendencies.

CHANGEUX: Would you mind first saying a little more about field theory?

CONNES: Not at all. As soon as one tries to put together quantum mechanics and special relativity, one has to deal with the fact that particles are automatically created and annihilated. The number of particles, contrary to what occurs in chemistry, isn't constant. In order to handle even very simple phenomena, it's necessary therefore to study fields, which depend on an infinity of variables, rather than isolated particles. This very complex theory has enjoyed immense success. But the analogy between the doctrine of functionalism in psychology and Heisenberg's theory of the *S*-matrix is striking. According to the latter doctrine, what happens at the moment when the particles collide is of little or no concern; the only thing that matters is the matrix that encodes the passage from the initial state of the system to its final state. Both states are characterized by a number of free particles, with specified mass and momenta. The theory attempts to analyze the properties of this matrix without there being anything precisely known about the mechanism that regulates the interactions at work at the moment of collision. To understand the *S*-matrix doesn't mean that one has therefore understood what's going on, but it does mean that one has a model to work with that gives results that fit with experimental reality—

CHANGEUX: In other words, a phenomenology.

CONNES: Yes.

CHANGEUX: The interactions occur in a "black box" that no one bothers with. The functionalists regard the brain as a box of the same color.

CONNES: Exactly. This step introduces a certain number of simplifications and complications. Problems can be formulated in a much simpler way because the details of the mechanism are left to one side; but because the number of possible solutions to the problem at hand is quite large, there's no real gain. This theory by itself won't do. But it remains a useful tool for understanding phenomena in the context of a more fundamental theory. It represents a point of view that therefore shouldn't be totally ignored—to the contrary, the history of physics shows it to have been a rich source of insight from time to time. String theory, which today is so much in vogue, issues directly from the S-matrix point of view, through the Veneziano model.

CHANGEUX: To my way of thinking as a neurobiologist, the functionalist approach is useful because it allows function to be better defined—ideally, in quantified form. In some sense this amounts to physiology: one measures the function from the outside, as it were, without examining the internal mechanism.

CONNES: Precisely. What's being analyzed is the output of the black box—what its capabilities are, in effect.

CHANGEUX: To my mind this is what a functional definition of a problem amounts to—it's fine as far as it goes, and neural models will have to do a better job of taking function into account in the future. And so I'm completely in agreement with you. I don't deny the interest of an experimental approach that quantifies functions; but I *am* opposed to an exclusivist position according to which the mere description of function is enough to explain it. This raises a problem we should pause to consider briefly. If the functionalist approach were correct, a cerebral function would be identified with one, or even several, mathematical algorithms. But can external reality be identified with mathematical objects? Do mathematical idealizations wholly describe observed phenomena? You yourself resist this idea. You think that the mathematical models used in physics don't give a complete, exhaustive representation of physical reality. Functionalism seems to me more a practical way of dealing with cerebral functions than an actual philosophy. But its defenders run up against a real epistemological obstacle, it seems to me, assuming as they do that it's possible to identify a mathematical algorithm with a physical property of the brain.

CONNES: In physics it's clear, in somewhat the same way, that to satisfy oneself with the S-matrix amounts to taking a step backward with respect to field theory. But the functionalists surely have good arguments to make when it comes to identifying which experimental results are reproducible and which quantities are significant.

CHANGEUX: Exactly. But they go further. They think, for example, that describing an argument or constructing a sentence by a calculation algorithm, and simulating such behavior by means of a Turing machine, suffices to understand how thought functions.

CONNES: We can show that's a huge exaggeration simply by considering the implications of the three levels of mathematical creativity we've been discussing. The faculty of being able to reproduce a sentence belongs to the first level: the mechanism required must be given in advance. Knowing how to change strategy when confronted with an error is altogether different, however. To believe that we understand the brain because we understand the first level couldn't be more wrong. Even at the first level the Turing machine solves nothing, since it fails to take into account the problem of algorithmic complexity.

CHANGEUX: Thus we dispose of functionalism!

CONNES: Not completely. It can be useful for specifying which quantities are worth analyzing. But while the evaluation of a theory in functional terms has a certain practical value, one can't be content to leave matters at that.

CHANGEUX: Not at all. It would amount to endorsing a very conservative, and misleading, point of view. History shows that by analyzing the levels underlying the one to be explained—getting inside the black box and taking it apart in order to reduce, and then reconstruct, a physiological process—knowledge has been systematically advanced in all areas of biology.

CONNES: That's true as well for field theory in physics.

CHANGEUX: It's satisfying to note that—for once at least!—our views converge. Let's move on then to the third and final point: the difference between the human brain and present-day thinking machines.

IS THE HUMAN BRAIN A COMPUTER?

CHANGEUX: The computers we have at our disposal today are very good at handling certain types of operations. They calculate extremely rapidly. They can carry out multiplication to ten places in a fraction of a second. But they're obviously quite limited in other respects. A computer would have enormous difficulties in recognizing a red poppy in a forest, for example, or a butterfly in the jungle—something a human being can do instantly! The point is often made as well that machines are devoid of affectivity, of the capacity for feeling that is so characteristically human. But above all they're incapable of anticipation, of intentionality—they can't write their own programs, they're helpless without a human master. Their capacity for self-organization is quite restricted, indeed nonexistent. Since you're someone who practices chess against a machine that can play as well, if not better, than most human beings, I'd very much value having your views on this point.

It seems to me that present-day computers lack two properties possessed by the human brain. First, both the brain's program and machine—to revert to Turing's model—exhibit from the first stages of development a very intricate interplay. It's difficult, perhaps impossible, to define a program independently of the cerebral machine's connectivity. Sense objects are successively deposited in long-term memory over the course of development. The hardware is constructed in stages as a function of individual genetic endowment, and also of the individual agent's constant interaction with the outside world. But above all—and this is the property that's crucial for the purposes of our discussion—the brain behaves as an *evolutionary* machine. It evolves in a Darwinian fashion, simultaneously at several different levels and on several different time scales. This is what, for me, separates the brain from computing machines as they're presently designed (with the exception of Edelman's)—apart, of course, from intentionality, a property closely linked to evolution that hasn't been closely examined by neurobiologists because it depends on the highest levels of cerebral organization. What in your opinion sets the human brain apart from present-day machines? Is it really possible to imagine a machine that would approximate the faculties of the human brain?

CONNES: Let's look first at machines that play chess. Here intentionality amounts to something quite simple: winning the match. Defining an evaluation function that estimates how far one is from achieving this object at any given point during the game is extremely simple as well. In principle, then, a machine can be built that uses an evaluation function conditioned by this well-defined form of intentionality. In the case of the brain, by contrast, intentionality changes when the problems presented to it change. The brain must therefore create its own evaluation functions, functions that suit different sorts of intentionality. More precisely, it must be able to determine if a particular evaluation function is well adapted to a given intention. It must therefore possess—how, I don't know—an evaluation function for evaluation functions.

CHANGEUX: This is what, following Granger, we've been calling strategic reason.

CONNES: Yes, but I wanted to set up a hierarchy. On the one hand, we've got evaluation functions. An evaluation function can be identified with a goal. To have an intention amounts in some sense to having an evaluation function. Obviously not all evaluation functions will do, since certain ones correspond to contradictory intentions, while others aren't suitable to any intention whatsoever. But an intention can be defined, more or less anyway, as a coherent evaluation function. The brain itself must be able to work out this kind of function in any given situation. It must therefore be able to create one, or, at the very least, choose among ones that already exist. And to do this, it must itself possess an evaluation function that's fixed once and for all, that enables it to know if the evaluation function it creates is well adapted to the end it is working toward.

CHANGEUX: The mechanism you describe assumes memory.

CONNES: That's right—memory, prior experience. The brain is evidently able to rely on analogies to compare the present situation with ones it has known previously.

CHANGEUX: On the one hand, there is genetic memory. The human organism in its present form is the result of many generations of organisms that have previously undergone similar experiences. When a new problem arises, then, the answer's already inscribed in the memory of the genes. On the other hand, since it's subject to the influence of external reality, the brain is able to draw upon long-term memory, which is built up over the course of postnatal experience.

CONNES: It's at the second level that the fundamental problem is located. What sort of mechanism enables the brain to choose an evaluation function appropriate to a given end? What criteria constrain its choice? So long as we fail to get a handle on *this* phenomenon, we'll have no choice but to resign ourselves to remaining stuck at the first level, a long ways away from the second. This is the problem present-day computers face.

CHANGEUX: Which is to say that they're nowhere near the third level.

CONNES: They're nowhere near escaping the first level! They're capable of carrying out addition, multiplication, and so forth (albeit extremely complicated forms of addition and multiplication and all the rest), or of playing chess. But the evaluation function— intentionality, so far as it exists—always has to be given in advance. No machine today is capable *by itself* of constructing an appropriate evaluation function for a given intention—

CHANGEUX: Computers right now can't even *think* of having intentions of their own!

CONNES: No, because they don't interact with the physical world in an evolutionary way. Though they've got memory in some sense, they haven't any past other than the one we impose upon them. They have a hard time changing in response to new circumstances. Affectivity certainly is a big part of adaptation: when one sets a goal for oneself, one perseveres—sees the thing through to the end—in order to be able experience the pleasure of achieving it more than anything else—unless, of course, one's a masochist!

CHANGEUX: I agree. The capacity for experiencing pleasure is itself determined by our evolutionary past. If self-destruction were pleasurable—believe me, the human species wouldn't be around any more!

CONNES: Of course not! But just the same I do think that any mechanism that allows us to judge whether an evaluation function is appropriate to a given end must presuppose affectivity. Affectivity is necessary in order for us to be able to appreciate what happens to us. How well an evaluation function is suited to a given end can't be measured solely by the pleasure or displeasure it generates, however. Imagine, for example, a chess player who's capable of computerlike calculation, but who nonetheless selects an inappropriate evaluation function. Obviously she's going to feel enormous frustration the moment she realizes that she's losing every match she plays. Choosing the wrong evaluation function will only cause her displeasure—but this will only become apparent to her at the end of a match, not before. The evaluation function she's selected will prevent her from realizing the weakness of her position during the course of the game, and from seeing that she's in the process of losing. Confronted with the final result, however, she'll realize she chose the wrong function.

CHANGEUX: As I say, this internal system for evaluating pleasure or displeasure is itself predetermined by the evolutionary past of the species (figure 31). The range of emotional reaction over a given population has already been conditioned by the aggregate sensitivity of its individual members to external and internal signals.

CONNES: All present-day machines operate on the basis of predetermined intentionality, on account of which they remain stuck at the first level.

CHANGEUX: How then are we to go about designing second-level machines?

Fig. 16. — *Cynopithecus niger*, au repos.
D'après nature, par M. Wolf.

Fig. 17. — Le même, caressé et exprimant sa satisfaction.

Figure 31. Expression of Emotions in the Monkey
The emotions felt and expressed by man have their own evolutionary history. Charles Darwin, in *The Expression of the Emotions in Man and Animals* (1872), analyzed in detail the outward manifestation of the emotions, particularly facial expressions in man, and showed that many of them are recognizable at an earlier stage in animals, particularly the monkey. This illustration is taken from the French edition of 1877.

A SELF-EVALUATING MACHINE THAT CAN SUFFER

CONNES: I can only try to give the problem a precise formulation. A machine of this kind should interact evolutionarily with the outside world. It should automatically create an evaluation function corresponding to an externally determined goal. It should therefore be able to evaluate its own strategy. Assuming the machine were to have sufficient memory and calculating power, it should end up with an evaluation function strong enough to make it a good chess player, for example.

CHANGEUX: But is this feasible? The concept is easy enough to formulate. Why then don't such machines exist? Is the obstacle theoretical or practical?

CONNES: I don't know. As far as I can tell, affectivity is the mechanism that permits human beings to gain access to the second level. Somehow a way has to be found to reproduce this quality in a machine.

CHANGEUX: One can imagine a machine that measures pleasure by a variable magnitude, with a threshold—a middle level, such that the machine optimizes—

CONNES: Once again, take the case of chess. Let's suppose that the machine isn't equipped with the evaluation function needed to play chess at a high level. It has at its disposal all the possible moves, the rules of the game, and great calculating power—but it lacks the will to win. How can this be built in to the machine? After each move a good computer evaluates its position, marks it on a scale, and selects from among all possible moves the one that maximizes the value of the evaluation function. The machine we have in mind doesn't have this function. Therefore we have to devise a system that would allow it to construct the evaluation function. The first step is to make sure that at the end of the game, when it's losing, or finds itself in a weak position, it would experience pain.

CHANGEUX: If it were to experience pain, you'd already have solved the problem.

CONNES: Not quite, since it reacts only to the final result of the game.

CHANGEUX: But if you've already built in the condition that when it loses, it suffers—you've got the answer you're looking for.

CONNES: No, because it suffers only at the end of the match.

CHANGEUX: But you've already got at least one part of the answer.

CONNES: Only a small part, because the evaluation takes place only at the end—when it's too late . . .

CHANGEUX: Wouldn't it be enough, then, assuming the brain had a bit of memory, if it "understood" what it had to do in order to attain its goal, and then was able to work out the strategy required, which of course would have to be tested? But if the machine were to suffer in the event of defeat, it seems to me that a good part of the problem would already be solved.

CONNES: If the machine were to suffer each time it played poorly, we'd have succeeded in finding the evaluation function.

CHANGEUX: That, I believe, would be possible only after a certain number of tests.

CONNES: You mean that it would gradually construct its evaluation function by correlating the various moves it's played with the result of each match? That seems reasonable to me.

CHANGEUX: The fact that your machine would suffer in case of defeat is very important in any case.

CONNES: It's a start anyway. The suffering felt at the end permits evaluation to begin. The resulting evaluation function would assign to the matches played a positive result in case of victory, and a negative one in case of defeat. The machine could also memorize games played by other players, evaluating them solely on the basis of their final result. But it must be realized that a game of chess is played locally, move by move. In a game comprised of forty moves for each player, the machine would have to begin to reflect well before the last one. It must do this locally, at each move. When we set a specific goal for ourselves, we don't wait until the last moment to reckon how far away we are from achieving it: we're constantly on the lookout, measuring the distance every step of the way. To the extent we succeed in advancing, we locally optimize our behavior as a function of past steps. Our machine would be stupid if it contented itself with saying, "I lose, I win, I lose, I win," without deducing any local consequences from its experience. As I see it, reflection serves as a mechanism for calculating the global result of all the matches stored in memory in order to create a local evaluation function. To the extent that particular moves stand out, memory refers back to matches won or lost—thus the evaluation function is created. If we were to succeed in building a machine equipped with this mechanism, we could modify the rules of the game and make it play again in order to observe if it adapts. That would be a good criterion.

CHANGEUX: Would this machine be able to generate hypotheses? Would it possess a "hypothesis generator"?

CONNES: Sure. It's already found in computers today.

CHANGEUX: So what do they lack?

CONNES: An evaluation function!

CHANGEUX: Then we've got to think harder about how one could be created.

CONNES: I think I can suggest a precise—but unfortunately very uneconomical!—proposition. It will suffice, however, in order to show that solutions to the problem exist. Let's suppose that the computer has a thousand chess games stored in memory, with the outcome of the game serving in each case as the sole evaluation of the game for each player. This primitive evaluation function would consist in saying 'X lost' or 'X won' at the end of the match; but the function is stupid for the simple reason that it isn't local. Let's try to define, then, an evaluation function over the set of *local* evaluation functions. By contrast with the primitive nonlocal evaluation function, it would compare the result of the match with the score that a given local evaluation function assigns to each player in the course of the game. If there's a correlation between the final result of the match and the result of the local evaluation function, the function is retained—if not, it's rejected. Since our computer has stored in memory a very large number of matches, the crude character of this estimate disappears, allowing each local evaluation function to be evaluated in turn. Thus a universal evaluation function has been defined that allows reflection to be localized.

CHANGEUX: This would come quite close to consciousness.

CONNES: No, not consciousness, because we're only at the second level. We're approaching the capacity for reflection, but we're not there yet.

CHANGEUX: Conscious reflection.

CONNES: If it weren't for the problem of complexity, we wouldn't be far from being able to propose a new model for adaptive computers. Building such machines remains impossible as a practical matter, however, in view of the fact that algorithmic complexity increases exponentially.

CHANGEUX: Where does this leave us with respect to the *third* level?

CONNES: As for that, well . . .

CHANGEUX: The notion of an evaluation function is certainly suggestive.

CONNES: It's absolutely essential.

CHANGEUX: One could also think of "consciousness" as a sort of perception of the perceived.

CONNES: What do you mean? I don't have any idea how to get past the level of simple reflection!

CHANGEUX: I'm aware of that—but doesn't reflecting upon reflection amount itself to a sort of awareness?

CONNES: No. As far as I'm concerned, reflection amounts to no more than an evaluation function over local evaluation functions—it's a long ways away from consciousness!

CHANGEUX: You don't see a way to fortify this function somehow?

CONNES: Frankly, no. The problem is that, faced with a set of possible goals, one has to be able to create *one's own evaluation function*. One therefore needs to be able to construct an evaluation function of local evaluation functions that compares local experience with the desired result—and the actual final result—over time. Locality is the critical thing. We don't really have any idea how to model it yet in an economical and efficient way.

CHANGEUX: I entirely agree. Neurobiologists are obsessed with the problem of understanding the local activity of neurons.

CONNES: At the second level, reflection is local in time—here, it's true, conscious thought is what does the reflecting. But at the third level, the mechanism is no longer the same.

CHANGEUX: How so?

CONNES: At the second level, one can adapt a strategy to a given goal. At the third—the level of genuine creativity—the goal itself is unknown. The characteristic property of creativity resides in the absence of a previously set goal.

CHANGEUX: I'm not sure I completely share your view on this. The creative mind only chooses among different *possible* goals. It simply operates at a higher level of intention.

CONNES: It often happens, in pursuing a given end, that one discovers something quite different than what one was looking for. What's essential, in any event, is recognizing the peculiar novelty and harmony of what one actually happens upon. It's no longer a question at that point of reflection, but almost of creating a new end.

CHANGEUX: Of accidental, rather than intentional, creation!

CONNES: Exactly. What I suggested earlier really doesn't apply to the third level, as it turns out. I was assuming a clearly defined end: the machine felt a certain pleasure at winning or a certain displeasure at losing. What I was trying to show there was how the selection function might be adapted to a well-defined end. But at the third level it's true, even in those cases where a provisional goal is given in advance, the very attempt to achieve it may suddenly lead to the recognition of an unsuspected harmony, which in turn may modify the goal itself.

CHANGEUX: Randomness plays a much more important role in these cases.

CONNES: I'm not entirely convinced it does. Bifurcations may occur, but the third level is characterized above all by the recognition of a harmony—

CHANGEUX: Yes, but first something has to exist—which then, by a process of incubation and lateral branching, gives rise to—

CONNES: Something else intervenes, I believe—the recognition of a harmony—that doesn't belong to the second level.

CHANGEUX: It operates at a higher level then.

CONNES: We've gone beyond the level of reflection at this point. The harmony is perceived, but by a mechanism of a qualitatively different type.

CHANGEUX: By a sort of integrating mechanism—this is the keystone we've been looking for to complete our edifice.

CONNES: Possibly this, or else some other process by which different neuronal ensembles similarly manage to achieve resonance.

CHANGEUX: In the case of aesthetic pleasure, one can speak of frontal cortex activity harmonizing, or resonating, with the limbic system—among other systems.

CONNES: Maybe so.

CHANGEUX: Pleasure is very important, as we've emphasized, at the moment of illumination.

CONNES: Yes. But whereas the mechanism governing reflection causes pleasure or displeasure to intervene only at the final stage to trigger a local selection function, everything occurs differently in the case of creation.

CHANGEUX: Just the same, one could imagine a machine of this kind being built.

CONNES: Perhaps—I don't know. We're back once more to our old problem: does there exist a preestablished harmony that human beings apprehend because they live in a harmonious world, or do they create it themselves? Do we discover this harmonious reality—or do we create the harmony out of the reality?

CHANGEUX: We are indeed back to our original problem—but now you present matters quite differently! Shouldn't we say: either there exists in the world a preestablished harmony—in which case we live in a platonic world; or we try merely to strengthen the harmonious resonance of the external world with our interior world—a world we build for ourselves?

7. The Real and the Rational

CHANGEUX: Throughout our previous conversations I've been arguing that our brains have created all of mathematics—as against your view that mathematical reality and the harmony that characterizes it exist independently of the human brain, and actually preexist the appearance of human beings on earth. This position, which I persist in calling "strong platonism," you share with a few other mathematicians, particularly in France. And so now, in our final conversation,[1] I'd like us to consider whether our positions are really as irreconcilable as they seem—to see whether in spite of all our disagreements we can't manage to find some common ground. One way for us to proceed, it seems to me, because the plausibility of the claim that mathematics existed prior to the appearance of human beings on earth can't be experimentally tested, is by agreeing to avoid all reference to what might be called the "mythology of origins." For this claim concerns after all as much the origins of matter, of the earth, and of life itself, as it does the origins of the human species—all of which have furnished innumerable religions and philosophies with the material for their founding myths. Perhaps as scientists we can succeed in freeing ourselves from the spell of these mythic cosmogonies, and attempt one last time to reach agreement on a few fundamental points. Let me propose then that we reexamine three questions: first, the nature of mathematical objects; second, mathematics, the child, and experience; and, finally, mathematics in relation to physics, and, in particular, the question of order in the world.

[1] See the translator's note, p. viii.

THE NATURE OF MATHEMATICAL
OBJECTS REVISITED

CHANGEUX: Let's see if we can't come up with a definition of mathematical objects that we can both agree upon *and* that will help us think more deeply about the nature of such objects. Obviously I don't use the word "nature" innocently. For me, as you know, mathematical objects are uniquely the product of the human brain—a position shared by Poincaré, I might point out, who notes that mathematicians proceed "by construction": they construct combinations of increasing complexity and then analyze the resulting sets of combinations—that is to say, they break them down (the original meaning of "analysis" in the Greek). Analysis of these sets allows mathematicians to perceive the relations among their elements, and so to deduce from these the relations among the sets themselves.

CONNES: From my point of view, Poincaré's description applies perfectly to our perception of mathematical reality.

CHANGEUX: Poincaré describes in detail the work of the mathematician, which he calls "invention." Note that he doesn't use the term "discovery." For him it is not a matter of the perception of mathematical reality, as you suggest, but of the description of the physical world by the mathematician.

CONNES: Poincaré's description fits perfectly with the actual invention *of conceptual tools*, which makes up a large part of what mathematicians do. As long as we leave to one side the problem of the existence of mathematical reality, I have no problem with this description.

CHANGEUX: The problem is that you introduce a distinction Poincaré didn't make, *and then* go on to accept that mathematics is uniquely the product of the human brain to the extent that you distinguish between tools and—

CONNES: I'll have to state my position on this point more clearly.

CHANGEUX: Do you then distinguish two categories of mathematical objects, all of which are produced by the human brain: object-tools, on the one hand, and objects in a more semantic sense, which would compose what you call mathematical reality?

CONNES: I distinguish between our perception and the external reality that is perceived. This is a point I think I can clarify by referring to something we haven't previously discussed. It will be necessary to use mathematical terms, but I'll explain them as I go along. The important distinction I want to make is between what may be called *inductive* and *projective* systems. Let me begin with an analogy. Suppose that you've got to find your name in a list of two thousand names. There are two ways to go about this. One is inductively, which consists in taking the names one by one until you come across yours. The other is projectively, which consists in first eliminating all those names that don't have the right initial letter, and then, from the remaining names, eliminating all those that don't have the right second letter; next, from the names that are left, eliminating all those that don't have the right third letter; and so on. It's obvious that these are two very different ways of attacking the problem. By going through the different names according to the first method, you get to know them individually and completely, you're familiar with each one in detail, but you haven't really looked at them as a whole—you've looked at the elements of the set one by one. With the second method, you've made a first division of the set into subsets corresponding to the first letter; then a finer division corresponding to the second letter; and so on. The distinction between the inductive and projective is really fundamental to the way we grasp the world. We come across it in everyday language. The word "chair" is clearly a case of projective labeling: many objects correspond to the noun *chair*, but the word itself doesn't unambiguously pick out a particular object. Proper names, by contrast, such as "Paris," pick out a particular object. This second kind of labeling, inductive labeling, is often historically influenced, and it would be very difficult to convert it into a projective labeling.

CHANGEUX: One may say, for example, that the world contains cities; that they have traits in common; that some of them are found in France; and that, among these ones, Paris is the capital. I think that it's a question of operational modes that, in one case, depend on hierarchical formal categories—the projective mode—and that, in another, are based on global apprehension—

CONNES: Not global: in the inductive mode, it's a question of isolating the individual elements of a set.

CHANGEUX: Of isolating particular units. In both cases we are dealing with "mental objects" produced by our brains to label an external reality.

CONNES: Yes.

CHANGEUX: This is an interesting distinction. I think that mathematical objects belong primarily to the second category—to the projective mode.

CONNES: Our conceptual apprehension of mathematical reality is projective in exactly the sense I've just described. Most of the conceptual tools used by mathematicians effect a projective division of what I want to call *archaic mathematical reality*.

CHANGEUX: But it seems to me that mathematical objects are projective by nature.

CONNES: No, the conceptual tools aren't to be confused with the mathematical reality itself. Let me explain. What I find fascinating about mathematical reality, and about the effort made by human beings to try to understand the objects that populate it, is that it's often possible to characterize a particular object up to isomorphism by its properties. I've already mentioned, for example, the "monster" group, the largest finite sporadic simple group. All of these adjectives—"largest," "finite," "sporadic," "simple"—correspond to a projective division in the sense I've described. It would be very difficult, I think, to make similar statements about external physical reality. How could even the earth, for instance, our own planet, be defined projectively? One could say that it's the third planet in a system revolving around a star situated in the spiral arm of a galaxy, but obviously this doesn't single it out from a great many other planets.

CHANGEUX: Its singularity arises from applying the projective method to the outside world—which is to say, from experience.

CONNES: In a way. What I find fascinating about mathematics is precisely that one is able to succeed—as, for example, in the case of finite groups—in isolating certain objects by their projective properties. It seems to me that mathematics accomplishes something that goes beyond what we're able to do in the real world.

CHANGEUX: I agree. I believe that these objects have been constructed—elaborated, in the literal sense of having been *worked out*. You say the same thing yourself: they are, to use your term, "projective"—that is to say, projected by the brain onto the external material world.

CONNES: What I said is that we construct our projective system, which is to say our system for perceiving mathematical reality, but not the reality itself.

CHANGEUX: It may be that what you call archaic mathematical reality is in fact a feature of physical reality. Let's come back to this point later. I think that we can agree for the moment at least upon your definition of projective mathematical objects, upon the fact that each one can be characterized by a set of unique properties that single it out from every other object. As a neurobiologist, I want to propose a hypothesis to you, then, a model: namely, that since mathematical objects are indisputably mental representations of the brain, they are therefore singular physical objects created by our brains and, by virtue of this, part of the physical world.

CONNES: Yes, this applies perfectly to the projective system that we construct.

CHANGEUX: Let me try to frame the problem more generally with reference to all kinds of mathematical representations. What I'm proposing involves two claims. First, that all mathematical objects are representations that the human brain projects onto the world. Second, that they are singular *physical* objects, built up within the brain with well-defined spatio-temporal properties.

CONNES: Arriving at a proper definition may be very difficult.

CHANGEUX: Mathematical objects are dynamic physical states of neuronal networks, characterized by the coherence of their patterns of activation and by some process of convergence among the neuronal connections that make up these networks. In other words, these brain states acquire their unified character through the "binding" of individual neuronal activities. It's known that certain brain lesions affect the use of mathematical objects, and that others don't. Certain regions of the brain are more specialized than others in the production, manipulation, and memorization of mathematical objects.

CONNES: Absolutely.

CHANGEUX: These activities are confined to certain clearly demarcated areas distributed throughout the brain; they possess a certain permanence, a reproducibility—in other words, they possess *invariant* properties. There must be invariance in the dynamic physical states of neuronal activation if we are going to be able to define the term "representation." This is why I speak of physical objects. But they're physical objects of a very particular kind.

CONNES: You can't push this point too far. *Everything* that the brain produces is a physical object.

CHANGEUX: Of course—which is exactly why mathematical objects fall in this category.

CONNES: I'd say then that the projective *perception* of mathematical reality accords perfectly with your view.

CHANGEUX: My point for the moment is that mathematical objects in general possess certain distinctive properties. I count four: let's try to define them one by one. First, they have *causal power*. That is to say, they can be used to carry out operations—in mathematics as much as in the world. For example, a numerical figure may be used to signify the value of an object in French francs. Imagine the object is sold at auction. Successive rounds of bidding establish a value. The auctioneer compares this value with the number he has in mind. He goes on or he stops. In this way an economy comes to be constructed on the basis of mathematical objects.

CONNES: Yes, of course, it's possible to use mathematics in this way, relying on its linguistic aspect. But this is only a very limited part of mathematical practice.

CHANGEUX: No, I think there's an essential semantic component involved here. I even think that mathematics actually came into being as a result of this particular process of signification: it developed as a sort of universal language for trading goods and defining their value. But there's more to the property of causality than the linguistic aspect, I agree. It also implies the notion of measure, that is to say the quantity attributed to an object, which can be added or subtracted.

CONNES: Quite so, but again this is only a small part of mathematics.

CHANGEUX: The second property of mathematical objects is that they are *universal*. That is to say, they're found in all human communities. They're universal mental objects, and therefore physical objects that represent relations among natural objects . . .

CONNES: It bothers me a bit when you say "mental objects, and therefore physical objects . . ." I would prefer it if we were to preserve the distinction between external physical reality—

CHANGEUX: It's a physical reality internal to the brain, not the actual physical world external to it.

CONNES: There I agree with you.

CHANGEUX: So we're in agreement after all. Bravo! Therefore we agree that these physical objects internal to the brain can be used to represent relations among natural objects, relations among mathematical objects themselves, and even the operations carried out among these. As the American philosopher Kitcher points out, language has a double function: it serves as a vehicle for the performance of mathematical operations, and also as the means for reporting these operations.

But this doesn't exhaust the properties of mathematical objects. Two other characteristics seem to me very important in defining the singular status of mathematical objects as physical objects internal to the brain. The third property I want to propose is that they possess what Granger calls *formal content*. In this they're unique, at least by comparison with physical objects belonging to the external world. For Granger, you'll recall, this formal content is constituted by the potential properties that these objects possess. Once a new result has been stated for the first time, the mathematician doesn't necessarily see everything that the statement contains, all the properties peculiar to the object. These are only discovered gradually—they're not necessarily explicit the day they're produced. Without entering into the definitional details of conjectures, postulates, and axioms, it's clear nonetheless that the work of mathematicians also consists in an internal exploration of these objects. Mathematical objects share a peculiar feature with the physical objects of the outside world, namely that in each case it takes a lot of work to unravel the multiple strands of which they are made up, all the properties that they possess. Here's where discovery comes in. Given that mathematical objects are physical objects that are internal to our brain, and assuming they can be circumscribed and delimited without too much trouble initially, the mathematician still faces the prospect of having to devote a great deal of time and energy trying to tease out their properties, to "de-nest" their potentialities, as it were. I think the fact that they possess such properties must enter into any definition of mathematical objects.

CONNES: We diverge on this point. You describe only our system of perception.

CHANGEUX: Your notion of perception is vague and therefore rather unsatisfactory from the standpoint of the physiologist. In fairness, however, I'm quite prepared to agree that mathematical objects have a certain reality—which I refer to as physical—that isn't apprehended all at once, but progressively, step by step. Next we have to identify which neuronal states possess *intrinsic* formal richness in our brains. If we can talk further about this, it may be possible for us to open up a new field of knowledge that will enrich neurobiology, if not also mathematics.

CONNES: I'm willing to qualify my position on what I call projective perception. I see the work of the mathematician, at least in so far as it concerns what goes on in his brain, as precisely a matter of grasping this raw mathematical reality I was talking about. He does this by constructing a projective system of concepts that involves the whole generative dimension of language and the whole deductive dimension as well.

CHANGEUX: We're not going to make much progress so long as you insist on restating the same position over and over again. We may agree on the notion of formal content, of potential properties that the mathematician only gradually discovers, but I cannot bring myself to share your opinion about the "subjective feeling" of what you call "raw mathematical reality." My sense is that a special effort of will is required if the mathematician is to succeed in consciously unraveling the properties of the raw mathematical *objects* his or her brain unconsciously creates. But you've just now touched upon the fourth, and final, characteristic of mathematical objects that I wanted to mention: their *generativity*. Not only do they possess this exceedingly rich form of "potentiality" that's unique to the products of the human brain; they're also capable of producing new objects, of originating new theories, of giving rise to an evolution that so far shows no signs of ever coming to an end. On this account mathematics finds itself in the singular position of being forever "open" to new mathematical representations. The edifice of mathematics, it seems to me, unlike that of any other branch of science, constructs itself—pulls itself up by its own bootstraps, as it were.

CONNES: Exactly. Mathematics is generative. But I want to make you see that it's unduly restrictive to say that it is *wholly* self-generating. Thanks to Gödel's theorem, for example, we know the integers will always have properties that can be neither demonstrated nor disproved but that are nonetheless properties of the integers.

CHANGEUX: They're an example of these potential properties—

CONNES: It's more subtle than that. If one were to construct a computer that had the deductive power of the human mind—that is, a computer that could tell whether one proposition follows from another on the basis of pure logic, one wouldn't be able to reduce the properties of the integers to a finite set of axioms. It's false to say that by this sole deductive procedure, this sole logical procedure, one succeeds in knowing all the properties of the integers. There's something quite striking about this, it seems to me, which marks off archaic reality from the projective, deductive procedure that we construct to perceive it.

CHANGEUX: Perhaps there's an analogy here with what we've said in connection with physical reality. Mathematical objects, we've already agreed, don't exhaust the whole of physical reality. Even so, it's quite possible that the reality of mathematical objects themselves may be difficult to exhaust, to the extent that they're physical constructions of our brains.

CONNES: It's here that I make a distinction between archaic reality and the projective system of perception that we construct. All the consequences, all the logical conclusions that we arrive at by deductive reasoning belong, in my opinion, to a projective system of thought. The true or not-true properties of the integers, by contrast, belong to archaic reality. What more can I tell you? This is the way I see it. I don't agree with you when you say that a dialogue with experience isn't really possible. Among the integers many curious features of mathematical reality can be observed—the existence of twin primes, for example (pairs of prime numbers, such as [3, 5], [5, 7], [17, 19], etc., that differ by two), or the fact that 8 and 9 are the only known consecutive integers that are nontrivial powers. These amount to experimentally verified facts about archaic reality. One advantage of present-day supercomputers, which have a computational capacity far superior to that of the most powerful human brain, is that they can carry out such experiments.

CHANGEUX: Experiments that take place in the computer—but they involve physical objects.

CONNES: These are really physical objects only in the sense that they're written in the computer program. But the numbers being investigated are much larger than the number of atoms in the universe.

CHANGEUX: It's an experiment, if you like, but one that takes place in an artificial brain. It's not an experiment based on the nature around us. It's an experiment based on mathematical objects, another sign of the generative power I was talking about—

CONNES: Which serves to mark off mathematical reality from physical reality.

CHANGEUX: Let's not get into that. The main thing is to get clear about the points on which we can agree. The computer exploits physical objects in order to explore the properties of the mathematical objects themselves or the properties of the outside world. It's a sort of artificial brain, but one that shows once again the very peculiar character of these mathematical representations by comparison with other representations. One can't do that with words taken from the dictionary.

CONNES: What I mean is this. Say you're trying to find out if there are integers that satisfy certain equations. Well, to do that, sometimes a computer can help—by doing calculations that the human brain would never be able to perform, and actually finding solutions.

CHANGEUX: Therefore this is an experiment that doesn't bear upon the world, but upon the computer, which is a sort of prosthesis of the human brain.

CONNES: For me it's an experiment that bears upon archaic reality. The result of the experiment doesn't depend on the type of computer that's used. If a result is found, well, that's it: we now know a little bit more about mathematical reality.

CHANGEUX: I don't disagree.

CONNES: What I mean is that the human brain is utterly incapable of arriving at the result in this way because of the limits to its computational power.

CHANGEUX: So one constructs a prosthesis, endowing it with capabilities that nonetheless are constructed by the human brain.

CONNES: Of course.

CHANGEUX: Let's go on then to the last point. Internal physical objects—

CONNES: Which is to say projective perception, or conceptualization if you prefer. You've got to be more precise if we're going to be able to understand each other.

CHANGEUX: Okay. They're the result of a certain process carried out by the brain.

CONNES: Obviously—a process of construction.

CHANGEUX: To avoid purely semantic confusion, let me reemphasize that I call mathematical objects "notional" objects (*objets idéels*) in order to avoid the term "ideal" (*idéal*), which has a certain teleological, even spiritualistic connotation. "Notional" is closer to "idea" than to "idealism." The basic question, which we've already discussed—but that it will be useful to take up again at this point—has to do with this business of selection. Poincaré used to say, "In mathematics the word 'exist' can have only one meaning: 'exempt from contradiction.'" Even if you don't agree with his definition—which is a bit reductionist, I admit—it's helpful for getting across the point that the difference between mathematical objects and other physical objects is related to a process that rather misleadingly is often called "idealization." This consists in passing objects through the "sieve of reason" in order to eliminate all contradictions. It is, in other words, a rational process of *selection* that assures the integration of a new object with the "cultural corpus" of current mathematics, which is itself the result of a sometimes quite erratic historical process of evolution. In mathematics, *the real is what is rational*—though usually this is apparent to us only after the fact! The collective, social aspect of mathematics as it's actually constructed, which has been studied by Arbib and others, hasn't been stressed enough in our conversations.

CONNES: From my point of view, it's clear that the conceptual tools of mathematics are created. But a new tool doesn't really acquire its social place in the mathematical world until the moment it permits us to force an opening that will reveal a small, hitherto undisclosed, unsuspected corner of the underlying archaic reality.

CHANGEUX: Let's forget the subjective aspect for the moment and look at what our positions have in common. The definition we're considering has a certain idealistic connotation, on account of this notion of filtering, of selection—on which nonetheless, I take it, we're agreed.

CONNES: Yes.

CHANGEUX: We're agreed too that mathematical objects have a certain generative power. From my point of view, this is connected with their "idealization," or, if you prefer, their formalization: the mathematician produces a certain number of definitions that restrict the content of the mathematical object, and, as a result, his brain confers new properties on these existing objects.

CONNES: The distinction we're making is very important in actual mathematical practice. Some people may imagine that mathematics is good simply for creating new tools and for studying them—

CHANGEUX: No, that's a trivial definition. Let's leave that aspect aside—we need to operate at a higher level. It's not a question merely of creating new mathematical objects, but also of discovering new concepts.

CONNES: But in order for these concepts to acquire common currency, even conversationally within the small community of mathematicians, they must pass a test: they have to reveal something new about archaic reality, not simply about the tools used.

CHANGEUX: No, I'd say that they have to have something new to add to the existing corpus, and that they have to enable mathematicians to make advances in knowledge. One can very easily do without this notion of archaic reality; the fact that you insist upon it so obsessively suggests that it's not as self-evident as you assume.

CONNES: No, one *can't* really do without it. Advances in knowledge are measured precisely by their impact on our understanding of archaic reality.

CHANGEUX: That's your definition. Not all mathematicians are obliged to accept it.

CONNES: One sees it commonly used in mathematical practice.

CHANGEUX: Perhaps so—but throughout human history people have believed in myths that were based on no objective evidence whatsoever. Be that as it may, let's talk about definitions we can agree on. We agree that there's a sort of sifting that occurs—a process of rational selection—and also that a special class of objects is produced by a process of "idealization"—

CONNES: Oh, by the way, let me mention one thing in passing. During that period of dreaming when one's aware that one is dreaming, one's very much aware too that the power of rational selection has virtually been suppressed.

CHANGEUX: That's quite true. A disconnection occurs among the mechanisms of rational selection, which itself is tied to the faculties of waking, to states of consciousness. The sifting process certainly involves the faculties of waking and consciousness, and, I'm tempted to say, a higher degree of attention and concentration than is usual in everyday life. I think we should therefore be able to agree on the following definition: mathematical objects are altogether "real" because they consist of specific cerebral physical states.

CONNES: Agreed. Projective representations of mathematical objects are certainly physical brain states, but reducing mathematical reality to these states would be like reducing literature to the chemical reactions of ink and paper.

CHANGEUX: We'll have to come back to this question of what you subjectively call archaic mathematics a little bit later.

THE CONSTRUCTION OF MATHEMATICS BY THE CHILD

CHANGEUX: In our earlier conversations we talked a lot about the problems the mathematician faces trying to deal with physical experience. It would be interesting to see what goes on in children. The mathematician possesses mathematical capacities only to a small degree at the time of birth. Human beings aren't born with the whole of mathematics in their heads, after all. Even if we could acquire mathematical ability as easily as Pascal, it would still be necessary to pass through a certain number of steps.

CONNES: "Ability" is the right word. I remember having a professor who used to say, "Too much knowledge, not enough know-how." Acquiring knowledge is one thing, but ability is something else again—it's a question of skill, of developing mathematical talent.

CHANGEUX: It's very difficult to tell by introspection alone how we acquire mathematics. There's an almost total amnesia when it comes to our earliest experiences as infants; in fact, we even forget how we learned to speak, or how we learned to walk, as young children. The child has no consciousness of the cerebral processes involved in the acquisition either of language or of mathematics. We can't appeal to introspection, to our personal experience. We have to rely on the observations of others about infant behavior. And speaking of "know-how," or ability, it's remarkable to note that infants only several months old possess the elementary capacity—known as *subitizing*—to tell the numbers from one to five apart. Many animals have this ability as well. A rat, for example, will respond to three taps, rather than two, or to five rather than three.

CONNES: At what level? Musical? Auditory?

CHANGEUX: Auditory and visual. The newborn child shares with certain animals the ability to discriminate among quantities. In this respect at least its brain resembles a primitive computer. Dehaene and I have tried to construct a rudimentary model of such a machine. The process of reckoning involves two types of operations. First there's the recognition of discrete objects, associated with the notion of the permanence of an object, which has been well defined by Piaget. Next there's an attempt to reckon the quantity of the objects that have been separated out. This requires a particular kind of mental effort that animals are capable of as well. If you put two piles of food in front of a rat, a small one and a large one, the rat's going to go for the large one.

CONNES: Does this reckoning lead to the realization that one pile is twice the size of the other, or only that it's larger than the other?

CHANGEUX: The rat can estimate a limited number of discrete objects, as can the machine Dehaene and I have sketched. It appears therefore that its brain can carry out elementary mathematical operations, almost as though this were an innate ability, although the possibility can't be excluded that some experience at a very early age is necessary. It's tempting to say that imposing categories upon the world is one of the techniques employed by both animals and humans for the purpose of exploring it. I think that we can agree that there is a perception of physical objects the permanence of which the child recognizes, and then a working out of the rules for classifying them. Initially the child organizes these objects in categories and devises a principle of abstraction by which individual traits can be selected that will allow them to be regrouped on the basis, say, of color or form. In distinguishing 3 from 4 or 5, the child recognizes their cardinality. Then it arranges them in increasing order of size, a sign the child recognizes the principle of ordinality. Next, using language, it creates recursive rules. Detecting equivalence among certain operations, the child proceeds gradually to construct the series of integers. This construction is made by means of an experiment performed upon the outside world. First, subitizing is assumed to apply. Then classification rules are introduced, along with equivalences among rules, or among rules of rules—all of which, of course, are mental representations. This is how Piaget conceived of the child's acquisition of mathematics, by stages, through a series of sensory-motor experiments upon the world, and the working out of a system of schemas that, because they are themselves subject to an ongoing process of selection, show a tendency toward increasing abstraction. Piaget sees this development as internal in its origins, with the child spontaneously experimenting upon the world. Vygotsky, by contrast, regards the child as subject from the very beginning to a social environment that imposes itself, and developing within this imposed framework the elementary mathematics it will use later in life. At an older age, the child will carry out these operations without having to refer to the outside world—without, for example, having to count on its fingers. They're now carried out in another world: the world of consciousness.

CONNES: I agree. This is a very important step. It seems difficult, however, to justify confining the development of mathematics, even in the case of the child, to its direct use in daily life. The following story was told to me recently. A father and his five-year-old son—obviously a quite gifted child—were walking together along a beach. The boy was unusually silent, concentrating very hard on something or other for rather a long time. Finally the child turned to his father and said, "Dad—there's no largest number, you know." The father (though he's a linguist rather than a mathematician) was amazed to realize that his son had perfectly grasped all by himself the proof that the set of natural numbers is infinite! He had grasped the fact that to any one of these numbers another could be added to produce a larger number!

But there's also another crucial step that's still more important, which we've already mentioned: the manipulation of objects (such as the p-adic numbers) that have nothing to do with external reality—

CHANGEUX: But that all the same have a physical reality internal to the brain.

CONNES: By all means. But even if this process of manipulation could be artificially modeled using a computer, such objects wouldn't have anything to do with the sensible world.

CHANGEUX: On this point we're in agreement then—except perhaps when you say they've got nothing to do with the sensible world. The brain's built out of neurons, after all. I'd say that the reason mathematical objects have nothing to do with the sensible world has to do instead with their generative character, their capacity to give birth to other objects. The point that needs emphasizing here is that there exists in the brain what may be called a "conscious compartment," a sort of physical space for the simulation and creation of new objects. These new mathematical objects are capable in turn of evolving by selection, as it were, with reference either to objects of memory or to cultural objects that have already been selected by mathematicians. In certain respects these new mathematical objects are like living beings: like living beings, they're physical objects susceptible to very rapid evolution; unlike living beings, with the particular exception of viruses, they evolve in our brain.

CONNES: The brain may be built out of neurons, but reducing mathematical objects to neurons is, as I say, like reducing literature to the chemistry of ink and paper. What I find striking is that we should be capable, thanks to the projective selection that the axiomatic method makes possible, of characterizing objects that are known only inductively.

CHANGEUX: Perhaps we'll talk about this a bit later. I don't want to get into the projective/inductive distinction at this point.

CONNES: The child operates by conceptualization, which amounts to projective selection. But I'd like to point out that projective selection works itself out in several steps. The final step, which for me is the special prerogative of mathematics, is the one that enables us to uniquely characterize the object. The object thus isolated is part of what I mean by archaic mathematical reality.

CHANGEUX: It's also part of the brain. At this stage, I don't see any difference.

CONNES: There is a difference, and an essential one at that. It's not possible, given our present state of knowledge of the outside physical world, to devise a method of projective selection sufficiently precise even to give a unique definition for our planet. What gives mathematics a surer handle on reality is the fact that, unlike physics, it can isolate objects projectively.

CHANGEUX: I agree entirely. But this doesn't in the least prove the preexistence of these objects.

CONNES: Of course not. But keep in mind that abandoning the myth-of-origins angle, as you suggested we do earlier, permits me to distinguish archaic reality as a separate category of existence.

CHANGEUX: All right, then. Let's go back to this archaic reality of yours again.

ORDER IN THE WORLD

CHANGEUX: To claim physical reality for mathematical objects, on a level with the natural phenomena we study in biology, poses a worrisome epistemological problem it seems to me. How can a physical state, internal to our brain, represent another physical state external to it?

CONNES: Be careful. On the one hand, this internal physical state is only one part of the brain's total physical state. On the other hand, your paradox is a paradox only to the extent that you reduce everything to physical states.

CHANGEUX: True enough. But let me go on. One answer might be that our representations of the world capture only very restricted features of external physical reality, that they don't fully represent this reality, that in some sense they are "reduced models." Poincaré worried at length about the *apparent* simplicity of the "laws" of physics. "And Newton's law itself?" he asked in *Science and Hypothesis*. "Its simplicity, so long undetected, is perhaps only apparent. Who knows if it be not due to some complicated mechanism, to the impact of some subtle matter animated by irregular movements, and if it has not become simple merely through the play of averages and large numbers?"[2] Reduced to the pertinent elements of external physical reality, the model loses in complexity—it "codes" only for definite *patterns*—but nonetheless gains in generality. Physical reality isn't rational. Only mathematical representations of the physical world can aspire to rationality.

A second reply is that the simplest way to go about encoding the outside world is to suppose that it's isomorphic with our mental representations—that an actual physical congruence obtains between that which encodes and that which is encoded. Now we both agree that there's no point trying to establish the strict identity of a physical object with its representation. But the notion that some restricted isomorphism might exist, at the level of certain areas of the cerebral cortex, between external stimuli and the distribution of electrical activity inside neuronal groups isn't in the least absurd. Certain images obtained using the activation marker deoxyglucose show an almost photographic similarity between the topology of an image of the outside world projected upon the eye and the topology of the neurons activated in the primary visual areas of the cerebral cortex.

In the course of evolution, perceptual capacities came to be supplemented by a capacity for abstraction, making it possible to model formal relations and simulate future events. The capacity for abstraction must have grown with lightning speed among the ancestors of *Homo sapiens* in the context of social behavior and collective activities such as hunting, for example. It goes without

[2] Henri Poincaré, *La science et l'hypothèse* (Paris: Flammarion, 1904), p. 176. The passage quoted here is from a reprint of the 1905 British edition, *Science and Hypothesis* (New York: Dover, 1952), p. 148.

saying that at a later stage in the history of the human species it was able to be turned to the advantage of a new language: mathematics. The prefrontal cortex, as I've said, helps relate objects to each other in space and time. It constructs associations of associations, as it were, as rules—as plans governing the translation of perceptions into action that occurs in sensory or primary motor areas. The isomorphism tends therefore to fade away in the primary areas of the cortex responsible for the successive association of objects to the prefrontal cortex. At this level, neurons and action potentials still serve to encode objects, but the almost exclusively associational character of their connections now makes it possible—allowing for learning, of course—for this coding to acquire the dimension of abstraction, or "secondariness," required to create mathematical objects.

CONNES: I agree that this is a plausible scenario.

CHANGEUX: Good. Under these conditions, then, there would have had to be a loss of isomorphism in favor of "new" mental representations. But such representations would have had to remain *simple* for two reasons: first, because of the genetic constraints imposed upon our cognitive apparatus; and, second, because of the modest margin of variability required by learning by selection and by the brain's use of acquired cultural knowledge. The mathematical encoding of the outside physical world would be a strictly internal affair, then, but it would be carried out in accordance with the brain's own innate modalities. Piaget's description of how the child progressively constructs the mathematics that it needs to apprehend the outside world fits very well with this picture.

Von Neumann noted more than thirty years ago that the nervous system constitutes an essentially statistical mechanism for transmitting messages, which therefore operates at very low levels of precision, whereas computers are reliable to a very high degree when it comes to arithmetic. The nervous system, on the other hand, possesses a relatively high degree of reliability in other areas, as if—as von Neumann remarked—a loss in arithmetical ability had been traded for improved logical ability. The repeated selection of mental representations, at ever higher levels of abstraction, is carried out in the human brain with ever greater logical "depth." In the end, arithmetic emerges as the *product* of these faculties of abstraction and reason, and not as its functional principle (unlike in the case of the computers we construct with the aid of these faculties). It shouldn't come as a surprise, then, that the representation of mathematics by the human brain turns out to be radically different from the representation implemented by computers. The encoding is a physical process, to be sure, but it's more a function of logic than arithmetic.

CONNES: I would put the point a bit differently: the encoding of mathematics is much more projective than inductive. What distinguishes this encoding from the way a computer functions is the existence of ordered hierarchical levels that control the brain's projective organization. It's because they're ordered hierarchically that our sensory perception of the outside world is less liable to gross error. This is the essential point that needs to be made, in my view, about the organization of our perception of the outside world.

CHANGEUX: Let's turn now to a problem that's harder to resolve, having to do with the regularities of the physical world. The physicist, like the mathematician who's interested in physics, looks to select the "idealized formal representation" that can be most closely adapted to this outside reality. But to define outside reality as an "inexhaustible source of information," as you do, really won't work; it amounts to endowing this reality with the voice of a human interlocutor—or of an infinity of interlocutors, emitting a ceaseless stream of messages all of which are immediately comprehensible by the human brain.

CONNES: It does seem to me that one indisputable feature of external reality is that it constitutes a constant source of information that, while not, of course, immediately comprehensible by the brain, isn't reducible to the past. In other words, the physics of an event can't be reduced to initial conditions, the conditions at a given instant, and to all that was known prior to that instant. It's impossible. Each second that passes in a given volume is going to produce a certain number of new bits of information that are irreducible to the past. If, for example, an atom of uranium disintegrates, there's a probability that a certain number of "ticks" will occur in a given period of time, but no one knows the exact moments when they will occur. And these moments represent a new piece of information that can't be reduced to the past. To me, this is one of the basic attributes of external reality. Each second brings something new, a quantity of information irreducible to the past.

CHANGEUX: Well, I'm relieved to realize that the idea I was trying to dismiss, of the physical world as a sort of interlocutor, isn't one that you actually subscribe to! It would amount to assigning specifically human qualities to external reality, a radical form of anthropocentrism—Penrose's point of view, certainly, if not yours. Penrose goes even further, in fact, claiming that the nature of our universe is such that humanlike observers *must exist*: "[T]he nature of the universe that we find ourselves in," he writes, "is strongly constrained by the requirement that sentient beings like ourselves must actually be present to observe it."[3] He's not alone, however, in elevating this idea to the status of a principle— what's known as the "anthropic principle"—which lands us back squarely in the realm of prescientific mythology, back to a sort of *pensée sauvage* that's got more to do with the social anthropology of Lévi-Strauss than the history of physics.

CONNES: I must admit I do not share this anthropomorphism.

CHANGEUX: It was Spinoza who said: "Nature proposes no end to its operations" and that "all final causes are only pure fictions imagined by men." The world around us hasn't been labeled, after all, to make it easier for us to read! It's our brain that does the work, that projects models onto the physical world, that cuts it up, classifies the pieces, and names them.

CONNES: I agree, with this qualification: I believe that not only does this physical reality exist, but that there also exists a mathematical reality.

[3] Roger Penrose, *The Emperor's New Mind: Concerning Computers, Minds, and the Laws of Physics* (New York: Oxford University Press, 1989), pp. 405–6.

CHANGEUX: We're coming to that. Nature itself has no meaning. Meaning is created by our brain, which stores it, first in long-term memory and later in the form of a still more stable cultural artifact. My view is that this physical reality isn't an inexhaustible source of information; it's an extremely rich source of questions.

CONNES: The one doesn't exclude the other. It's possible for something to be a source of uncoded bits of information, and at the same time a source of questions. These aren't mutually exclusive ways of interpreting the world. Reality is a source of information in the sense that there are things constantly coming into existence that can't be reduced to past events—things that are really *new*.

CHANGEUX: I think we've managed to agree on the fact that our models, even if they refer to cerebral physical states, don't exhaust physical reality. Let's move on, then, to a trickier point. It's undeniable that this reality, despite its extreme complexity, exhibits intrinsic *regularities* that the physicist discovers, represents in the form of simple equations, and states in the form of *laws*. I've already mentioned Poincaré's view on this point. The existence of such regularities poses a problem for me, however. What would you say to the idea that the various regularities of the physical world might not be anything more than the product of the history of the universe, of an evolution that's still in the process of unfolding? It's a simple enough idea, and not in the least original: you find it in Descartes, Buffon, Laplace, and more recently Prigogine. On this view, the order that the biologist discovers in physical reality is homologous with that of the physicist, only at the very different levels of organization that have appeared among living beings during the time it's taken for the various species to evolve. The mechanisms involved are, of course, quite different. But why not extend a sort of Darwinian mechanism to the evolution of matter itself? Obviously one can't talk of "survival" in the same way that one can in the case of living beings, but one can talk of existence, or rather of stability in time and space. Max Delbrück begins his work *Mind from Matter* by describing the genesis of the elements of Mendeleev's table of elements in red giant stars. It's in these stars, after all, that all the atoms we know were formed from the hydrogen atom, by a process of diversification operating combinatorially upon elementary particles. Selection manifests itself by the spatiotemporal *stability* of certain combinations, with the unstable ones disappearing. Matter is therefore spontaneously organized, step by step, through a process of variation-selection, from which spatiotemporal *patterns* emerge, exhibiting the peculiarly "material" regularities that the physicist discovers—with his brain, mind you—and sets up as laws. But perhaps this is only a simple metaphor. What do you think?

CONNES: It is, as you say, a very tricky question. The problem with extending the Darwinian mechanism to the evolution of the universe itself is that its explanatory power depends entirely on the notion of time. Without a better understanding of time, there's a risk of becoming trapped in circular arguments. We've already mentioned the fact that a number of theoretical physicists are currently trying to devise a "theory of everything." The problem they're trying to solve, the problem of quantum gravity, involves the apparent incompatibility of quantum field theory and general relativity. Certain elementary principles developed as part of the theory of measurement in quantum mechanics show that because the observer is now considered part of the system itself, the answer—if there is one—can indeed be thought of as involving everything. It is also clear, however, that because of the full covariance required by general relativity, the notion of time becomes very problematic. At the moment, string theory—a beautiful mathematical theory that marks at least the beginning of a solution to the problem of quantum gravity—is the most promising attempt to resolve the difficulties involved. It has already yielded a number of interesting applications in mathematics, but the string theorists are really a new breed of theoretical physicist. An amusing article was written about them some years ago by a well-known particle physicist, pointing out that it's hard to say in what academic department they belong. In physics? Not really, because what they theorize about—levels of energy that, so far at least, are totally unrealizable—isn't susceptible to experimental test. Nor do they belong in mathematics departments, because they aren't really interested in proving results with the rigor that's necessary in mathematics. The author's conclusion was that they belong in religion departments.

CHANGEUX: Indeed! But it's not so farfetched when you stop to think about it: like theologians, these physicists are working on first things.

CONNES: The problem is that their work relies only to a very small degree on experimentally verifiable results. They're trying to guess a priori what the fundamental principle should be. One aim of the theory is to be able to show that a suitably low energy limit will allow the standard model of electroweak unification and strong forces to be reproduced, which would in turn allow predictions to be made about achievable levels of energy. But for the moment this is a dream, nothing more. From a philosophical point of view, the string theorists' approach differs sharply from the more pragmatic, far more modest attempts of traditional physicists to construct increasingly refined models that hardly pretend to exhaust all of external reality; but the new approach is quite well motivated, given the beauty of the mathematics it uses.

CHANGEUX: I understand your reasons for preferring the more traditional approach. Even so, I'm interested in learning a little bit more about string theory. It strikes me as a serious scientific attempt, at least, to answer the question of origins.

CONNES: String theory isn't a sufficiently mature theory yet to have much to say about a question of this type. Even though certain principles (such as elimination of anomalies) make it possible to constrain the number of possible solutions, no background-independent action functional yet exists for comparing the various solutions. So the theory is still rather difficult to use. However cosmologists and particle physicists, working in collaboration, certainly do have partial answers—they're both interested in knowing what can be deduced from simple models of the beginning of the universe. There are several excellent and well-known books summarizing this approach: Steven Weinberg's *The First Three Minutes*, for example, and Stephen Hawking's *A Brief History of Time*.

CHANGEUX: Isn't the fundamental question we're talking about whether order in the universe—which I don't deny exists—can emerge spontaneously from such models?

CONNES: Indeed it is, but when you talk of order emerging you're implicitly making use of the notion of time. In simple models of the universe, time figures as one of the coordinates of four-dimensional space-time. Selection occurs among various universes, through an action functional and the functional integral approach, unlike Darwinian selection. Time is probably the hardest concept in all of physics to understand. Hawking's book is a good introduction to the difficulties one encounters.

CHANGEUX: Are you suggesting that evolution follows a unique path?

CONNES: Not at all.

CHANGEUX: Therefore selection occurs.

CONNES: One can't really say that. Keep in mind that a four-dimensional universe is *completely* given: its entire evolution over time is fixed. Selection occurs among universes instead.

CHANGEUX: You could say the same thing about human evolution—that man is contained potentially in the mouse!

CONNES: No. Because when you talk of human evolution, time is implied.

CHANGEUX: Not everything that's possible actually comes to pass. Variation occurs. As a result there's a role to be played by what might be called chance. Organization nonetheless emerges through selection.

CONNES: The chance you're talking about assumes temporal evolution.

CHANGEUX: I think I see what you're driving at, but I confess I haven't thought enough about the question from this point of view to form an opinion really. What troubles me is how matter came to be organized in the first place. One can say that we don't know: *ignoramus*. But can one say *ignorabimus*: that we shall not

know? No, we can't say that we will never succeed in compre-
hending the fundamental causality of the physical world. You say
that in the beginning, in the earliest moments of the universe,
time didn't exist. To me this suggests that your definition of time
is inappropriate; but in any case it doesn't alter the fact that later
on elements formed inside red giant stars, and that their development can be traced as a function of time.

CONNES: That we understand the manner in which certain things
evolve is clear. But the problem is otherwise: when one talks of
causality, time is implied. The very notion of causality is a temporal notion.

CHANGEUX: You still haven't told me where you stand on the question of order in the universe. All that you've told me is that the
metaphor of the Darwinian model doesn't apply because this
model contains a temporal dimension and that in the beginning
time doesn't exist—which is exactly what I dispute in the case of
red giant stars.

CONNES: The universe, at least as far as we currently understand it,
is a universe at the beginning of which—that is to say, prior to the
Big Bang—time has no meaning. And so the notion of causality
disappears, and all the mystery is concealed in the initial conditions. Various suggestions have been made for solving this problem, such as the Hartle-Hawking "no-boundary" proposal. In
trying to think about the problem, one has to come to terms somehow with the question of what reality consists in, in the absence
of time. At this point, clearly, one has to make use of philosophical tools in order to try to define what is meant by the term "reality." I consider that external reality has a sort of intuitive and
archaic existence, and that one understands a piece of it only
when, by a process of projective division, this piece can be
uniquely characterized with respect to the whole. From this point
of view, mathematical reality can be more firmly grasped than
physical reality. Its existence is comparable to that of physical
reality but distinct from it, as I have tried to explain using various
examples.

CHANGEUX: There we are! At bottom, your archaic mathematical reality is constituted by the primitive stages in the organization of the physical universe that we were talking about a moment ago.

CONNES: Not quite. You conceive of my external mathematical reality as a part of the external physical world. What I'm about to tell you is going to come as a surprise, then. For me, it's just the opposite: external physical reality is a part of archaic mathematical reality.

CHANGEUX: If you insist on this we may find it harder to reach some sort of final agreement.

CONNES: Well then, let's say that these two sorts of reality are on the same level—

CHANGEUX: With the human brain evolving afterward to constitute a new internal physical reality?

CONNES: Exactly. To me, our ability to comprehend the external physical world implies that there exists an archaic mathematical reality, a reality that exists on the same footing as external physical reality.

CHANGEUX: It's what constitutes this intrinsic organization, this internal order you were describing.

CONNES: In a way. The thing that's extraordinary about mathematical conceptualization is that we're able to conceive of the universe as a four-dimensional object, and that, in order to picture it, we don't have to situate it within a larger dimensional space. We can picture it intrinsically, as it were—in its own terms.

CHANGEUX: But you don't assign any necessary role to causality in mathematics?

CONNES: There's no longer any causality, because there's no longer any time! Once you adopt this way of looking at the outside world, the notion of causality is simply one of the features of the mathematical model of the universe. There's no longer any obstacle to conceiving of this archaic mathematical reality as something that exists alongside the universe—

CHANGEUX: It's not alongside, it's *inside* the universe.

CONNES: No, and that's where we differ. From my point of view, it would be nearer the truth to say that it's the physical universe that's inside archaic mathematical reality.

CHANGEUX: If you regard archaic mathematical reality as the definition of those regularities that exist as intrinsic features of the world around us, then I think that we can nonetheless agree, even if you do introduce a slight distinction.

CONNES: It's a crucial distinction, I'm afraid. But I'd like to continue with my reply to your question, if I may, and say a few words about my philosophy of how our understanding of the mathematical world can be reconciled with our understanding of the external world in which we live. In a naive way perhaps, I see the physical world around us as a struggle between two main influences, the discrete and the continuum.

CHANGEUX: You're setting yourself outside the human brain here—you're describing the outside world independently of yourself.

CONNES: Yes, I know. Let's take, for example, the room we're in right now, or, better yet, a landscape. This contains a mixture of two kinds of things: on the one hand, we find objects that have been constructed by human beings—parallelepipeds or artifacts or whatever—according to the laws of geometry and the laws of physics involving the continuum; and, on the other hand, we find natural objects such as trees, which have branches, which have leaves, which have ribs, and so on—all of *these* objects are the result of an iterative process. By "iterative process" I mean all those biological processes that in order to pass from one generation to the next require the genetic encoding of discrete bits of information and the development of the genes that do the encoding. For me, external reality is a struggle between the loss of information due to friction with the outside world—the continuous, physical world—on the one hand, and, on the other, the biological phenomenon constituted by duplication of discrete information in the process of genetic transmission. These two tendencies, I believe, are opposed to each other.

CHANGEUX: But that just the same are themselves physical phenomena.

CONNES: Yes, which can be built into our understanding of the outside world by physics. But I am opposing the ever-increasing quantity of discrete information concentrated in life with the general principles of classical continuum physics. The important progress now being made in understanding the process of biological iteration shows that we can now encode many quite complicated and apparently nongeometric objects found in nature using a very small number of parameters.

CHANGEUX: Possibly this technique applies to the structure of the atom and the elements as well.

CONNES: Not really. The chemical elements are perfectly understood thanks to quantum mechanics. Mendeleev's table is accounted for quite nicely by the laws of physics. The formation of trees, by contrast, is very poorly understood. Now, because of recent work by Mandelbrot and others on fractals, we know that with a small number of parameters it's possible to encode forms that are quite strangely similar to real trees. And because we're now well on our way to being able to understand such iterative phenomena, we can have confidence that we shall eventually arrive at a mathematical picture of the outside world that incorporates this genetic component. It would be wrong to suppose that mathematics makes it possible to encode only geometrical, continuous physical phenomena; understanding iteration also makes it possible to encode the living forms of the natural world.

CHANGEUX: And even the functioning of our brain. . . .

CONNES: I hope so. But we've still got a very, very long way to go. In this oversimplified model of the natural world I've just described, the role of the discrete is just as important as that of the continuum. One can similarly give an oversimplified picture of the geography of mathematical reality, as I tried to do earlier. There one of the main unsolved problems involves developing the right geometric concepts for understanding a space that mathematicians call the *arithmetic site*. The geometric understanding of this set should contain many of the regularities observed in the sequence of prime numbers. It's by no means unimaginable that the new geometry required by physicists for the understanding of quantum gravity will turn out to be the same as the one required by mathematicians for the understanding of the arithmetic site. If this turns out in fact to be the case, it would go a long ways to demonstrating how intricate the relation between physical reality and what I like to call "archaic mathematical reality" really is.

Epilogue:
Ethical Questions

IN SEARCH OF THE NATURAL
BASES OF ETHICS

CHANGEUX: The development of scientific knowledge poses new ethical questions for biology and mathematics alike. Though the popular press frequently discusses the conflicts that arise between science and morality, there is seldom any attempt to inquire into the foundations of moral judgments. First we need to examine the relation between ethics and morality. Since Kant, philosophers have tended to make a distinction between the two, usually according a privileged status to the former. Morality is taken to bear upon the actions of individuals: it codifies the various prescriptions that regulate behavior at a given moment in the history of a society. Ethics, on the other hand, has a more general aim. Its object is to provide foundations for the rules of behavior laid down by morality—to construct, as it were, a *rational theory of good and evil.*

The neurobiologist is directly concerned with ethical problems, beginning with his daily work. As a practical matter, when it comes to exploring the human brain, not everything is possible. Severe limits are imposed upon experimentation. Moral dilemmas arising from new research are argued before ethics committees made up of scientific figures and representatives of the major religions and various philosophical groups. Occasionally the recommendations of this "moral magistracy" assume legislative form as codes of professional conduct, which are widely acknowledged and for the most part respected. But advances in genetic engineering and biotechnology have given rise to a novel set of questions that are more difficult to define in jurisprudential terms: What does it mean to be a living creature (e.g., is the human spermatozoid a living creature)? Can a person be said to be brain-dead (e.g., does a flat electroencephalogram indicate death)? How is human personhood to be defined (e.g., would *Homo erectus*, if he lived today, have the same human rights as *Homo sapiens*)? All these have now become subjects of vigorous debate in the humanities and the life sciences.[1]

All these questions inevitably lead us to inquire into the foundations of moral rules. Are these the product of dogmatic consensus, founded upon certain metaphysical principles common to most religions—a sort of "pact" among religious authorities? Or are they the expression of simple common sense, of a collective desire reflecting the popular will, untainted by metaphysical prejudice? Or, in contrast to each of these alternatives, is it possible that ethics may one day find itself elevated to the rank of a science as a result of the search for objectivity that animates the current debate? Trained as I've been in the school of André Lwoff, Jacques Monod, and François Jacob, I can't dismiss this latter possibility. Even if some reject the idea that ethics rests *exclusively* upon objective knowledge, it seems to me essential today that we draw upon it in constructing a new theory of ethics. It is true that the aims of science and of ethics are unambiguously at odds with each other; at the same time, we should keep in mind Spinoza's dictum that *knowledge* of the essence of things is the supreme virtue. We must therefore take the data of anthropology, history of religions, law, cognitive psychology—and therefore neuroscience—as our point of departure at every stage of analysis. Since it's now possible to proceed in a rational manner, constructing testable, revisable models, there's no excuse for failing to do so. Rational method and objective knowledge are a surer basis for discussion than metaphysical postulates or beliefs, which are perpetually in conflict either with common sense or with the most elementary physics.

---

[1] For a lucid summary of the legal and bioethical issues in this emerging debate see John A. Robertson, *Children of Choice: Freedom and the New Reproductive Technologies* (Princeton: Princeton University Press, 1994).

I would even go so far as to endorse Jacques Monod's remark that the incessant quest for truth—the driving force of science in his view—constitutes a de facto ethics—historically perhaps the most widely respected ethics of all, even if now and then the behavior of certain scientists seems to argue otherwise. A great many philosophers have remarked upon the rigors of the quest, implied by the fact that free inquiry requires ever deeper research—once again we encounter an authentic ascesis! Do we have the necessary courage, the necessary strength? The situations we face in life are often contradictory, and further complicated by the existence of so many conflicting motives. Searching for objective foundations of morality, for moral rules based on an analysis of accepted scientific facts, is an immensely difficult thing—how much easier, after all, to appeal to a priori transcendental truths than to the sometimes fleeting facts of science! The task of devising precise rules of conduct is made all the harder by the fact that it assumes a body of knowledge and reflection that with each passing day becomes more difficult to master. Will we find ourselves having to rely therefore upon applied mathematics in the form of computers, with their gigantic data bases? Sooner or later will we have to ask computers to make moral judgments?

This quite obviously is a question of interest to mathematicians as well. Whatever the answer may be, the situation is the same with respect to ethics as to mathematics: you and I, as representatives of the animal species *Homo sapiens*, possess a brain that determines the acceptance or refusal of moral rules. But it also constructs these rules in a specific social environment, at a definite moment in the cultural history of mankind. The scientist who refuses to succumb to the comfortable mental dichotomy of the religious believer, who wishes to remain true to himself, and who consistently rejects all forms of metaphysical explanation, will be obliged sooner or later to inquire into the natural and cultural bases of ethics. In one sense, of course, this amounts only to following the trail already blazed by the Lumières and the heroes of the French Revolution—with the considerable advantage that today we have at our disposal a number of powerful results in neuropsychology, cognitive science and social anthropology.

Gunther Stent, a very respected molecular biologist, organized a Dahlem Conference in 1978 on morality as a biological phenomenon. Its aim was to attack the ideological presuppositions of the then-infant discipline of sociobiology, but without abandoning research into the biological basis of morality—quite the opposite. In fact, the conference revived a fundamental disagreement that goes back (as is so often the case) to Greek antiquity, where already two opposing arguments had developed similar to those we've discussed in connection with the foundations of mathematics. The idealist position, defended by Plato, can be simply stated: moral conduct must be in harmony with principles belonging to the world of Ideas. Now this world, as we have discussed at length, is assumed to contain the mathematical laws governing both the universe and human knowledge. Wisdom, for Plato, consists in apprehending them. For Democritus, however, and Epicurus (and, later still, Lucretius)—all of whom saw human beings as an animal species rather than as shadows of the Forms of an eternal world—wisdom consists in repudiating platonist fantasy, in acquiring knowledge of the terrestrial world, in ridding oneself of all those prejudices responsible for human unhappiness. Two contrary points of view, then, not easily reconciled. I don't propose to try. My sympathies—I dare say this won't come as a surprise to you!—lie on the side of Democritus. I propose to make his case on the basis of modern science, but in the same spirit, adopting a naturalist position that makes no reference whatsoever to metaphysical assumptions. I don't pretend to have succeeded in constructing a coherent system. I'd simply like to sketch a few preliminary reflections in outline form, asking your indulgence in advance in the hope you won't hold me too strictly to account!

The first problem requiring our attention is whether or not there are such things as universal moral rules. On the platonic view, a universal ethics must exist, just as a universal mathematics exists. If you're a platonist in mathematics, then you've got to be one in ethics. Now there is considerable diversity among cultures, as anthropology shows. Important variations exist from one culture to another in modes of thought, in social organization and, on this account, in ethical judgments (figure 32). Every society constitutes a "cultural other" that remains effectively incomprehensible to the "outsider." The ethnic conflicts of recent decades—between Sunni and Shi'ite Moslems in the Iran-Iraq war, between Protestants and Catholics in Northern Ireland, between Jews and Moslems in Israel, between Hindus and Buddhists in Sri Lanka, between Hindus and Moslems in Pakistan, and so forth—all testify to a mutual cultural impenetrability that, sad to say, sustains religions scarcely deserving any longer of the name because they divide more than they unite (recall that the word "religion" derives from the Latin *religere*, meaning "to bind together"). This moral relativism—or, rather, the *relativity* of morals—follows naturally from the diversity of languages, of cultural representations, of beliefs and of laws that we observe in the world.

To the extent that moral prescriptions and norms vary from one community to another, it isn't easy to settle upon a sure criterion, the objectivity of which would make it possible to evaluate the ethical superiority of such-and-such a belief, or such-and-such a behavior. Each culture defends its own morality tooth-and-nail, as the best justified of all moralities. Each one is convinced that its morality is the most "natural"! Together they make up a virtual symphony of blindness and mutual intolerance, in which each one is persuaded of the justice of his part. The Japanese, now our principal scientific and economic partners, for millennia have practiced a morality whose historical foundations are utterly different from those of the Judeo-Christian tradition of the West. Why should their morality be inferior or superior to ours? Especially when we witness, as in the case of Rwanda in 1994, the most Christianized population in Africa engaged in the most horrifyingly inhumane genocide? Social anthropology places the naturalist in an extremely difficult position—the naturalist who wishes, as I do, to try to develop a *humanistic ethics*—because it calls attention to the diversity, rather than the universality, of

Figure 32. The Tower of Babel

This seventeenth-century painting by François de Nome of Lorraine (known also as "Monsu Desiderio") illustrates the phenomenon of cultural relativism. It recalls the celebrated episode of the Tower of Babel, which, according to biblical mythology, was erected by the sons of Noah in order to reach heaven. The diversity of languages spoken by the workers participating in its construction is said to have prevented them from reaching their goal. This diversity of cultures and languages is accompanied by a diversity of often mutually incompatible moralities that constitute an inexhaustible source of conflict. (Reprinted from "Entretien avec le docteur F. Sluys," *Connaissance des Arts* [October 1957]) moral rules. It seems very hard, taking into account all the rules that exist or have existed in different cultural communities, to extract precise "moral universals" from them.

SOCIAL LIFE AND THE FRONTAL LOBE

CHANGEUX: The chief universal that emerges with certainty, however, is the very existence of morals and of ethical reflection across so many different cultures—what might be called, again following Kant, the universality of the ethical urge (figure 33), a term that can be understood to cover the entire set of rules of interactions among the individual members of a social group. On this assumption, ethics proceeds from the very fact of society. This is the first point: the naturalist must demonstrate a connection between the existence of morals and ethics and the phenomenon of social life, keeping in mind that this phenomenon is not unique to human communities.

In fact, social bonds are far stronger among certain animal species (insects, for example) than they are in human beings. Among honey bees, for instance, as everyone knows, sterile female workers assume responsibility for the feeding of the queen, who alone is capable of reproduction. Certain species of wasps build extremely complex common structures with a degree of coordination and efficiency that far surpasses our own architectural abilities. What are called social behaviors in mammals are overlaid by *antisocial* behaviors (such as familial attachment, territoriality, or intraspecies aggression) that enter into competition with more general interests and so affect the survival of the species. The manner in which social bonds are expressed in human beings displays a number of singular features due to the fact that, of all living animal species, our cognitive faculties are the most developed. In *Homo sapiens* the social and the rational come into contact and become joined together.

Under such circumstances, ethics tends to coincide with the rationality of those obligations toward other people that impose themselves on everyone in a particular social group. It seeks to

Figure 33. Liberty and Equality United by Nature

Anonymous engraving from the late eighteenth century, allegorically illustrating the natural foundations of the two primary concepts of the Declaration of the Rights of Man. Equality, to the left, holds as her attribute the caliper gauge, while Liberty, at right, is identified by her Phrygian cap. Nature is represented in the form of a seated goddess with multiple breasts, her hair piled atop her head, girded with cornucopia and dressed in a skirt decorated with the signs of the zodiac. She bids the union of the other two allegorical female figures, who are shown shaking hands. (Musée Carnavalet; photograph by J. E. Bulloz) define a set of guiding maxims consistent with the needs of reason and cooperation among members of the community. And so, first of all, it bears upon the ways in which members of the social group communicate with each other. This is not only a question of understanding speech acts, but also of recognizing the *intentions* behind speech acts—of constructing what philosophers and anthropologists call an inferential model of communication, after the work of Grice, Sperber and Wilson, and others. This ability to make inferences about the beliefs of others leads us to consider certain cognitive faculties characteristic of the human species: first, the ability to attribute beliefs, knowledge, and emotions both to oneself and to others—to have what David Premack calls a "theory of mind." These cognitive faculties include the capacity to build up a representation of another person's mental states, a theory of the theories that he or she constructs to deal with the future. There is also the ability to create representations of the organization of social groups, and of the individual mental states contributing to such organization.

The basis for such a faculty is found in the neural architectures of the brain, which include levels of organization similar to those you've defined as the second and third levels involved in the practice of mathematics. Now the importance of the frontal lobe in the majority of these cases has long been known. Clinical research on frontal lobe lesions furnishes proof, in fact, of disturbances in social behavior, indeed of the "moral sense." Harlow, in 1869, described the extraordinary case of Phineas Gage, a young railroad worker who survived a gruesome injury caused by a metal tamping rod that passed clear through his skull, entering the head through the cheekbone, passing upward into the brain and exiting via the frontal lobe. While Gage miraculously suffered no impairment of his physical faculties, his "mental equilibrium" was destroyed: whereas prior to the accident he was by nature calm, courteous and respectful, afterward he was given to crude outbursts and violent displays of temper. Luria describes the case of a frontal patient contemplating Klodt's painting *Last Spring*, which represents a dying young girl, seated in a chair. The patient interprets the scene as a marriage because of the girl's white dress. He no longer understands the emotional elements of the painting; he can't situate them correctly in their social context. Not without reason does Luria call the frontal cortex the "organ of civilization"!

Other areas of the brain, such as the temporal cortex, play quite different roles. Here again cases of dysfunction yield fascinating insight into function. One case (documented by Geschwind and confirmed by Gazzaniga) of epilepsy of the temporal lobe involved a curious intensification of religious convictions, marked by strange and unexpected transitions from one system of belief to another, accompanied by a furious desire to write—graphomania—and a taste for bizarre sexual practices. The frontal cortex, like the temporal cortex, is in constant interaction with other areas of the cerebral cortex, as the Damasios have emphasized. It's clear that the brain contains no single "center" of ethical behavior; instead it appears that hierarchical and parallel sets of neurons contribute to the cognitive functions that jointly construct a code of right action. This neural predisposition to ethical behavior is common to the human species, and is one of the traits that distinguishes man from other animal species. It's therefore subject to the same genetic constraints that define what may be called "human nature." The origin of what is universal in ethics—of something that might form the basis for a "Declaration of the Rights of the Human Species"—is to be sought in the expression of our common genetic heritage.[2]

PROSOCIAL BEHAVIOR IN THE CHILD AND ITS CULTURAL IMPRINT

CHANGEUX: These genetic determinants express themselves, progressively and sequentially, in the course of embryonic and fetal

---

[2] For the first systematic and comprehensive mapping of this genetic heritage, see the monumental work of L. L. Cavalli-Sforza, P. Menozzi, and A. Piazza, *The History and Geography of Human Genes* (Princeton: Princeton University Press, 1994).

development as the broad lines of cerebral architecture are laid down and, in particular, the primacy of the frontal cortex is established. The child interacts with "the other" from birth. *Prosocial behaviors* develop that assure its harmonious interaction with the other persons in its environment. From the age of three months it exchanges affection with its mother and father; from the age of one, the child learns to share. It spontaneously shows objects to other people, which it offers to share in the hope of entering into communication with them. At eleven months, it shows signs of taking care of others: it feeds dolls with imaginary food and drink, for example. At two to three years, it is capable of conversation. Quite early it displays feelings of friendship and affection as well, the characteristic tokens being smiles and kisses. It shows interest in others, but sometimes fear of strangers. Finally, between the ages of four and six, it acquires a theory of mind with the capacity for attribution I mentioned—the ability to "put oneself in the place of others."

But the ability to share the emotions of others appears rather earlier on. As I say, this is a vitally important ability, one that underlies the representation of another person as someone like oneself—not only as an individual, but as a person with feelings and emotions, capable of suffering. A more primitive form of sympathy, in the sense of behavior intended to relieve the discomfort of another, manifests itself between nineteen and thirty-six months, after which the notions of obedience and of conscious responsibility appear. Well before this, between nine and twelve months, the child begins to follow the orders of its mother, and at seventeen months to teach itself. The young child becomes progressively more capable of helping and cooperative behaviors, collaborating with others in joint action directed at a common goal. Prosocial attitudes therefore undergo a gradual development that very probably supposes an important number of innate behaviors.

Just the same, the child's interaction from birth with its physical and social environment leaves traces that will mark its individuality as an adult at least as decisively as any genetic heterogeneity. Hubel and Wiesel have shown that suturing the lid over one eye of young monkeys (or, as in Blakemore's experiment, raising kittens in an environment of alternately light and dark vertical bars) sharply modifies the functional specificity of the neurons of the visual cortex—a result that probably applies to other regions of the brain, the frontal cortex in particular. In the embryo, spontaneous neural activity can play a considerable role in the epigenesis of the nervous system. The development of individual cognitive performance, and of emotional states, is very probably subject to a significant degree to epigenetic selection, as we have already seen. Beliefs and moral rules are fixed simultaneously, and perhaps in analogous ways, with the acquisition of a native language. The child's brain becomes impregnated with moral rules, as it were, along with a language specific to the familial and cultural environment in which it's raised. This environment imposes in a rather authoritarian—indeed, a totalitarian!—way a particular cultural relationship that will mark the child for decades to come, and from which it will detach itself only with difficulty, if at all, in later years. The neurocognitive basis for the establishment of beliefs remains unknown for the most part, of course. It will furnish the basis for a good deal of fascinating research in the years to come.

Thus it appears essential to be able to specify which behavioral regularities are due to faculties imposed upon us by our genetic heritage—faculties that, in forming a sort of generative ethical grammar, determine the principal stages of prosocial behavior. The next step would be to distinguish those moral rules peculiar to a definite culture that give it its special character. But this remains a very hard distinction to make, given how deeply the genetic and cultural components of our heritage are bound up with each other in the course of successive stages of development. However this may be, the liberation of a fringe of connectionist variability from genetic domination as a result of specific patterns of growth and, of course, the epigenetic stabilization of synaptic connections, is what permits a particular morality to be established in a definite social milieu at a given moment in its history.

THE FUNCTIONS OF MORALITY

CHANGEUX: The factors determining the establishment of a moral code in human communities have given rise to contradictory theories. The quite controversial arguments of sociobiologists such as E. O. Wilson are based on research carried out on insects—typically ants, wasps, or bees—whose social behavior is subject to an extremely strict genetic determinism. As a theoretical matter, the geneticist Hamilton has shown that the gene determining self-sacrificing behavior in insects can become widespread throughout a population, and serve evolutionarily to introduce "altruistic" behavior in the population if the suicide saves five brothers or sisters, or ten second cousins—whence the idea that the function of morality is not only to assure the survival of the species, but also to propagate those genes determining social behavior, particularly prosocial behavior in the infant.

The problem arises in extending this idea directly from insect to human beings. Wilson maintains, for example, that the brain's sole justification for existence is to assure the survival and multiplication of the genes that govern its development, and that marriage rules are to be understood as "strategies of genetic transmission." In support of such arguments the various bans on inter-religion marriage are often cited, or the celibacy imposed upon Catholic priests (to the benefit, by the way, of moral rules that oppose contraceptive methods or the interruption of pregnancy, which results in more children being born—and therefore in the propagation of the genes of the very people who adopt these doctrines!). The possibility isn't ruled out, of course, that mechanisms of this type might have intervened in the course of the evolution of insects, whose behaviors are rigidly determined—though as yet there's no proof of this. To suppose that such mechanisms might have operated during hominization, however, poses an additional problem for population geneticists. They have to explain how the spectacular growth in cerebral complexity observed from *Australopithecus* to *Homo sapiens* was achieved in the space of several million years, even less, by genetic mechanisms that remain largely unknown.

Personally, I've always been very skeptical of arguments that assume too simplistic a relationship between genes and social behavior. Not only do they conveniently skip over epigenesis, they ignore above all the fact that in humans one of the major functions of ethics is to reconcile social behavior with reason—a function that hasn't developed in insects! Even though the sociobiological argument may have some plausibility as far as the biological evolution of the early ancestors of *Homo sapiens* is concerned, there do exist examples of moral prescriptions and rituals whose consequences are the opposite of the ones I've just mentioned. One of the most spectacular is the cannibalistic practice found in New Guinea responsible for spreading *kuru*, an illness caused by a slow virus (or prion) that leads to very serious cerebral deterioration in adults. In most cultures, the moral rules adopted are genetically neutral with respect to brain development. This naturally tends to favor a multiplicity of beliefs and moral rules. There's no evidence whatsoever to suppose that in present-day societies a relation exists between the moral rules peculiar to a culture and some Darwinian propensity for transmitting the genes that would determine such rules. It's much more plausible to assume that morality operates epigenetically.

Even though it's genetically neutral, and arbitrary in its prescriptions, the function of morality on the social level can be thought of as regulating interactions among individuals, and, as a consequence of this, directly or indirectly affecting the survival of the species. But this regulation applies first of all to the smaller cultural community to which the individual belongs. The survival of a given cultural group is strikingly different from that of the human species. With the development of a more elaborate ethics, morality has the effect of facilitating inferential communication among members of the community by shortening the time required to translate intentions into behavior. By abbreviating an intermediate series of logical steps, morality functions as a system of rights and duties—and so supplies a sort of condensed rationality, in Granger's sense, reducing the burden placed upon thought and providing *ready-made* responses to future behavior.

IN DEFENSE OF A REVISABLE, RATIONAL, AND NATURAL MORALITY

CHANGEUX: Once one has accepted, on the one hand, the idea of a neurocognitive basis for ethics that is universal for the human race, and, on the other, the incontestable existence of moral relativism across cultures, the question arises as to which principles will serve in practice as a guide for elaborating moral rules. How, specifically, are we to tell the difference between good and evil? The American philosopher Thomas Nagel has grouped different ethical theories together in two distinct sets: *deductive* theories, founded on a priori or self-evident axioms of good and evil; and *inductive* theories, which imply the repudiation of everything a priori, whether metaphysical or ideological. According to Nagel, the archetypal deductive theory is Kant's categorical imperative, as it relates to rules of action: "Act solely in accordance with that maxim which, at the same time, you can will to be a universal law." The same is true as well of *utilitarian* arguments, such as those of Bentham, which take utility for their moral foundation— the "principle of the greatest happiness," according to which those actions that tend to increase happiness (identified with pleasure and the absence of pain) are good, and those that tend to produce the contrary are bad. Utilitarian ideologies, so far as they are universalist in character, often in practice contradict their own principles, even if at first sight they seem to be justified. Moral universalism thus comes into conflict with the diversity of cultures, utilitarianism with the happiness of the individual as against that of the community. Deductive moral theories lend themselves to dogmatism, fanaticism—and, in the worst case, to unchecked authoritarianism—because they require the individual to bow down before theoretical postulates purporting to promote the "happiness of all mankind"!

With Spinoza, for whom good is identified with that which leads us *to truly understand things* and evil with that which distances us from true understanding, interest shifts away from deductive theories toward inductive theories. Inductive theories hold that ethical principles are to be adopted and revised on the basis of their plausibility, and of their capacity to explain more particular judgments. They therefore take into account the cultural evolution of society, of scientific knowledge—that is, the joint evolution of technology and culture in response to the "universal predispositions" of the human brain. Naturally I adopt the inductive point of view. Of all the available approaches it seems to me the most acceptable because it recognizes the possibility of revising moral norms, as a function both of the appearance of new practical problems and of the growth of knowledge. In this respect it bears a certain analogy with Rawls's theory of justice. In a nutshell, Rawls argues in favor of a method known as "reflexive equilibrium," according to which judgments are developed and then submitted to test a posteriori with an eye to achieving maximum internal coherence and objectivity. Each judgment generates a tension between criticism of existing principles and justification of new ones. If a society's economic system is redistributive, for example, if it redresses the misfortunes arising from social or natural contingencies, the result is an ethics founded on the critique and continual revision of moral norms, an ethics intended to liberate new forms of behavior. Personally, I find such a philosophy seductive because it's consistent with the search for the neural bases of moral behavior, and because, by aligning itself with the cause of science, it offers protection against the ultimately totalitarian consequences of deductive ethical theories. It's an unpretentious philosophy, gradualist in that it resolves problems on a case-by-case basis—an ethics of small steps, as it were, that doesn't ground itself on entirely inapplicable a priori postulates.

From the point of view of such a philosophy, it's no longer a question of submitting science to the imperatives of beliefs, to the authoritarianism of revealed dogmas or of some ideology, but of developing a *critique of beliefs, ideologies and moral norms*, as a function of the development of objective knowledge, in order to derive satisfactory rules of conduct. Conversely, such rules, once established, may serve to place limits on permissible scientific experimentation (particularly experimentation involving human beings) and help define also the purposes to which scientific knowledge is to be put at the level of society as a whole. My own view is that the inferential model of communication—of how we recognize the intentions of others, how we evaluate the rational coherence of intentions and monitor the development of a reflexive equilibrium within social groups—makes it possible to devise a dynamic ethics—what might be called an "open morality"—founded both on a natural, neurocognitive basis and on open, rational debate, avoiding all recourse to metaphysical presuppositions.

THE "ENLARGEMENT OF SYMPATHY" AND THE FUNCTION OF AESTHETICS

CHANGEUX: The primary task of science, in its attempt to arrive at objective knowledge, is to try continually to ferret out the irrational. It devises theoretical representations of the world in accordance with the facts of observation. Even if there exist severe limits to this quest for objectivity, their consequences are less serious than the subjectivity of beliefs. Many beliefs persist, even spread, in spite of their being unverified and physically or historically implausible, with the result that their "fundamentalist" character becomes more pronounced—a paradox in a world where objective knowledge doesn't cease to advance. Despite the dogmatic and unrevisable character of belief systems, both social anthropology and the history of religion provide evidence of an evolutionary dimension as well. Religions are succeeded by other religions, and ideologies by other ideologies, often abruptly and violently. While moral prescriptions, and the law founded on these systems of belief, unquestionably represent *contracts* between human beings and the institutions that impose them, as

Epicurus suggested long ago, they are contracts of a special kind, having formidable and often exclusionary implications: belief systems constitute the essential foundations of racial prejudice, for instance. The antagonisms they create among ethnic groups are at least as pronounced as the differences in the color of their skins or the shape of their eyes, differences that are exploited for ideological ends by politicians. Why, we may ask, do they persist with such force?

Beliefs, which constitute a particular category of mental representation, can be said also to belong to the class of public cultural representations. A belief may be defined as a specific state of nerve cell activity characteristic of an individual's interaction with others of his kind, a sort of model constructed inside the brain on a biological—that is to say, a physical, *material*—basis. Such models, as we've discussed at great length, are distinct from scientific models. They don't aim at testing or verification; in fact, they usually contradict the most elementary common sense! Nonetheless they can propagate from one brain to another, and spread "infection" much as viral attacks do, suggesting comparison with epidemics. The invasive character of this battle of beliefs recalls the Darwinian "struggle for life"—without, however, having any necessary consequences at the genetic level, because, as I've already indicated, it takes place on a different level of organization and a different time scale than biological evolution. Given our present level of knowledge, the conditions under which certain beliefs rather than others come to be culturally selected, or "stabilized," can only be guessed at. Even so, let's indulge ourselves in a bit of speculation.

One possibility is that beliefs function as substitutes for scientific explanation, either because objective data can't be obtained at a given moment in the history of knowledge, or because there are obstacles to obtaining access to knowledge in a particular social milieu owing to insufficient education or information, or both. The diverse myths regarding the origin of the material world, of animal species, and of man, all testify to a refusal to bow down before the unknowable—to the characteristically human urge to understand that is the prelude to taxonomy, to a preliminary ordering of the universe: the first sign, in Lévi-Strauss's phrase, of "a timid and stammering science." These early substitutes for causal explanation sufficed at a given moment in history (and may still suffice in many parts of the world today, in the absence of more readily assimilable data), to fill in disturbing gaps in existing knowledge. Then as now, the child who's been trained to think critically and rationally, and who from a very early age is familiar with the basic facts of science, enjoys important selective advantages in the incessant struggle between beliefs, which is part of a larger struggle between subjective belief and objective knowledge.

But beliefs and ideologies can also become entrenched in human communities, at an intermediate level between the individual and the species, as a result of their usefulness to political authority in its various forms. When the first humans of the type *Homo habilis* came to be differentiated from their neighbors on the plains of Africa, the human population probably added up to about one hundred thousand members, spread out over thousands of square kilometers—a far lower density than today. The enormous increase in population that accompanied the emergence of man had the effect of dividing society into groups marked off from one another by distinct cultural characteristics. This segregation of cultures seems to have first appeared in *Homo erectus* with the domestication of fire, about four hundred thousand years ago, when culturally distinct groups began to organize themselves around institutions and other forms of authority whose identity was founded, at least in part, on systems of belief. The survival of this institutionalization of beliefs and ideologies long ago made it inevitable that the critique of beliefs would be extended to include the still more difficult critique of institutions. (Socrates, to take only one famous example, paid for this with his life.) The question is wholly political because it bears upon the relation between knowledge (that is, science—in the original and broadest sense of the word) and power; but this relation, like that of morality or law to politics, is contradictory from the first.

Homicide is condemned among individuals *within* a state, but glorified *between* states; in some states it is justified in cases of blasphemy, but not of polygamy. Moreover, the morality of the state is frequently at odds with the morality of the citizen, on the one hand, and that of the species on the other. The Universal Declaration of Human Rights constitutes one of the first bulwarks of the human species against states, beliefs and ideologies; and the defense of a revisable, noncontradictory morality is therefore an aspect of a larger political struggle.

Of course, a revised critique of beliefs and ideologies that re-establishes moral norms on a scientific basis isn't by itself enough to construct a morality founded upon neurocognitive facts. The enormity of the problem is such that to defend the rights of human beings—as persons—appears altogether insufficient, and often seems actually *contrary* to science rather than based upon it. Adam Smith, the Scottish philosopher of the Enlightenment, now known mainly for his works on economics, was one of the first modern thinkers inspired by Epicurus to look for a secular explanation of morality. In the *Theory of Moral Sentiments* Smith considers the chief element to be *sympathy*, which he holds operates in such a way as to make us aware of the effect of our actions on others, and to compare our actions with the sentiments that "provoke" them. For Smith, sympathy isn't a faculty in the sense in which we've tended to use this term, but a product of social life that has gradually developed over the course of human history.

Darwin revives this thesis in *The Descent of Man*, arguing that sympathy is an essential part of the "social instinct," something distinct from love, innate, produced by natural selection and shared by human beings with other animal species. But he holds too that man is "a moral being," which is to say capable of comparing his motives and his actions, and of approving or disapproving them. With the growth of civilization and the aggregation of smaller social units into larger ones, sympathy becomes extended not only to the members of one's own community (including "the infirm, idiots, and other useless members of society"), but also to the members of other nations and races. This argument on behalf of the "enlargement of sympathy" clears Darwin, it should be noted by the way, of various allegations of racism that have been made against him, and plainly dissociates him from the inegalitarian positions subsequently adopted by certain of his contemporaries, notably T. H. Huxley. Kropotkin, in a fascinating work published at the turn of the present century, *Mutual Aid: A Factor of Evolution*, takes up Darwin's points again, developing and enriching them by a great many observations borrowed from the animal world and from "primitive" human societies and their history. For him, cooperation plays a far more important role than conflict in the evolution of civilization: the greater the degree of cooperation among individuals, the greater the chance that the species will survive and that knowledge will flourish. The instinct to render mutual assistance he considers to be an "instinct of solidarity and human sociability" and the basis for the "higher moral sentiments." Chief among these sentiments are justice and morality, which "lead the individual to consider the rights of every other individual as *equal* to his own."

The position of Darwin and Kropotkin hasn't been weakened in the least by recent developments in cognitive science. I've already noted that sympathy manifests itself, along with a predisposition toward helping and cooperating with others, in the prosocial behavior of the child at definite moments in the course of development. It's possible, therefore, to conceive of a logic of "good and evil" according to which things that tend to enlarge sympathy and facilitate mutual aid are regarded as good, and things that tend to restrain and render these things difficult as bad. An ethics of this type, faced with limited and restricted choices (which lead to the incessant revision of norms called for by Rawls), counsels us to adopt—to rationally *select*—those judgments that locally at least favor mutual aid rather than individual or collective struggle, and that tend to reinforce the natural disposition toward sympathy. This disposition may be a positive factor in the evolution of human societies. If sufficiently enlarged, it might serve in the future as the basis for a morality for the entire human species—a morality capable of putting to an end its division into distinct cultural groups, and so bringing about the reconciliation between the social and the rational that historically has been so much desired.

Unlike theological belief, the evolutionary secularization of morality can take advantage of a *space of variability* that allows us to escape the consequences of morality's supposedly sacred origins, above all the creationist authoritarianism of dogmas and ideologies. We've already discussed how a diversity generator might operate at high levels of cerebral organization to assist the creation of mathematical objects. Clearly it's capable of operating at the level at which mental representations are produced of moral prescriptions that bear upon social or individual behavior. These Darwinian variations of social representations stand then to be propagated from one brain to another, selected at the level of the community, and finally retained in the minds of lawmakers, for example, who as a result are now disposed to legislate on the basis of enlarged sympathies and a desire to promote "mutual aid" rather than "reciprocal struggle." This reminds me of Henri Lefebvre's question: can a "right to difference" be asserted? Naturally I want to answer in the affirmative, with the qualification that the right to difference means accepting variability with its *random* component. For there can't be evolution without variability at every one of the levels of organization that I've discussed—not just at the genetic level alone, nor only at the level of neuronal connectivity in the developing brain. I'd even say that revolution can't occur without preexisting variation, whether it involves the shape of the body or the productions of the brain, which include the models it conceives of human society. To block every process of variability by some form of dictatorship would amount, I think, to blocking the anticipatory function that is peculiar to the human brain. It would also limit the brain's capacity to absorb information from its cultural environment in order to produce the models and novel ideas that contribute to its process of evolution. It's therefore legitimate, I think, to insist upon random variation as a component of any natural ethics that purports to be evolutionary. After all, what more dynamic definition of liberty could be imagined than the "right to imagination"?

Are these three elements—the rational critique of beliefs and ideologies, the enlargement of sympathy, and the right to imagination—enough to constitute the basis for an ethics free from irrationality? I don't pretend to know the answer. Beliefs are often found to be associated with emotional states that bind members of a social group to one another. The rupture of this bond creates feelings of distress. The neural and chemical bases of this fundamental emotion of social interaction have been studied using animal models. Cries of separation or distress provoked by isolation, in both the child and adult, can be calmed by morphine or aggravated by pharmacological agents that selectively block the effect of opiates. But rites and beliefs are liable to appear, as Lévi-Strauss observes, merely as expressions of an "act of faith in an unborn science," as a first attempt at taxonomy that possesses an "eminent aesthetic value." The pleasure that both human beings and animals derive from classifying the objects of the world around them is also found at a more sophisticated level in mathematical creation, as you've repeatedly emphasized, and in scientific creation in general. Scientific knowledge involves a kind of pleasure that's perfectly comparable with the pleasure that religions provide.

But one may ask whether art doesn't play exactly this role as well. Having served in the past as a vehicle for beliefs and ideologies, can't it be imagined as taking the place of religion one day as a unifying force for universal and rational communication? Can't it transcend the diversity of cultures and consolidate sympathy by providing an authentically collective pleasure that integrates this diversity, rather than introducing a source of divisiveness in the manner of religions, which by their nature are intolerant? Schiller, in his *Letters on The Aesthetic Education of Mankind*, dreams of an aesthetic utopia that would supply the foundations for true political liberty by reconciling the "laws of reason" with the "interests of the senses." I've discussed the plausible neural and cultural bases of aesthetic pleasure and art at length elsewhere;[3] here I want to conclude by taking the liberty of dreaming, with Schiller, of a "universal aesthetic State" that could free mankind from its enslavement to arms and the irrational. Alas, as Spinoza wrote at the conclusion of his *Ethics*, "All that is fine is as difficult as it is rare."

There you have, then, the ethical reflections—rather hasty and disorganized reflections, I admit—of a neurobiologist. As a mathematician, what do you make of them?

ETHICS AND MATHEMATICS

CONNES: I want to begin by responding to your main point. You say, "If one adopts the platonic point of view, there must exist a universal ethics, just as there exists a universal mathematics. If you're a platonist in mathematics, then you've got to be one in ethics." I'm afraid I can't bring myself to share this view. As I explained earlier in connection with Gödel's Theorem, my belief in the existence of a raw mathematical reality, as an inexhaustible source of information, is the result of long personal experience, not of reading Plato—whose ideas I don't necessarily agree with in any case.

I don't believe in a universal ethics, and it seems to me that mathematics confers no special competence for speaking about ethics in general terms. The idea of a mathematical ethics scarcely makes sense. For this reason I wholeheartedly approve your criticism of deductive ethical theories founded on a priori principles that are, in fact, ideological in character. Let me illustrate the relevance of your argument by an example that is well

---

[3] J.-P. Changeux and B. Grinbaum, eds., *Raison et Plaisir* (exhibition catalogue for "De Nicolo del Abbate à Nicolas Poussin: Aux sources du classicisme") (Meaux: Musée de Meaux, 1988), p. 158. For a more extended discussion, see the recent book of the same title by Changeux (Paris: Editions Odile Jacob, 1994).

known to mathematicians: public key cryptography. This depends upon certain quite sophisticated results in number theory, among other branches of mathematics, and makes it possible to manufacture unbreakable codes that can be exploited—for good ends and bad—by governments and their intelligence services, and by police authorities. The mathematician therefore can't hide away in an ivory tower, pretending that the purity—the other-worldliness—of mathematical research prevents it from ever providing a basis for this kind of public application.

A deductive ethical theory denying pure mathematics any application beyond the private sphere of civil society would lead to a hopeless impasse. The mathematician who wished to remain faithful to such an ethics would have to renounce working, or, at the very least, refrain from publishing his results. He would therefore enter into contradiction with the de facto ethics of science noted by Monod, which, as he rightly states, consists in an incessant quest for truth. The dangers posed by official abuse of public key cryptogram technology to democratic freedoms are, of course, quite real, and it would certainly be premature to dismiss out of hand the possibility that some variation on Orwell's nightmarish "Big Brother" prophesy could become a reality. But with a little perspective, it can be seen that public key cryptograms may also be of great benefit to society. Already they've become essential to the protection of the individual citizen against computerized invasions of privacy, particularly the falsification and misuse of personal medical records and other confidential information. It's by no means unimaginable that in the future people will sign their names in mathematical form in order to guard against just such transgressions. Mathematicians, no less than other scientists, must therefore exercise vigilance in assessing the possible applications of new results on a case-by-case basis, without thereby endorsing a deductive ethics that would cripple them in their work.

These then, very briefly, are the few thoughts I feel justified in allowing myself to express on ethical matters. Mathematicians can no more take refuge in an ivory tower than they can subscribe to a deductive ethics; to the contrary, they must join with other scientists in cultivating a spirit of scientific responsibility. But what matters most to me, personally, is being able to communicate to others my sense of what mathematical research is all about—the quest for truth and the inner joy that comes from surrendering oneself to it. From the first, my part in these conversations has been devoted to this purpose, and nothing else.

Glossary of Mathematical Terms

Algebra — An algebra consists of a set X together with specific laws of addition and multiplication satisfying the usual rules of elementary algebra, with the possible exception of the commutativity of products (i.e., $xy = yx$).

Algebraic extension — Given a field k, a (finite) algebraic extension of k is a larger field K containing k and having a finite dimension when viewed as a vector space over k.

Algorithm — A finite procedure leading to a determinate result by means of a finite number of operations, without regard to the initial values assumed.

Algorithmic complexity — A concept permitting the time required to carry out an algorithmic procedure to be estimated.

Anomalous magnetic moment — A correction to the electron's intrinsic magnetic moment introduced in the theory of QUANTUM ELECTRODYNAMICS (QED), the branch of QUANTUM FIELD THEORY (QFT) that accounts for the electromagnetic interactions of electrons and photons.

Asymptotic freedom — A field theory is said to be asymptotically free when the effective interaction decreases at very high energy or, equivalently, at very short distance. The asymptotic freedom of the theory of strong interactions (QCD) is established.

Axiom of choice — An axiom of set theory according to which, given a set X, it is always possible to choose a MAP f which to each nonempty subset A of X assigns an element $f(A) \in A$.

Bell inequalities — Inequalities allowing the hypothesis of HIDDEN VARIABLES in QUANTUM MECHANICS to be tested. Experiments have confirmed the predictions of quantum mechanics.

Bijection, or *one-to-one map* — A bijection from a set X onto a set Y is a MAP f that assigns to every element x of X an element y of Y, such that for every element y of Y there exists one and only one element x of X such that $f(x) = y$.

Braid — A braid of n strands is an element of the FUNDAMENTAL GROUP of the topological space formed by the n-tuples of distinct points in the Euclidean plane.

Brownian motion — A stochastic process introduced in mathematics by the American Norbert Wiener (1894–1964) as a model of the random motion of colloidal particles observed by the British botanist Robert Brown (1773–1858).

Cardinality — Two sets X and Y have the same cardinality if there exists a BIJECTION from X onto Y. A cardinal is a class of sets having the same cardinality. The AXIOM OF CHOICE implies that the set of cardinals is totally ordered (see WELL ORDERING below).

Central function — See FUNCTION.

Chromodynamics — See QUANTUM CHROMODYNAMICS.

Compact space — Compact topological spaces are characterized by a certain property of finiteness that makes them comparable to FINITE SETS. For every given degree of approximation (technically, every open COVER), a compact space appears finite (technically, a finite cover can be extracted from the original open cover). A topological space X is locally compact if for every element of X there exists an open set V of X containing this point, whose closure is compact (i.e., the smallest closed set containing the open set V is compact).

Conditional probability — A concept describing the changes in probability due to some partial information on the results of events. For example, the probability of obtaining 2 as the sum of the outcomes of a roll of two dice is 1/36; if it is known a priori that the roll of the first die is a 1, then the conditional probability of getting 2, given this information, is 1/6. Were it known in advance that the result of the first roll would have been some number other than 1, the conditional probability of getting 2 would of course be zero.

Connected space — In topology, a space is said to be nonconnected if it is the disjoint union of two topological spaces. If any two points in a topological space can be joined by a continuous arc, the space is connected.

Constructivism — A doctrine closely allied to the INTUITIONISM of Brouwer, whose interpretation of the ontological status of mathematical objects was a reaction against the FORMALISM of Hilbert and others. According to constructivist theory, the class of mathematical objects is limited to those objects that can actually be constructed.

Continuous mapping — An application between two TOPOLOGICAL SPACES such that the inverse image of any open set is open.

Continuum hypothesis — A conjecture advanced by the German mathematician Georg Cantor (1845–1918), as part of the theory of SETS, that every infinite subset of the real line R is either COUNTABLE (i.e., has the same CARDINALITY as the set of positive integers N) or has the cardinality of the continuum, which is that of R itself. A theorem of the American mathematician Paul Cohen (1934–) shows that this hypothesis is independent of the other axioms of set theory.

Countable — A set X is countable if there exists a bijection from X onto the set N of natural numbers. The set X is then said to have the same cardinality as N.

Cover — A family of subsets A_i of a set X constitutes a cover of X if every element of X is found in at least one of the subsets A_i. If the members of A_i are open subsets of the topological space X, the cover is said to be open. If the set of indices i is finite, the cover is said to be finite.

Curvature — Numerical quantity defined at every point of a surface embedded in space and depending only on the intrinsic metric properties of the surface. The geometry of the surface at a point of given curvature is comparable to that of a sphere with the same curvature if the latter is positive; and to that of a pseudosphere if the curvature is negative.

Discrete — A topological space is discrete if every subset A of X is both open and closed or, equivalently, when the notion of convergence becomes trivial.

Eigenvalue — A scalar λ, for a linear transformation T on a vector space V, for which there is a nonzero member v of V for which $T(v) = \lambda v$. See HILBERT SPACE.

Elementary particles — See PAULI EXCLUSION PRINCIPLE.

Euler-Poincaré characteristic — An invariant of a topological space, calculated very simply in the special case of a SIMPLICIAL COMPLEX as the number of vertices less the number of edges, plus the number of triangles, less the number of . . . , etc. Named for the work of the Dutch mathematician Leonhard Euler (1707–83) and the French mathematician Henri Poincaré (1858–1912).

Factor — A certain class of algebras of operators in a HILBERT SPACE. Factors have been classified by the American mathematician F. J. Murray (1911–) and von Neumann (see GAME THEORY below) into types I, II, and III. See SUBFACTOR.

Field — 1) In algebra, a field is an associative algebra in which every nonzero element x has an inverse $1/x$. A field is finite if the underlying set is finite. Every finite field is commutative (i.e., $xy = yx$ for every x and y). 2) In physics, a field is a scalar or vectorial quantity $\psi(x)$, whose value depends on the position x in space or in space-time.

Field theory — See QUANTUM FIELD THEORY.

Finite group — A concept based on the early work of the French mathematician Évariste Galois (1811–32) on algebraic equations. A GROUP Γ is said to be finite if the underlying set is finite. A sporadic finite group refers to a finite simple group that does not belong to any of the classical series; see MONSTER.

Finite set — A set X is finite if the number of its elements is finite. Then there exists an integer N and a bijection from X onto the set $\{1, \ldots, N\}$ of the natural numbers smaller than N. The number N is called the CARDINALITY of X.

Formal series — An infinite sum of terms having no property of convergence. Such series are manipulated in the same way as convergent series in the case of calculations that involve only a finite number of terms at a time.

Formalism — A theory of mathematics, associated with Hilbert, according to which mathematics can be reduced to a formal language and a train of logical deductions.

Free group — Elements of a GROUP that can generate all other ones using the composition law of the group are called "generators" of the group. A group is said to be free if there is no nontrivial word in the generators whose product in the group is equal to the identity.

Fuchsian functions — Named after the German mathematician Lazarus Fuchs (1833–1902), these are meromorphic functions defined on a half-plane that possess periodicity properties relative to certain discrete groups of isometries of the POINCARÉ HALF-PLANE.

Function — An association of precisely one object of one set (the "range") with each object from another set (the "domain"); the term MAP is used synonymously (also "operator," "transformation"). A scalar function refers to a function f over a set X that is a map of X to the set R of real numbers or C of complex numbers. If X is a group, f is said to be central if the value of f at $x \in X$ depends only on the conjugacy class of x (i.e., if the value is unchanged if x is replaced by $gxg^{-1}, g \in X$).

Functional integral — A formal definition, attributed to the American physicist Richard Feynman (1918–88), permitting a very simple interpretation of the perturbation expansion derived from QUANTUM FIELD THEORY. The possibility of substituting a true integration over an infinite number of dimensions for this formal definition led to the development of constructive field theory.

Fundamental group — A group associated by Poincaré with every sufficiently regular topological space. It governs the classification of coverings of the topological space (i.e., mappings from Y to X that are local HOMEOMORPHISMS). An element of this group is a HOMOTOPY class of continuous paths in X.

Game theory — The mathematical theory of decision making under conflict, first developed by the Hungarian-American mathematician John von Neumann (1903–56).

Gauge theory — A large class of QUANTUM FIELD THEORIES possessing an infinite-dimensional symmetry group for the LAGRANGIAN FUNCTION. The classic examples are QUANTUM ELECTRODYNAMICS, YANG-MILLS THEORY, and GENERAL RELATIVITY.

General relativity — See RELATIVITY.

General topology, or *point-set topology* — A branch of TOPOLOGY dealing with general topological spaces up to homomorphism. It is concerned with the concepts of limit, continuity, and neighborhood.

Geodesic — The shortest path from one point to another in RIEMANNIAN SPACE.

Gödel's proof — A landmark theorem stated in 1931 by the Austrian-American mathematical logician Kurt Gödel (1906–78). Relying upon a complicated mechanism of SELF-REFERENCE, Gödel was able to show that not every true statement involving a set of axioms broad enough to generate arithmetic can be derived from them. It is more generally understood to demonstrate that the consistency of a logical system cannot be proven within the system.

Group — A group Γ is a set together with a map $(g_1,g_2) \rightarrow g_1,g_2$ of $\Gamma \times \Gamma$ to Γ, called the "composition law," which satisfies the following conditions:

1) Associativity: $g_1(g_2g_3) = (g_1g_2)g_3$ for all g_1, g_2, and $g_3 \in \Gamma$; and
2) For every pair a, b of elements of Γ, there exist unique x, $y \in \Gamma$ such that $ax = b$, $ya = b$.

Heisenberg uncertainty principle — A principle attributed to the German physicist Werner Heisenberg (1901–76), specifying an absolute limit to the precision with which two observable complementary quantities can be measured, such as position and momentum, or time and energy; thus $\Delta q \Delta p \geq h$, $\Delta t \Delta E \geq h$.

Hidden variables — A hypothesis formulated as an attempt to account in classical terms for the probabilistic character of experimental results in QUANTUM MECHANICS.

Hilbert space — Infinite dimensional real or complex metric vector space named for the work of the German mathematician David Hilbert (1862–1943) on EIGENVALUES.

Homeomorphism — Given two topological spaces X and Y and a map f from X to Y, f is said to be a homeomorphism if it is a continuous bijection and if its inverse f^{-1} is also continuous. All the topological properties of a space are unchanged by a homeomorphism. A sphere, for example, is homeomorphic with an egg-shaped surface but not with a doughnut.

Homotopy — Given two topological spaces X and Y, and two continuous maps f_0 and f_1 from X to Y, f_0 and f_1 are said to be homotopic if there exists a continuous map from X to the product space $Y \times [0,1]$, which yields f_0 and f_1 when evaluated at 0 and 1, respectively.

Hyperbolic geometry — A NON-EUCLIDEAN GEOMETRY in which the curvature is constant equal to −1. A two-dimensional model is given by the POINCARÉ HALF-PLANE.

Hyperbolic group — A class of discrete groups that appear as FUNDAMENTAL GROUPS of negatively curved spaces.

Infinite sequence — An infinite countable set of quantities. The upper (or lower) limit of an infinite sequence of real numbers is the largest (or smallest) number such that there is an infinite number of terms in the sequence arbitrarily close to it.

Information theory — A branch of probability theory concerning the quantitative analysis of the optimal transmission of signals through a given communication channel, such as a telephone line.

Injection — A map f from a set X to a set Y is an injection if for any x in X the knowledge of $f(x)$ determines x.

Intuitionism — A doctrine propounded by the Dutch mathematician L.E.J. Brouwer (1882–1966), related to CONSTRUCTIVISM, objecting to the unrestricted use of Aristotelian logic in mathematics in connection with infinite sets. In particular, it objects to reliance upon existence proofs purporting to show that there exists an integer satisfying a certain property merely by showing that the opposite assumption for all integers leads to a contradiction.

Invariant — See TOPOLOGICAL INVARIANT.

Knot theory — A simple closed curve in the sphere S^3 is called a "knot." Two knots that differ by a homeomorphism of S^3 are said to be equivalent.

Lagrangian function — A local function of fields and their derivatives that serves as the starting point for FIELD THEORY, named in honor of the French mathematician Joseph Louis Lagrange (1736–1813).

Liar's paradox — The earliest known mechanism of SELF-REFERENCE. It is conventionally attributed to Epimenides of Crete, who is supposed to have said, "All Cretans are liars." In its simplest and most general form ("I am lying"), it involves the paradox that if the speaker is telling the truth, he is lying; and that if he is lying, he is telling the truth. A modern variant is the problem known as "prisoner's dilemma," an aspect of GAME THEORY.

Lie group — Deriving from the work of the mathematician M. S. Lie (1842–99) and designating a particular class of topological groups (i.e., of topological spaces endowed with a group structure). The study of such groups is related to that of Lie algebras, which furnish the basis for classifying them.

Locality — Principle according to which physical interactions are always transmitted by fields whose dynamics are governed by a LAGRANGIAN FUNCTION.

Locally compact — See COMPACT SPACE.

Map — As a term, identical to FUNCTION.

Measure — A measure μ on a COMPACT SPACE X is a continuous linear form defined on the space of continuous functions on X. A measure is positive if $\mu(f) \geq 0$ for every positive function $[f]$ on X.

Measurability — A subset A of a COMPACT topological space X equipped with a positive MEASURE μ is measurable if, for every given $\varepsilon > 0$, two compact spaces $K_1 \subset A$ and $K_2 \subset A^C$ (the complement of A) can be found such that the measure of the complement of $K_1 \cup K_2$ is smaller than ε.

"Monster" — Nickname of the SPORADIC FINITE SIMPLE GROUP having the greatest number of elements of all the sporadic simple groups.

Non-Euclidean geometry — A geometry (first discovered by Gauss, Bolyai, and Lobachevsky) in which all the Euclidean axioms are true except the fifth, which is concerned with the uniqueness of parallel straight lines. See HYPERBOLIC GEOMETRY.

Open and closed sets — In an abstract TOPOLOGICAL SPACE, the family of open sets is given by definition as verifying three specific conditions. Closed sets are those whose complement is open. On the real line R, assuming the usual topology, open sets are defined as the arbitrary union of open intervals (a, b).

Order — The order of a FINITE GROUP is the number of elements belonging to the group.

P-adic field — Name of the LOCALLY COMPACT field obtained by the completion of the field of rational numbers with reference to the p-adic metric. The p-adic metric is defined in such a way that, given two rational numbers x and y, the greater the power of the prime p by which their difference $(x - y)$ is divisible, the nearer x and y are to each other.

Partial differential equation — An equation involving one or more functions in several variables $(x_1, \ldots, x_n)$, and their partial derivatives, evaluated at the same point.

Pauli exclusion principle — A principle of QUANTUM MECHANICS named for its inventor, the German physicist Wolfgang Pauli (1900–1958), according to which a given quantum state cannot be occupied by more than one fermion. The most common application of this principle is to the case of an electron, which is a fermion.

Periodic table of the elements — The standard arrangement of simple chemical elements devised by the Russian chemist Dimitry Mendeleev (1834–1907). The elements are arranged in order of their atomic numbers in such a way that elements having similar properties occur at regular intervals and form groups of related elements.

Poincaré half-plane — Named for the French mathematician Henri Poincaré (1854–1912), and consisting of the upper half-plane $\{(x, y); x, y \in R \ y > 0\}$ with the Riemannian metric $dx^2 + dy^2 / y^2$.

Prime number — An integer p other than 0 or ± 1 divisible only by ± 1 and itself. The number of primes is known to be infinite, but no general simple formula for generating them has been discovered.

Quantum chromodynamics (QCD) — The part of QUANTUM FIELD THEORY that deals with strong interactions between QUARKS, by introducing a new gauge group, the color group, and new gauge bosons, the gluons.

Quantum electrodynamics (QED) — A theory independently developed by Feynman, Schwinger, and Tomonaga (who shared the Nobel Prize in 1965), and Dyson to explain the radiative corrections to the electromagnetic interactions of electrons and photons.

Quantum field theory (QFT) — The physical theory of weak, electromagnetic, and strong interactions.

Quantum gravity — A physical theory, not yet satisfactorily worked out, whose goal is to quantize gravitational waves; in its present form, it is not renormalizable and yields no observable physical result.

Quantum mechanics — A method for interpreting subatomic physical phenomena, based originally on the discovery by the German physicist Max Planck (1858–1947) that radiation from a black body is emitted in discrete quanta of energy.

Quarks — Six ELEMENTARY PARTICLES whose first three, the *u*, *d*, and *s*, were postulated by the American physicist Murray Gell-Mann (1929–) as the basis of all matter.

Quasi-crystals — Although the periodic structure of crystals is incompatible with fivefold SYMMETRY in a plane, for example, there exist quasi-periodic structures that are compatible with such a symmetry.

Random sequence — A sequence of zeros and ones, for example, that cannot be defined using a shorter sequence. The periodic sequence 010101 . . . is an example of a sequence that is not random; the sequence of winning lottery numbers, on the other hand, probably is.

Relativity — A physical theory of gravity due to Einstein (1879–1955), according to which the presence of mass is intimately related to the curvature of the geometry of space-time.

Renormalization — A procedure used in QUANTUM FIELD THEORY to eliminate divergences arising in the calculation of the perturbation expansion. See FEYNMAN INTEGRAL.

Riemannian space — Named after the German mathematician Georg Riemann (1826–66), Riemannian space designates a metric space in which the length of the arcs is locally calculated as the square root of a differential quadratic expansion.

Ritz-Rydberg principle — A combination principle in spectroscopy establishing that the sum of certain pairs of frequencies of an atom is also a frequency of the atom.

Russell's paradox — An inconsistency in SET THEORY detected by the English mathematician and philosopher Bertrand Russell (1871–1969).

S-matrix (or scattering matrix) — A concept introduced in field theory by Heisenberg, taking the form of a table giving the probability amplitude of going from given initial conditions to a specific final result during an experimental procedure.

Schrödinger's equation — An equation in QUANTUM MECHANICS formulated by the Austrian physicist Erwin Schrödinger (1887–1961) that governs the evolution over time of the wave function of a quantum system.

Self-reference — A concept referring to methods of proof used to formalize paradox, technically defined as a proposition yielding mutually contradictory implications. An ancient instance is the LIAR'S PARADOX. More recent examples include two of the most famous results of modern mathematical logic, RUSSELL'S PARADOX and GÖDEL'S PROOF.

Simple group — A homomorphism θ of a group Γ_1 to another group Γ_2 is a map from Γ_1 to Γ_2 that respects the composition law (i.e., $\theta(gg') = \theta(g)\theta(g')$ for g and g' in Γ_1). A group Γ is simple if every homomorphism θ of Γ to an arbitrary group Γ_2 either is constant (i.e., $\theta(g) = e$ for all $g \in \Gamma$) or is an injection (i.e., $\theta(g) = e$ only for $g = e$).

Simplicial complex — A combinatorial object with which a topological space is naturally associated (cf. SIMPLICIAL TOPOLOGY).

Simplicial topology — A branch of TOPOLOGY concerned with the study of polyhedrons. A (finite) simplicial complex consists in the specification of a (finite) set X and a family Σ of finite subsets of X such that 1) if $s \in \Sigma$ and $s' \subset s$, then $s' \in \Sigma$, provided s' is not equal to the empty set; and 2) every subset of X containing only a single element belongs to Σ. To every SIMPLICIAL COMPLEX there corresponds a topological space, called its "geometrical realization" or "associated polyhedron."

Singularity — A point in a space X is singular if it can be recognized as such by the intrinsic nature of the space in its neighborhood.

Sporadic group — A SIMPLE GROUP that does not naturally fall into any classical series of simple groups.

Stationary principle — Principle of QUANTUM MECHANICS and geometrical optics according to which the important contribution to an oscillatory integral can be evaluated solely on the basis of the critical points of its phase function.

Statistical mechanics — The theory of the evolution of macroscopic quantities obtained by the probabilistic theory of the evolution of microscopic quantities in a mechanical system.

String theory — a recent QUANTUM FIELD THEORY of extended objects suggesting that particles are string-like objects (i.e., extended and one-dimensional). It is hoped that on the basis of this theory a satisfactory account can be given of QUANTUM GRAVITY.

Subfactor — Involutive subalgebra of a FACTOR, which is itself a factor.

Symmetry — In physics, a transformation that leaves the form of the LAGRANGIAN FUNCTION unaltered. The German mathematician Emmy Noether (1882–1935) has shown that every symmetry has a corresponding conserved quantity that is a constant of motion (for instance, the fact that the laws of physics stay the same over time—that symmetry is preserved over time—is associated with the conservation of energy).

Topological invariant — A well-defined quantity associated with a topological space not altered by a HOMEOMORPHISM. The EULER-POINCARÉ CHARACTERISTIC of a SIMPLICIAL COMPLEX is an example of a topological invariant of the underlying topological space (an example, in fact, of a homotopy invariant).

Topological space — A pair consisting of a set X and a family of subsets of X, called "open subsets" (or more often simply OPEN SETS) of X. These subsets satisfy the following conditions: 1) the empty set $\varnothing$ and X are open; 2) an arbitrary union of open sets is open; and 3) a finite intersection of open sets is also open.

Topology — That branch of geometry which deals with the topological properties of figures (i.e., those properties of a given figure A that hold for every figure into which A may be altered by elastic deformations, such as stretching or twisting, or other transformations of shape; alternatively, properties that do not rely explicitly on a notion of distance between points in the set). These include connectedness and compactness, and the condition of subsets being open or closed.

Trace — If A is an algebra over a field k, a trace on A is a linear map τ from A into k, verifying that $\tau(ab) = \tau(ba)$ for every pair (a, b) of elements of A.

Turing machine — A universal computing machine, first imagined by the English mathematician Alan Turing (1912–54).

Ultraproduct — A form of Cartesian multiplication establishing results about compactness in logic and mathematics.

Wave function — A FIELD $\psi(x)$ defined in space that describes a particle in QUANTUM MECHANICS. Its evolution over time is given by SCHRÖDINGER'S EQUATION, and its norm $|\psi(x)|^2$ can be interpreted as a probability density for the particle to be found at the point x.

Well ordering — A total ordering on a set X is the result of a choice among two distinct elements x, y for every pair of elements (x, y) of X. Where x is the element chosen, this is denoted $x > y$. It is supposed that if $x < y$ and $y < z$, then $x < z$. A totally ordered set is said to be well ordered if, for every subset Y of X, there exists an element y_0 of Y such that $y_0 < y$ for every element y of Y different from y_0.

Yang-Mills theory — The natural gauge theory that generalizes QUANTUM ELECTRODYNAMICS for non-Abelian gauge groups.

Glossary of Neurobiological Terms

Acetylcholine — One of the first neurotransmitters discovered; its effect at the neuromuscular junction is blocked by curare.

Adenosine triphosphate (ATP) — Small molecule produced by cell metabolism and used in storing and transferring energy.

Agnosia — A defect in the recognition of sensory stimuli that is not due to a change in the body's basic sensory mechanisms or to a lowered state of attention.

Allosteric protein — Regulatory protein (enzyme, gene repressor, or pharmacological receptor) carrying at least two distinct categories of binding sites, which interact, indirectly, via discrete conformational transitions of the protein molecule.

Amino acids — Organic compounds containing amino and carboxyl groups that form the essential structure of proteins and are also active as neurotransmitters. Some examples are glutamic acid, aspartic acid, and gamma-aminobutyric acid (GABA).

Aphasia — A defect in the production and/or comprehension of written and/ or spoken language due to a brain lesion.

Aplysia — The sea slug, a mollusk of the gastropod class whose very simple nervous system has been the subject of important studies at the cellular level.

Axon — A single fiber growing out of a neuron, along which impulses travel from the cell body to the axon terminal. It is the output channel of the nerve cell and terminates in branches, at the end of which synapses form.

Basal ganglia — A large group of neurons in the floor of the forebrain.

Brainstem — An important part of the brain from the medulla to the midbrain.

Catecholamines — A family of chemical substances with a catechol nucleus to which an amine group is attached. Several of them act as neurotransmitters—for example, noradrenaline and dopamine.

Category — The smallest possible grouping of cells of the same morphology and biochemical type.

Cellular crystal — An ensemble of nerve cells of the same category organized in a regular pattern, such as the Purkinje cells of the cerebellum.

Cerebellum — An outgrowth of the hindbrain that is specialized for motor coordination; it contains only a small number of neuron categories, including Purkinje and granule cells.

Cerebral cortex — The layer of gray matter forming the outer shell of the cerebral hemispheres; it is highly developed in mammals, particularly the *neocortex*.

Chromosome — A rodlike body in the cell nucleus containing DNA and visible by microscopy during cell division.

Clone — An individual (or cell) derived from a single individual (or cell) by asexual reproduction.

Corpus callosum — The large fiber bundle connecting the cerebral hemispheres.

Cortical areas — Distinct zones of the cortex characterized by their cellular architecture and function. Classically, one distinguishes the primary *sensory* areas, responsible for receiving input from the sensory organs; the *motor* areas, dealing with motor commands; and the remaining *association* areas.

Cyclic AMP — A small cyclic molecule derived from ATP and used as an internal signaling mechanism in the cell.

Dendrites — Multiple, branched outgrowths of a neuron that receive numerous synaptic contacts from axon terminals, thus collecting signals and transmitting them to the cell body.

Deoxyribonucleic acid (DNA) — The molecular basis of heredity, made up of linear chains of nucleotides, themselves formed of an organic base, a sugar (deoxyribose), and phosphate. Usually two complementary DNA chains form a double helix.

Dopamine — A catecholamine neurotransmitter that is implicated in one theory of schizophrenia.

Enkephalin — A peptide neurotransmitter that acts like morphine. There are two types: leu-enkephalin and met-enkephalin.

Gamma-aminobutyric acid (GABA) — An amino acid that acts as an inhibitory neurotransmitter.

Gene — A segment of the chromosome composed of DNA and with a defined function. Structural genes code for proteins, while regulatory genes govern the activity of structural genes.

Genome — All the genetic material (DNA) of a cell.

Genotype — The genetic constitution of an individual.

Graph — A mathematical expression providing a rigorous description of the geometry of a network.

Hippocampus — A cortical structure in the medial part of the mammalian temporal lobe; it results from the infolding of an "old" cortical area found in reptiles and primitive mammals. It does not have the typical six layers of the neocortex.

Homoeotic — Describes genes whose mutation (in invertebrates) causes the replacement of one organ by another. For example, in the *opthalmoptera* mutation a wing appears in the place of an eye.

Hypothalamus — A cluster of neurons in the forebrain beneath the thalamus. Despite its small size, it plays an important role in "vital" functions, including feeding, drinking, sexual behavior, sleep, temperature regulation, emotion, and hormone balance.

Ion — An atom or molecule carrying an electrical charge, such as sodium (Na+) or chloride (Cl-) ions.

Ion channel — The pore through which ions cross the cell membrane. There are several categories, defined by their ion specificity and their electrical sensitivity. The propagation of a nerve impulse involves sodium-selective channels.

Isogenic — Describes individuals with the same genotype, like identical twins.

Lateral geniculate nucleus — Thalamic nucleus relaying the visual pathways.

Limbic system — A group of primitive structures important for the control of emotional behavior, including the hippocampus, parts of the thalamus and hypothalamus, and related nuclei of the septum and amygdala.

Locus coeruleus — Nucleus in the central part of the brainstem whose neurons contain noradrenaline.

Mauthner cell — A giant neuron; only two are situated in the medulla of fish. It is involved in the flight reflex.

Membrane — A continuous lipid and protein film delimiting and enveloping all cells, including nerve cells. Among its constituent molecules, there are molecule channels, enzyme pumps, and neurotransmitter receptors.

Membrane potential — The difference in electrical potential across the cell membrane due to a difference in concentration of ions inside and outside a cell.

Mutation — A spontaneous or induced modification, transmissible by heredity, of the genetic material (DNA).

Myelin — The lipid substance forming a sheath around certain nerve fibers.

Neocortex — See CEREBRAL CORTEX.

Neuron — The nerve cell, formed of a cell body (or soma) containing the nucleus, and outgrowths of two types: dendrites, converging toward the cell body, and a single axon leaving it.

Neurotransmitter — A chemical substance involved in the transmission of the nerve signal at a chemical synapse. There are probably dozens of such transmitters in the brain.

Noradrenaline (norepinephrine) — A catecholamine neurotransmitter with multiple functions in the central and peripheral nervous systems.

Peptide — A linear chain of amino acids, like a protein, but shorter (up to twenty amino acids). Some examples are enkephalin, substance P, and LHRH.

Phenotype — The cluster of apparent, observable characteristics of an individual resulting from the interaction between the genotype and the environment in which the individual develops.

Planum temporale — A cortical area near the auditory cortex.

Pleiotropic — Describes the capacity of a gene to influence several distinct characteristics in the phenotype; for example, the albino gene affects both skin pigment and the anatomical organization of the visual pathways to the brain.

Postsynaptic — On the "downstream" surface of a synapse, the part usually formed by a dendrite, a muscle, or a gland.

Presynaptic — On the "upstream" side of a synapse, normally formed by an axon terminal.

Protein — The fundamental cell component; it is a "macromolecule" formed of linear chains of a large number of amino acids (sometimes more than a thousand.) The amino acid sequence is characteristic of each type of protein. Enzymes, receptors, molecule channels, and antibodies are all proteins.

Pump — An enzyme that uses ATP to actively transport ions and create a concentration gradient across the cell membrane.

Purkinje cell — A neuron characterized by its bushlike dendritic tree; it is the principle cell category in the cerebellar cortex.

Pyramidal cell — The main cell category in the cerebral cortex, out of which it sends its axon.

Receptor — A term for two different receivers: the sensory *cells* of the sense organs (e.g., the rods and cones of the retina); and the *molecules* that recognize specific substances such as neurotransmitters or hormones (e.g., the acetylcholine receptor).

Repressor — An allosteric protein regulating the expression of structural genes as proteins.

Reticular formation — Groups of cell bodies in a bed of nerve fibers in the ventral part of the brain, from the medulla to the thalamus. In fact the groups are discrete; the best known contain catecholamines like noradrenaline or dopamine.

Ribonucleic acid (RNA) — A linear macromolecule related to DNA and important in transcribing and translating DNA to produce proteins.

Septum — A group of neurons related to the limbic system.

Serotonin — A neurotransmitter derived from an aromatic amino acid, tryptophan.

Singularity — The distinguishing characteristic of each cell in a given category based on the precise set of connections that it gives and receives.

Soma — The cell body of a neuron, containing the nucleus and cytoplasm, together with mitochondria and other organelles.

Stellate cell — A cortical neuron whose axon remains within the cortex.

Substance P — A peptide neurotransmitter involved in the handling of pain messages in the spinal cord.

Superior colliculus — A paired nucleus in the roof of the midbrain responsible for certain visual reflexes.

Synapse — The junction between neurons or between neurons and other cells, such as muscles and glands. At a synapse the membrane of the axon terminal and that of the postsynaptic surface are juxtaposed, but not fused. There exist electrical synapses, where electrical signals are transmitted directly, and chemical synapses, which use a transmitter to cross the intercellular cleft.

Thalamus — A group of nuclei in the forebrain, beneath the cortex. Most pathways entering or leaving the cortex relay in the thalamus, and it receives fibers from the cortex in turn.

Index

ability, 192
acalculia, spatial, 105
acetylcholine, 95, 247
acetylcholine receptors, 95–97
adenosine triphosphate (ATP), 247
aesthetics, function of, 226–33
agraphia, 105
alexia, numerical, 105
algebra, 237
algebraic extension, 237
algorithm, 237
algorithmic complexity, 237
allosteric protein, 3, 247
Alzheimer's disease, 106
amino acids, 58–59, 247
analog calculator, 164
analogy, reasoning by, 142–43
anarithmetic, 105
anomalous magnetic moment, 237
aphasia, 247
Aplysia, 247
Arbib, M. A., 190
archaic mathematical reality, 182, 183
Archimedean law, 8
Archimedes' brain, 104
Aristotle, 38
arithmetic site, 208
armillary spheres, 45
Artificial Intelligence (AI), 153
ascesis, intellectual, 25
asymptotic freedom, 237
asymptotic problem, 35–36
ATP (adenosine triphosphate), 247
Avogadro's number, 92
axiom of choice, 237; countable and uncountable, 42–43
axiomatic method, 18–19, 30, 156–61
axons, 92, 247

Babel, Tower of, 215
Bach, Johann Sebastian, 29
Bacon, Francis, 7

Barlow, H. B., 131
basal ganglia, 247
Beethoven's Seventh Symphony, 29
beliefs, 117, 227; in mathematics, 38–40
Bell inequalities, 69, 237
Bentham, Jeremy, 224
Big Bang, 205
bijection, 43, 237
Binet, Alfred, 75
biology, mathematical models in, 57–64
bionics, 97
Birman, J., 47, 50
Blakemore, C., 221
body-mind dualism, 55–56
Bohr's atom, 28
Boulez, Pierre, 29
braid, 237
braid group, 47
brain: as computer, 168–71; levels of organization of, 82–97; mathematics and, 3–24; organization of, xi–xii
brainstem, 247
Broca, Paul, 119
Brownian motion, 68, 237
Buchner, Eduard, 83
Buffon, George Louis Leclerc, Compte de, 201

Cabanis, P.J.G., 155
calculation, faculty of, 122
Calder, A., 41–42
Cantor, Georg, 11
cardinality, 194, 238
catecholamines, 247
category, 247
causal power, 184
cellular crystal, 247
cerebellum, 247
cerebral cortex, 106, 247–48
cerebral function, 26
chemistry, ink and paper, 195
Chevalley, Claude, 20–21

chromosome, 248
Church-Turing thesis, 164
circuits, elementary, 99
clone, 248
closed sets, 243
cognitive abilities, evolution of, 14, 15
cognitive science, 4
Cohen, P., 158–59
compact space, 238
computer, brain as, 168–71
computers, 86–88; and chess, 125–27, 173–75
conceptual Darwinism, 124
conditional probability, 238
conditioning, 143–44
connected space, 238
consciousness, 80, 123–24
constructive interference, 144
constructivism, 238; formalism and, 42–44; realism versus, 11–17
constructivist mathematics, 41–46
continuous mapping, 238
continuum hypothesis, 158–59, 238
corpus callosum, 248
cortical areas, 248
Courrèges, P., 111
cover, 239
cryptography, public key, 233–34
cultural imprint, prosocial behavior and, 219–21
cultural representations, 31; mathematical objects as, 32–35
curvature, 239
cyclic AMP, 248

D'Alembert, Jean le Rond, 7
Damasio, A. R., and H. Damasio, 219
Danchin, A., 111
Darwin, Charles, 229–30; mathematicians and, 122–52
Darwin tree, 37
Darwinian schema, utility of, 122–27
Darwinian-style analysis, 80–82
Darwinism, 147; conceptual, 124; generalized, 107; mathematical, 143; of mathematical objects, 35–38; neural, 112–13. See also mental Darwinism

Death, and the brain, 211
Declaration of Human Rights, Universal, 229
Declaration of the Rights of Man, 217
deductive theories, 224
Dehaene, S., 80, 104, 115–16, 146, 193
Delbrück, Max, 201
Democritus, 26, 27, 213
dendrites, 248
Denis, M., 75
deoxyribonucleic acid (DNA), 248
Desanti, J. T., 25–26, 75; subframeworks (submodels) of, 25, 79
Descartes, René, 6, 7, 11, 20, 201; and mind-body dualism, 55–56
destructive interference, 144
dialogue form, xii
Diderot, Denis, 6–7
Dieudonné, Jean, 74
diffraction phenomenon, 66, 67
digital calculator, 164
discrete, 239
disorder, organization versus, 125
diversity generator, 80
DNA (deoxyribonucleic acid), 248
dopamine, 248
dreaming, 191
Drosophila, 109
Dyson, F. 8

Edelman, G. M., 88, 107
EEG (electroencephalographic recording), 14
eigenvalue, 239
Einstein, Albert, 51–52, 56
electroencephalographic (EEG) recording, 14
emotions, expression of, in monkey, 172
encoding, neuronal, 99, 134; and isomorphism, 197–99
enkephalin, 248
Epicurus, 229
epigenesis, 109
Epimenides, the Cretan, 156; see liar's paradox
epistemology, strong materialist, 26, 82
ethical questions, 210–35

ethics, xii, 210; humanistic, 214; mathe-
    matics and, 233–35; natural bases of,
    210–16
Euclid, 13
Euclidean geometry, 14, 18–19, 23
Euclid's prime number theorem, 22, 34
Euler-Poincaré characteristic, 134, 136,
    239
evaluation function, 81, 118, 144, 175–
    78
Everett, H., 71
evolution, term, 38

facial recognition, 131–34
factor, 239
Feynman, Richard P., 8
Feynman's integral, 9, 144
field, 239
finalism, 36
finger pointing in monkey, 98–101
finite fields, 13
finite group, 19–20, 239
finite set, 239
first-order representations, 117
Fodor, J. A., 82
formal content, 20, 185
formal series, 239–40
formalism, 240; constructivism and, 42–
    44
Foucault, Michel, 74
fractals, 208
free group, 240
Freudenthal, H., 11
frontal lobe, social life and, 216–19
Fuchsian functions, 19, 240
function, contrasted with structure, 240
functional integral, 240
functionalism, 166–67; S-matrix and,
    165–68
fundamental group, 135, 240

GABA (gamma-aminobutyric acid), 248
Gage, Phineas, 218
Galilei, Galileo, 26
Galois, Évariste, 20
game theory, 240
gamma-aminobutyric acid (GABA), 248

ganglions, 98
gauge theory, 53, 240
Gauss, Karl Friedrich, 19
Gazzaniga, M. S., 219
Gelfand, I., 5
gene, 248
general topology, 240
generalized Darwinism, 107
genetic influence, 109–10
genetic memory, 170
genome, 248
genotype, 248
geodesic, 139, 141, 241
Georgopoulos, A. P., 98
Geschwind, N., 219
Gestalt theory, 128
glossary: of mathematical terms, 237–
    46; of neurobiological terms, 247–51
Gödel's incompleteness theorem, 154–
    62, 187, 233
Gödel's proof, 241
Gordian numbers of knots, 48–49
grandmother cell theory, 131
Granger, G.-G., 20, 89–90, 123, 169,
    185, 224
graph, 248
group, 241

Hadamard, Jacques, 74–76, 148; theory
    of mathematical creativity, 75–81,
    143–52
Hamilton, D. W., 222
Harlow, J. M., 218
harmony, 177–78
Hartle-Hawking hypothesis ("no-
    boundary" proposal), 205
Hawking, S., 204
Hécaen, H., 105
Heidmann, T., 97
Heisenberg, Werner, 61
Heisenberg uncertainty principle, 70, 72,
    241
hidden variables, 241
hidden variables model, 68–69
Hilbert, David, 159–60
Hilbert space, 241
hippocampus, 248

Hodgkin-Huxley model of nerve impulse, 57, 58, 63, 71, 153
homicide, 229
homoeotic, 248
homeomorphism, 241
homotopy, 241
homotopy type, 135
Hubel, D. H., 110, 221
humanistic ethics, 214
Hume, David, 12
Huxley, T. H., 230
hyperbolic geometry, 139–42, 241
hyperbolic group, 241
hyperbolic simplicial complexes, 138–39
hypothalamus, 249

idealism, and Plato, 11, 23–4, 190, 213
illumination, 75, 76, 80, 118, 143, 147, 148–51
incompleteness theorem, Gödel's, 154–62
independent, defined, 28
indeterminacy, 65–58, 70–73
inductive system, 181
inductive theories, 224
infinite sequence, 241–42
information theory, 242
injection, 242
intellectual ascesis, 25
intelligence, creating, out of matter, xi
intentionality, 144, 169
interference, constructive and destructive, 144
intuition, 31
intuitionism, 242
ion, 249
ion channel, 249
isogenic, 249

Jacob, François, 55, 94, 154–55, 211
Jacob's ladder, 48
Johnson-Laird, P. N., 82, 164
Jones, V., 47–49
Judeo-Christian tradition, 214

Kant, Immanuel, 41, 84, 122, 210, 216; three-level theory of knowledge of, 84–89, 99; categorical imperative of, 224
Kepler's Laws, 151
Kitcher, P., 185
Kline, Morris, 121
knot theory, 47–51, 242
knots, Gordian numbers of, 48–49
knowledge, 211; advances in, 191
knowledge acquisition apparatus, 25
knowledge level, 85
Kosslyn, S. M., 75
Kropotkin, Piotr Alekseyevich, Prince, 230
kuru, 223

Lacan, Jacques, 127
Lagrangian function, 63, 242
language, mathematics as, 7, 9–11
Laplace, Pierre Simon, 210
lateral geniculate nucleus, 249
learning, 95
Lefebvre, Henri, 231
Leibniz, Gottfried Wilhelm, 6, 7
Leucippus, 27
Lévi-Strauss, Claude, 55, 200, 232
Levinthal, F., and C. Levinthal, 110
Lhermitte, F., 106
liar's paradox, 242
liberty, concept of, 29–30
Lie group, 20, 242
limbic system, 249; pleasure and, 118–20, 145
locality, 242
Locke, John, 12
locus coeruleus, 249
logical apparatus, 17
long-term memory, 127; organization of, 138–42
Loyola, Ignatius, 74
Lucretius, 213
Lumière, Louis Jean, and Auguste Lumière, 212
Luria, A. R., 105, 106, 218–19
Lwoff, André, 211

magnetic resonance imaging (MRI), 14, 104, 116
map, 242
Mandelbrot, B. B., 208
Markov, Andrei Andreevich, 50
material reality, mathematical reality versus, 22
materialism, 44; platonism and, 25–40
mathematical creation, mental Darwinism and, 116–21
mathematical creativity, enlargement of, 149
mathematical Darwinism, 143
mathematical knowledge, 33–34
mathematical logic, 43
mathematical models in biology, 57–64
mathematical objects: as cultural representations, 32–35; Darwinism of, 35–38; existence of, 18; natural selection of, 146–52; nature of, 3–6, 180–92
mathematical reality, 43, 125; archaic, 182, 183; material, physical reality versus, 22, 206–09
mathematical terms, glossary of, 237–46
mathematicians: Darwin and, 122–52; neuronal, 74–121
mathematics: beliefs in, 38–40; brain and, 3–24; construction of, by child, 192–96; constructivist, 41–46; defining, xi; ethics and, 233–35; as language, 7, 9–11; neuropsychology of, 105–7; psychoanalysis of, 30–32; relation between physics and, 51–56; "unreasonable effectiveness" of, xi, 47–51; and pleasure, 81, 173–79, 235
Mathieu, Émile Léonard, 20
matter, creating intelligence out of, xi
Mauthner cell, 249
Mayr, Ernst, 38, 39–40
measurability, 42–43, 242–43
measure, 242
membrane, 249
membrane potential, 249
memory, 77–78; genetic, 170. See also long-term memory

memory objects, 128. See mathematical objects, thought objects
Mendel, Gregor, 60
Mendeleev's periodic table of elements, 9, 61, 62
mental Darwinism, 113; mathematical creation and, 116–21
mental objects, neuronal circuits and, 97–104
mental representations, 128
mental rotation experiments, 5
Michelangelo, 151
Mill, John Stuart, 17
Milner-Pétridès ("Wisconsin cardsorting") test, 102, 104
mind, 82
mind-body dualism, 55–56
models, 46
Mokobodski, G., 158
monkey, finger (hand) pointing in, 98–101
Monod, Jacques, 3, 211–12, 234
"Monster," 20, 148, 182, 243. See Finite group
moral rules, universal, 213–14
morality, xii, 210; functions of, 222–24; revisable, rational, and natural, 224–26; in Japan as different from Judeo-Christian tradition, 214
MRI (magnetic resonance imaging), 14, 104, 116
mutation, 249
myelin, 249

Nadal, J.-P., 115
Nagel, T., 224
natural bases of ethics, 210–16
natural selection of mathematical objects, 146–52
nature made to order, 41–73
nerve impulse, Hodgkin-Huxley model of, 57, 58
nervous system, levels of organization in, 85
neural architectures of reason, 104
neural Darwinism, 112–13

neural phenotype, 112
neurobiological terms, glossary of, 247–51
neurocognitive approach, 153
neuromimetics, 154
neuronal circuits, mental objects and, 97–104
neuronal mathematician, 74–121
neurons, 90, 92, 249; response-specificity of, 132–33; types of, 91
neuropsychology of mathematics, 105–7
neurotransmitters, 63, 95, 249
Newell, A., 84, 85
Nietzsche, Friedrich, 27
non-Euclidean geometries, 18–19, 243
nonmeasurable functions, 42
nonreproducibility, term, 69
noradrenaline, 249
notional objects. *See* mathematical objects

objects. *See* mathematical objects; mental objects; thought objects
open sets, 243
order, 243; in the world, 196–209
organization: disorder versus, 125; level of, notion of, 83
Orwell, George, "Big Brother" prophecy of, 234

P-adic fields, 16, 243
Papez, J., 119
parallel universes, 71–72
partial differential equation, 243
Pasteur, Louis, 83
Pauli exclusion principle, 9, 61, 243
Penrose, Roger, 200
peptide, 249
perception, collective, hallucinatory, 32; inner, 123
perception, projective, 186
perceptual maps, 5
periodic table of the elements, 61, 62, 243
PET (Positron Emission Tomography) scan, 14, 104

phenotype, 250
physical phenomenon, 68
physics, relation between mathematics and, 51–56
Piaget, Jean, 193, 194
Planck, Max, 64
planum temporale, 250
Plato, xi, 11, 23–24, 33, 213, 233; allegory of the cave, 12
platonism: materialism and, 25–40; realism and, 31; strong, 179
pleasure, limbic system and, 118–20
pleiotropic, 250
Poincaré, Henri, 19, 74, 75, 122, 180, 197–98, 201
Poincaré half-plane, 243
Popper, Karl, 108
positron emission tomography (PET scan), 14, 104
postsynaptic, 250
Premack, D., 218
presynaptic, 250
Prigogine, I., 201
prime numbers, 12–13, 243
projective perception, 186
projective system, 181
prosocial behavior, 220; cultural imprint and, 219–21
protein, 250
psychoanalysis of mathematics, 30–32
pump, 250
Purkinje cell, 250
Pygmalion, xi
pyramidal cell, 250
Pythagoras, 4, 33

QCD (quantum chromodynamics), 243
QED (quantum electrodynamics), 154, 244
QFT (quantum field theory), 53–54, 244
quantum chromodynamics (QCD), 243
quantum electrodynamics (QED), 244
quantum field theory (QFT), 53–54, 244
quantum gravity, 244

quantum mechanics, 64–73, 244
quarks, 244
quasi-crystals, 244

random sequence, 244
rational, real and, 179–209
rationality, "condensed," 50, 224
Rawls, J., 225
real, rational and, 179–209
realism, 23–24; constructivism versus, 11–17; platonism and, 31
reality, defined, 32
real-valued functions, 42
reason: level of, 99; neural architectures of, 104
reasoning by analogy, 142–43
receptors, 250; presynaptic and postsynaptic, 97, 100
relativity, 51–52, 244
religion, 214; as distinguished from scientific inquiry, 229–33
renormalization, 8–9, 244
replication-translation-amelioration process, 142
representations, Sperber's classification of, 117; mental, 128; linking, within frameworks of thought, 143–46
repressor, 250
response-specificity of neurons, 132–33
reticular formation, 250
ribonucleic acid (RNA), 250
Riemannian space, 244
rigidification process, 36
Ritz-Rydberg principle, 61, 244
RNA (ribonucleic acid), 250
Russell, Bertrand Arthur William, 3rd Lord, 160–61
Russell's paradox, 160–61, 244

S-matrix, 52–53, 244; functionalism and, 165–68
Sartre, Jean-Paul, 74
Schiller, Johann, 232–33
Schrödinger's equation, 9, 61, 66, 245
Schwinger, Julian, 8
sciences, hierarchy of, 6–11

second-order representations, 117
selective synaptic stabilization, 109
self-evaluating machine, suffering, 173–78
self-reference, 245
septum, 250
serotonin, 250
Shakespeare, William, 14
Shallice, T., 104
Shepard, R. N., 5, 75; mental rotation experiments of, 5
Simon, H. A., 84, 85
simple group, 245
simplicial complexes, 128–30, 245; hyperbolic, 138–39
simplicial topology, 245
simplicity, 29
singularity, 245, 250
Smith, Adam, 229
social bonds, 216
social life, frontal lobe and, 216–19
Socrates, 12, 27, 228
sodium ion-selective channel structure, 58, 59
soma, 250
song learning in swamp sparrow, 114, 115
Sperber, D., 117, 218
Spinoza, Baruch, 38, 42, 200, 233; on Knowledge, 211, 225
spontaneous generation, 83
sporadic groups, 20, 21, 245
stable forms, coding, 127–38
stationary phase principle, 144
stationary principle, 245
statistical mechanics, 245
stellate cell, 251
Stent, G., 213
Stern-Gerlach experiment, 72
string theory, 245
strings, 53–55
strong interactions, analyzing, 52–53
strong platonism, 179
structure, contrasted with function, 60–61, 83–84, 164–67
subdivision, 130

subfactor, 245
subitizing, 193
subjectivity, 32
substance P, 251
superior colliculus, 251
Suslin problem, 156–57
swamp sparrow, song learning in, 114, 115
symbolic level, 99
symmetry, 245–46
sympathy, enlargement of, 226–33
synapses, 90, 251; synaptic efficacy, or strength, 95–97, 109

tactical reason, 123
Taine, Hippolyte, 74–75
thalamus, 251
Theresa, of Avila, Saint, 147
thinking machines, 153–78; possibility of, 153–54; Turing's, 162–64
Thom, René, 3, 5, 128
't Hooft, G., 53
thought, linking representations within frameworks of, 143–46
thought objects, 46
thought tools, 13, 35
Thurston, W. P., 142
Tits, J., 20–21
Tomonaga, Sin-itiro, 8
topological invariant, 128, 246
topological space, 246
topology, 134–35, 246; general, 240; simplicial, 245

trace, 246
Turing, Alan M., 162–63
Turing machine, 162–64, 246
twin primes, 188

ultraproducts, 43–44, 246
understanding, level of, 99
universal machine. *See* Turing machine
universal moral rules, 213–14
utilitarianism, 224
utilization behavior, 106–7

Valéry, Paul, 26
Vanini, Lucilio, 26
variability, theorem of, 112; space of, 231
Veneziano model, 52, 166
Vesalius, Andreas, 26
visual system, 92–93
Von Neumann, John, 198
Vygotsky, Lev, 194

wave function of electron, 66, 67, 246
Weinberg, S., 204
well ordering, 246
Wiesel, T. N., 110, 221
Wigner, Eugene, xi, 47, 51
Wilson, D., 218
Wilson, E. O., 218, 222
Wisconsin card-sorting test, 102, 104
wisdom, according to Plato, 213

Yang-Mills theory, 246

Jean-Pierre Changeux is Director of the Molecular Neurobiology Laboratory at the Institut Pasteur in Paris and holds the Chair of Cellular Communications at the Collège de France. Among his works translated into English are *Neuronal Man: The Biology of Mind* (Pantheon/Oxford).

Alain Connes holds the Chair of Analysis and Geometry at the Collège de France. Winner of the 1982 Fields Medal, he is the author of *Noncommutative Geometry* (Academic).